CREATION LEGENDS OF THE ANCIENT NEAR EAST

By the same author:

THE CREATION OF MAN, by *Michelangelo*

In this noble representation of the culminating act of the Biblical account of the Creation, the great Florentine artist seems to have drawn on both pagan and Christian ideas. The spherically inflated mantle of God the Father is reminiscent of the 'world mantle' or 'mantle of heaven', with which Zeus or Caelus (heaven) is sometimes invested (e.g. on the breastplate of the statue of Augustus of the Prima Porta, Rome). It has been suggested that the figure of the angel or *putto*, about whom the left arm of God rests, represents the Christ Child as the Second Adam to be. A profound symbolism also appears to be implied by the touch of the Creator's hand—perhaps the infusion of life into the as-yet inert figure of Man. (See C. de Tolnay, *Michelangelo*, II, pp. 135–7, and figs. 311–19, Princeton University Press, 1945.)

Frontispiece: The Creation of Man, by Michelangelo, from the fresco in the Sistine Chapel, Rome. (Photo: Anderson.) For description, see over.

CREATION LEGENDS

OF THE

ANCIENT NEAR EAST

by

S. G. F. BRANDON, M.A., D.D.

Professor of Comparative Religion
in the University of Manchester

HODDER AND STOUGHTON

PREFACE

On reflection it appears perhaps not strange that the Christian world waited until the sixteenth century for the mighty drama of the Creation to be adequately depicted in art. Although mediaeval artists sought, often with an attractive naïvety of conception, to portray certain scenes of the *Genesis* story, it took the daring genius of Michelangelo to translate visually on to the walls of the Sistine Chapel the whole majestic imagery of the ancient Hebrew writers. The secret of the achievement surely lies in Michelangelo's character, for in a very real sense he was the typical Renaissance man. In this great Florentine artist the reviving spirit of classical culture blended with, and stirred to a new vision, the long established Christian estimate of life. Hence the essential humanism that pervades the great Sistine frescoes, which is evident not only in the frankly, though superb, anthropomorphic rendering of God the Creator, but also in the manifest concentration on the destiny of Man the Creature.

The impressive, and fundamentally noble, representation which the ancient Hebrew account of the Creation received at Michelangelo's hands is symptomatic of the place which that account held for so long in minds nurtured in the traditions of Christian civilisation. It is perhaps in turn also symptomatic that in this modern age, when science has taught us the essential relativity of both ourselves and the earth upon which we live in the scheme of the universe, that research has also shown the relativity of the Hebrew creation story by unveiling other more ancient accounts of the origin of things that were once current in the Near East. If, through this transaction, the Hebrew account has lost much of its former prestige, however, for our understanding of our common humanity there has been much gain. As it is hoped will be evident in the following pages, the study of the creation legends of other peoples of the ancient Near East has a supreme interest, because it affords an insight into the first recorded speculations of mankind about its own origin and that of the world

v

in which its members found themselves living. Moreover, when seen in this wider context, the Hebrew cosmogonies acquire also a fresh and perhaps an even deeper significance; for, by noting what they had in common with other contiguous traditions and wherein they differed from them, a sounder appreciation of their true uniqueness is achieved.

In seeking to understand ancient ideas, set forth in difficult and sometimes still imperfectly known languages, and often preserved in very fragmentary form, it is inevitable that many complicated issues have to be investigated and their problems discussed; and this is even more necessary in a work such as this which may fairly claim to be the first comprehensive study of the ancient Near Eastern cosmogonies. However, in the following pages, while endeavouring to do this in an adequate manner, I have sought to keep such intricacies limited to the footnotes in view of the wide human interest of the subject. I should like to take the opportunity here also to anticipate a possible point of criticism by saying that I am aware that I have nowhere attempted to define what I mean by the term 'legend', and that I have sometimes used the term as almost synonymous with 'myth'. My reason for so doing is that I have felt it to be wiser not to attempt a more precise formulation, since, after much study of the issues involved, I know of no really adequate *general* distinction between these two terms.

It remains for me to express my sincere thanks to the following of my colleagues in the University of Manchester: to the Reverend D. Howard Smith for kindly reading the manuscript and making many useful suggestions; to Professor F. F. Bruce and Dr. R. A. Kraft for their valuable help in checking the proofs. To Professor H. W. Fairman of Liverpool University I am indebted for his kind provision of material not easily available to me. The skill and kind cooperation of Miss E. A. Lowcock of the Department of Geography, Manchester University, have provided the line drawings; and my thanks are due also to Mr. S. Roberts, Deputy Librarian, and Mr. G. A. Webb of the Arts Library, Manchester University, for arranging the reproduction of certain photographs. Mr. T. Burton Brown, Keeper of Egyptian Antiquities, Manchester Museum, kindly provided the photograph of the statue of Ptah. I am also deeply grateful to Miss Linda Shepherd for the devoted and efficient manner in which she has interpreted and typed a difficult manuscript—indeed she has often divined my meaning when it has subsequently eluded me myself. And to the Publishers my thanks are especially due for their interest and kind invitation to me to undertake this study. To my wife I am indebted for her assistance in preparing the indexes.

The University of Manchester,   S. G. F. BRANDON
February 20th, 1963.

ACKNOWLEDGMENTS

THE author gratefully acknowledges the permission kindly given by the following institutions and publishers to quote from the works indicated or to reproduce the illustrations specified:

The American Philosophical Society and Professor S. N. Kramer (S. N. Kramer, *Sumerian Mythology*); The British Museum (Keeper of the Department of Egyptian Antiquities (Plate I)); The Syndics of the Cambridge University Press (G. S. Kirk and J. E. Raven, *The Presocratic Philosophers*); The Chicago University Press (A. Heidel, *The Babylonian Genesis*); The Clarendon Press, Oxford (R. C. Zaehner, *Zurvān: A Zoroastrian Dilemma*); The Edinburgh University Library (Plate XIII); Messrs. W. Heinemann Limited [Loeb Classical Library] (Homer, *The Iliad*, Hesiod, Diodorus Siculus); Messrs. Macmillan and Company Limited (Plates III, IV, reproduced from H. Frankfort, *Cylinder Seals*); The Manchester Museum (Plate II); N. V. Uitgeversmaatschappij Elsevier, Amsterdam (Plate X); The Reading Museum and Art Gallery (Plate II); The Oriental Institute, Chicago University (Plate XII); The Princeton University Press (*Ancient Near Eastern Texts*, ed. J. B. Pritchard); Die Staatliche Museen, Berlin (Plate XI).

CONTENTS

THE PHOTOGRAPHS

LIST OF ILLUSTRATIONS IN THE TEXT

xii

ABBREVIATIONS

Ae.R.T.B.	= *Die aegyptische Religion in Text und Bild*, eingeleitet und übertragen von G. Roeder, 4 Bände, Zürich/Stuttgart, 1959–1961.
Ae.Z.	= *Zeitschrift für ägyptische Sprache und Altertumskunde*.
A.N.E.T.	= *Ancient Near Eastern Texts relating to the Old Testament*, ed. J. B. Pritchard, Princeton University Press, 2nd ed., 1955.
B.J.R.L.	= *Bulletin of the John Rylands Library*, Manchester.
B.A.S.O.R.	=*Bulletin of the American Schools of Oriental Research*.
B.S.O.A.S.	= *Bulletin of the School of Oriental and African Studies*, London.
B.W.A.N.T.	= *Beiträge zur Wissenschaft vom Alten und Neuen Testament*.
B.Z.A.W.	= *Beihefte zur Zeitschrift für alttestamentliche Wissenschaft*.
C.A.H.	= *Cambridge Ancient History*.
C.T.	= *The Egyptian Coffin Texts*, ed. A. de Buck.
E.R.E.	= *Encyclopaedia of Religion and Ethics*, ed. J. Hastings, 12 vols. and Index vol., Edinburgh, 1908–1926.
E.T.	= English translation.
H.G.R.	= *Histoire générale des Religions*, ed. M. Gorce et R. Mortier, 5 tomes, Paris 1947–1952.
I.A.A.M.	= *The Intellectual Adventure of Ancient Man*, ed. H. & H. A. Frankfort.
I.C.C.	= *The International Critical Commentary*, ed. S. R. Driver, A. Plummer, and G. A. Briggs.
J.A.O.S.	= *Journal of American Oriental Society*.
J.E.A.	= *Journal of Egyptian Archaeology*.
J.N.E.S.	= *Journal of Near Eastern Studies*, University of Chicago Press.
J.S.S.	= *Journal of Semitic Studies*, Manchester University Press.
L.R-G.	= *Lehrbuch der Religionsgeschichte* (Chantepie de la Saussaye, hrg. A. Bertholet u. Edv. Lehman), 4 Aufl., 2 Bände, Tübingen, 1925.
M.A.W.	= *Mythologies of the Ancient World* (ed. S. N. Kramer), New York, 1961.
O.C.D.	= *Oxford Classical Dictionary*, Oxford, 1949.
P.W.	= A. Pauly, G. Wissowa, u. W. Kroll, *Real-Encyclopädie d. klassischen Altertumswissenschaft*.

Pyr.	= *Pyramid Texts.*
R.A.	= *Revue d'Assyriologie et d'Archéologie orientale.*
R.A.C.	= *Reallexikon für Antike und Christentum.* hrg. T. Klauser.
Reallexikon	= *Reallexikon der aegyptischen Religionsgeschichte,* by H. Bonnet, Berlin, 1952.
R.G.G.	= *Die Religion in Geschichte und Gegenwart,* 3. Aufl. hrg. K. Galling.
R-G.L.	= *Religionsgeschichtliches Lesebuch,* hrg. A. Bertholet, Tübingen, 1908–
R.H.P.R.	= *Revue d'Histoire et de Philosophie religieuses.*
R.H.R.	= *Revue de l'Histoire des Religions.*
S.B.E.	= *Sacred Books of the East,* ed. F. Max Müller.
T.L.-Z.	= *Theologische Literaturzeitung.*
Wörterbuch or **Wb.**	= *Wörterbuch der aegyptischen Sprache,* hrg. A. Erman und H. Grapow.
Z.A.T.W.	= *Zeitschrift für alttestamentliche Wissenschaft.*

CHAPTER ONE

THE DAWNING CONCEPT OF CREATIVITY

THE idea of the creation of the world or the universe, and all that it contains, is one with which all Western peoples are familiar from childhood. The Biblical story of the Creation is part of our cultural heritage, and, despite the scepticism engendered by the nineteenth century clash of theologian and scientist over the truth of the *Genesis* record, that story still powerfully affects our imagination. From it we surely derive that profound conviction that the world had a beginning. So profound indeed is this conviction that it might fairly be regarded as instinctive. For, even if we are disposed to see mythological elements in the *Genesis* account of the Creation, it rarely occurs to us to regard the idea itself, namely, that the world had a beginning, as a strange one for human beings to entertain. Yet, as we shall see on analysis, the idea is truly a strange one and it requires explanation. One obvious line of explanation can, however, be ruled out at the start. It might be suggested that the sacred authority with which the Biblical story of the Creation became invested, together with its dramatic quality, have so influenced the Western tradition of thought that we have come to accept its basic idea as axiomatic. But, powerful as the influence of the *Genesis* account has undoubtedly been, its concept of a beginning to the world is not unique. The idea itself is found, though presented in diverse forms, among many peoples, both in ancient times and today, whose cultural origins are quite unconnected with the cultural tradition of the Hebrews.[1]

If we can make the effort to overcome our familiarity with the idea that the world had a beginning, and so look at it afresh, we shall find that it could never have been an idea that might naturally have suggested itself to men through their experience of the world. In the first

---

[1] Cf. the comprehensive summaries of cosmogonic traditions under 'Cosmogony and Cosmology' in *E.R.E.*, IV, pp. 125–179, see also *ib*, pp. 226b–229b; *R.G.G.*, V (3 Aufl.), 1469–1473 ('Schöpfung', by C.-M. Edsman).

place, of course, mankind could not have witnessed the beginning of the world. Even the earliest creation myths, as we shall see, describe the creation of the earth as being accomplished before that of man, although they relate the two events very closely in time-sequence. Then, it needs scarcely to be said that modern scientific opinion is agreed that our species, which we dignify as *homo sapiens*, and even its hominian precursors, appeared late in the course of geological time, and that, when it did appear, the major structure of the earth had long been completed. Further, even if the surmise be made that some remote members of our race may have witnessed great cataclysms towards the end of the Pleistocene Age, when the landscape was drastically changed perhaps by flooding as the polar ice caps diminished, it is still difficult to see how even this experience could have prompted the conception of the beginning of the world.[1] What such a spectacle would most likely have suggested, it being granted that these hypothetically remote ancestors of ours were capable of conceptual thought and deductive reasoning, would have been a realisation of the destructive power of water as it rose and obliterated the land—indeed the impression left by such experience would have been more calculated to inspire speculation about the onset of chaos than about the formation of a cosmos.

From speculation about such a hypothetical situation we shall be better advised to turn to consider a matter of which we can be tolerably certain. It is that to primitive man his physical environment must have seemed unchanging. Despite brief seasonal changes, the landscape had an abiding sameness of appearance which was far more likely to have suggested permanence than to have prompted the idea that it had had a beginning, and, hence, had not always existed. Further, the constant succession of day and night, and, at least in lands of more stable climate, the unceasing spectacle of the rising and setting of the sun, the steady rhythm of the moon's phases,[2]

[1] Cf. J. G. Frazer, *Folk-Lore in the Old Testament*, pp. 74–5, 137–8, 142–3.
[2] The moon had, of course, an ambivalent symbolism. Its waxing, waning, disappearance and reappearance are suggestive of impermanence; yet the change to which it is subjected follows a constant pattern and suggests an eternal rhythm of birth, growth, death and rebirth. Cf. M. Eliade, *Traité d'Histoire des Religions*, pp. 142–4, 153–4, 155–8; *Patterns in Comparative Religion*, pp. 154–6, 163–4, 171–4. It is interesting to note that in our earliest extant collection of mythological texts, i.e. the *Pyramid Texts*, the moon is not prominent; cf. P. Derchain in *Sources orientales*, V, pp. 55–6.

and the enduring pattern of the stars,[1] were all calculated to give the impression that the structure of the universe was fixed and abiding. Accordingly, from experience of his physical environment primitive man would surely have been led to deduce that things had always been such as he himself saw them. To have thought otherwise would require a degree of mental abstraction from the evidence of present experience and the ability to envisage the existence of a wholly contrary situation such as would appear most unlikely in the earlier stages of human culture. Moreover, the very conception of the beginning of the world involves a high order of detachment from one's physical environment, as well as the power to contemplate that environment as an integrated whole in terms of its duration backward in time beyond the range of personal memory, indeed to its imagined far-off beginning.

We are brought thus to ask how came man to acquire the idea of 'beginning'; because his initial conception of the beginning of the world must have arisen from what he understood 'beginning' to mean. Now, since 'beginning' essentially connotes a happening or event, its conception obviously involves some awareness of time as exemplified in the three basic categories of past, present and future. In other words, the human mind, in the course of its development, must have reached such a degree of time-consciousness as to permit the selection and definition of some past happening as constituting an 'event' of initial significance relative to present interests. This means, so far as we are concerned here, that to be able to think of a 'beginning', men must already have achieved detachment of attention from 'here-now' interests, so that they could survey mentally a range of past experience and identify some particular event as marking or producing a new situation with which they were concerned.[2] To avoid our becoming further involved here in an abstract terminology, we may perhaps put the issue simply in the form of a question: what

[1] The evidence of the *Pyramid Texts* (656c, in Sethe, *Die altägyptischen Pyramidentexten*, I, p. 360) shows that the ancient Egyptians had been impressed by the unchanging appearance of the circumpolar stars, which they called the 'Imperishable Ones', and sought to join them in order to assure themselves of eternal existence. Cf. H. Bonnet, *Reallexikon*, p. 749; S. G. F. Brandon, *Man and his Destiny in the Great Religions*, p. 38.

[2] Cf. S. G. F. Brandon, *Time and Mankind*, pp. 15–16, 25. On the philosophical implications see B. Russell, *Human Knowledge*, pp. 91–2, 95, 349, 471 sq.

happenings or objects within the world of their experience were likely to have given the earliest peoples the idea of 'beginning'? The most likely phenomenon seems surely to be that of birth— whether human birth or that of animals. The emergence of a living, though minute, being from the body of the mother afforded the most striking ocular demonstration of a 'beginning'.[1] How the infant came to be in the womb was undoubtedly a mystery to primitive man. The evidence of Palaeolithic representations of pregnant women and animals clearly attest a knowledge of the gestation;[2] but it is uncertain whether the process of generation was understood. Some ithyphallic figures have been found, and there are representations of a male bison following a female.[3] However, in view of the period that separates impregnation and birth, it seems probable that the significance of gestation and birth was appreciated long before it was realised that these phenomena were the result of conception following coition. Accordingly, although knowledge of gestation must have caused birth to be regarded as its consequence, the phenomenon of birth itself would surely have afforded primitive man his most graphic and obvious example of the 'beginning' of an individual living being, whether human or animal. There would, of course, have been one

[1] "The riddle of time is the riddle of the beginning", G. van der Leeuw in *Man and Time* (Papers form the *Eranos Yearbooks*), p. 325; "Before the eschatological consciousness arises, there is no real beginning to time", H. Plessner, *ibid*, pp. 233–4. The concern of these writers with the repetitive element in what they define as 'primordial time' seems to have prevented them from considering the significance of biological birth as the basic datum for primitive man's conception of 'beginning'—of course, the continuous recurrence of the phenomenon would suggest the idea of 'an eternal beginning' upon which they have laid emphasis. See below p. 117. Cf. M. Eliade in *Sources orientales*, I, pp. 490–1.

[2] Cf. R. Pittioni, *Die urgeschichtlichen Grundlagen der europäischen Kultur*, Abb. 27, p. 66; H. Breuil, *Quatre Cents Siècles d'Art pariètal*, p. 279, fig. 317; G. R. Levy, *The Gate of Horn*, pl. 6 and pp. 56–7; E. O. James, *Prehistoric Religion*, pp. 145–8; J. Maringer, *The Gods of Prehistoric Man*, ill. 27–34, pp. 97–8; E. & J. Neustupný, *Czechoslavakia*, pp. 32–3, pl. 10–11. See pp. 6–7.

[3] Cf. Maringer, ill. 14, 36, figs. 25, 26; H. Kuhn, *Die Felsbilder Europas*, pp. 15, 16. Maringer (pp. 99–100) is convinced that fertility rites, centring on phallic symbols, were celebrated in the Upper Palaeolithic period. One of the bas-reliefs in the 'sanctuary' at Laussel has been interpreted as a representation of the act of coition (cf. Th. Mainage, *Les Religions de la Préhistoire*, p. 287, n. 10; Breuil, p. 280: it is differently interpreted by Miss Levy, p. 60 and pl. 7(d)). See also James, *Prehistoric Religion*, pp. 146–7; *The Cult of the Mother Goddess*, p. 15.

other instance of biological beginning for the observation of primitive man, namely, the emergence of the chick from the egg.[1] Whether he was quick to relate this phenomenon to parturition in humans and other mammals as a variant of the same biological process cannot be known; but we shall see that the idea of the egg provided some stimulus to later cosmogonic speculations.

It would appear, therefore, from these *a priori* considerations that the phenomenon of biological birth most probably supplied the human mind with its initial conception of 'beginning'.[2] Such a biological pattern would mean, in ignorance of the cause of generation, that 'beginning' would essentially connote the emergence of a pre-existing but immature individual being from the womb of a mature individual of the species concerned. The process of parturition would be seen as initiating a separate individual existence. As a conceptual image of beginning, biological birth would, accordingly, have been applicable only to animals; whether it was imaginatively extended by early man to explain the origin of other forms of organic life such as trees we cannot know. It would certainly seem, at least to our minds, that experience of biological 'beginning' was unlikely to have prompted speculation about the beginning of the world or to have supplied the imagery for its conception. In this connection, too, it should be noticed that, whereas Palaeolithic art provides abundant evidence of primitive man's concern both with his own kind and with the animals which constituted his main source of food, there is apparently a complete absence of interest in the physical environment —no representations are found of the heavenly bodies, the sun, moon or stars.[3]

Palaeolithic culture, as it is known to us through archaeological research, does, however, suggest another source of stimulus than that of biological birth for the conception of 'beginning'; moreover,

[1] On the symbolism of the egg in later myth and ritual see Eliade, *Traité d'Histoire des Religions*, pp. 353–5; *Patterns in Comparative Religion*, pp. 413–6; in *Sources Orientales*, I, pp. 479–83. See also below pp. 44 f., 184 f.

[2] It must be asked whether the phenomenon of the kindling of fire suggested the idea of 'beginning'. It seems that even the sub-human hominid *Sinanthropus pekinensis* knew the use of fire. Cf. G. Clark, *From Savagery to Civilisation*, pp. 33–4.

[3] Cf. Brandon, *Man and his Destiny in the Great Religions*, pp. 22–5. For probable representations of celestial bodies in later prehistoric art see Maringer, fig. 36 (Mesolithic), fig. 49; Kuhn, Tafel 70.

5

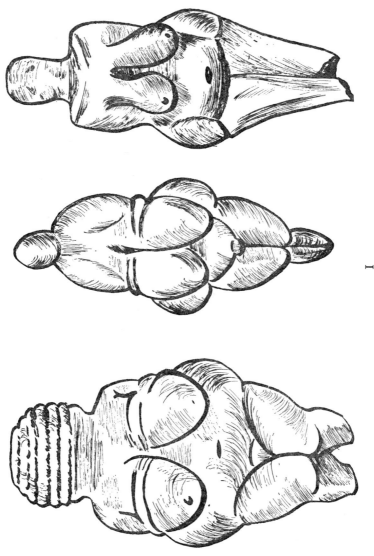

I

Female figurines of the Upper Palaeolithic period, found respectively at Willendorf (Austria), Lespugue (France), and Vestoniče (Czechoslovakia). The emphasis upon the maternal attributes, while the faces are left featureless, is surely significant of the concern of the makers of these figurines. (See p. 4.)

'beginning' here is associated with creativity. The stimulus concerned is that which might reasonably be assumed to have come from Palaeolithic man's technical and artistic ability. To have taken a flint-pebble or a piece of bone and to have fashioned from the one an arrow-head or from the other a harpoon was to create a new thing in form and

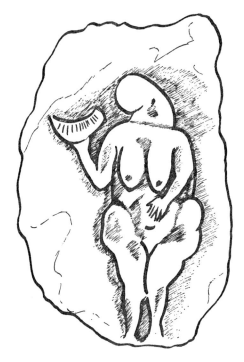

II

The so-called 'Venus of Laussel' (Dordogne). This sculptured figure, which holds a bison's horn, formed what appears to have been the central object of a Palaeolithic sanctuary. Like the figurines, the face is blank.

purpose. But even more stimulating to the imagination would surely have been both the praxis and the achievements of artistic activity. The Palaeolithic artist who drew upon the blank wall of a cave the figure of an animal instinct with life, or carved from shapeless stone the figure of a woman, was a creator. He must have felt, and his fellow tribesmen must have recognised, that he was possessed of a marvellous power to bring into being a new and significant form—moreover, in terms of intent, these artistic creations were not mere depictions but were believed to be endowed with magical efficacy.[1]

[1] Cf. P. Wernert, "La signification des cavernes d'art paléolithique", in *H.G.R.*, I, pp. 89–97; Kuhn, pp. 12–23.

7

For us the contemplation of the products of Palaeolithic art prompts many questions of great importance from the point of view of our subject; but we can only frame them with no expectation of finding answers to them. However, the exercise will be of value for our subsequent study.

First, we may ask whether the Palaeolithic artist would have conceived of himself as a creator and so have been led, as would also those who saw his work, to imagine another source or mode of 'beginning' than that which they recognised in the process of biological birth? And, if such a conception were attained, would there have been any speculation about the nature of this creativity or creative power? Since the creations of Palaeolithic art were the combined product of a personal creative ability operating on a pre-existent material, were the minds of some Palaeolithic peoples stimulated thereby to seek an analogical explanation for the objects of their physical environment either singly or as a whole—in other words, were they led on to imagine some transcendent creator who had similarly fashioned the world?[1] Or, further, a question that might to some degree affect that which has just been asked: how did the Palaeolithic artist differentiate between his own representations of women or animals and actual women and animals? This is not the idle question that it may well appear at first sight, because, as we have already noted, this art was motivated by magical belief. Hence, the pictures and the carvings were no inanimate depictions, but objects of great potency and so may have been further suggestive of some primaeval act of the creation of both men and beasts.[2] Finally there is the problem constituted by the fact that where men appear to be represented in the earliest examples of this art, they are never drawn realistically—their forms are either crudely schematic or they seem

[1] Maringer, p. 43, on the strength of seeing in a certain bone found in the Salzofen cave a phallic symbol, has suggested that certain bear-hunters in the Lower Palaeolithic era may have conceived of a 'lord of the beasts', to whom sacrifices were made for the replacement of the animals killed in the hunt. He neglects to ask himself whether at this very remote period the facts of biological generation were thus known; see also n. 3, p. 4 above.

[2] Even the ancient Egyptians were so convinced of the magical potency of a depicted figure that sometimes in tomb inscriptions they felt it necessary to damage the hieroglyphic sign of a snake or crocodile, thus to render it innocuous to the owner of the tomb. Cf. F. Lexa, *La Magie dans l'Égypte antique*, I, pp. 77, 78, 88.

8

to wear an animal disguise.[1] If the Palaeolithic artists were male, as they are usually assumed to have been, although without actual evidence, the interesting question thus arises: why did they represent the male form in this strange manner while rendering the female realistically?[2]

It would seem, however, that from a consideration of Palaeolithic art at least one inference may be safely drawn. It is that the exercise of this art, involving as it did the formation of a mental image and then its translation into a concrete linear or plastic form, must have given rise to the notion of creativity. In other words, Palaeolithic man would have been acquainted thereby with the idea of 'beginning' as due to a personal act of creation. Whether he sought to relate this form of 'beginning' to that with which he was familiar through the phenomenon of biological birth, we cannot, of course, tell. If, as it appears, he did not understand the process of procreation, it seems improbable that the concept of creation that stemmed from his experience as an artist would have helped him to account for the origin of embryonic forms of living beings in the womb before birth. Consequently, it would appear that at the earliest stage of human culture, such as it is known through the archaeological record, two distinct conceptions of 'beginning' would have been current which derived respectively from the phenomenon of biological birth and artistic creation. Since each of these conceptions was concerned with the 'beginnings' of living beings, whether actual or in image, it seems unlikely that they would have prompted Palaeolithic man to speculate about the origin of his physical environment and so lead on to the formation of some primaeval cosmogony.

In our search so far for those factors which seem most likely to have furnished the earliest peoples with their notions of creativity we have confined our enquiry to such evidence as has seemed relevant in Upper Palaeolithic culture, i.e. to the earliest known forms of human culture. However, between this primaeval evidence and the first

[1] E.g. see the famous Lascaux picture of the bird-headed man being killed by a wounded bison (Breuil, pp. 131, 134-5, 148, 150-1, fig.) and the so-called Dancing Sorcerer of the Trois Frères cave (Breuil, pp. 166, 176-7). Cf. Kuhn, pp. 15-17.

[2] From the contrast in treatment, further evidence could be deduced that the Palaeolithic peoples saw only in the woman the source of new beings of their kind.

recorded cosmogonies stretches the immense period of time during which human culture passed through its Mesolithic and Neolithic phases. It was during the latter stage of development that certain discoveries or inventions were made which were fundamental to the establishment of civilised ways of life. This new knowledge gradually wrought those profound changes in the economic and social ordering of life that have aptly been described as constituting 'the Neolithic Revolution'.[1] Briefly it meant that man changed from being primarily a 'food-gatherer', existing upon what he found or got by hunting, to one who obtained his food by cultivating it. Now, by becoming an agriculturalist, man necessarily became closely acquainted with the generative powers of Nature as exemplified in the seed-corn. In turn he must have become more intimately associated with the land itself than when he merely wandered over it in search of game. He was now profoundly concerned with its fecundity, and was taught to observe its reaction to the climatic changes that the rotation of the seasons brought. Hence he became also more urgently interested in the signs of the heavens than he had been before when his interest had been concentrated upon the animals which constituted the chief source of his food. The movements of the sun, and the moon and the stars now began to command his attention, and from long and careful observation his first calendars, so necessary to the life of the agriculturalist, were in time constructed.[2] Moreover, this increasing preoccupation with his physical environment as a vital factor in his own well-being was calculated to change man's attitude towards it from that of an original unthinking acceptance to one of lively concern about its fundamental nature and the various changes to which it appeared to be subjected. The earth itself was no longer just inanimate matter; it possessed the power to germinate the seed, and to nourish the plant so that it produced its fruit and also the seed whereby to continue the annual miracle of generation and growth upon which the life of man depended.

[1] See V. G. Childe, *Man Makes Himself*, chap. V ('The Neolithic Revolution')

[2] Cf. Childe, pp. 103–4. Childe suggests (p. 51) that even as a hunter, man had to 'decipher the calendar of the heavens'. He may have done so; but Palaeolithic art, as we have seen, shows no concern with celestial phenomena. It would seem more likely that the Palaeolithic hunters would closely have followed the animals in their annual migrations in search of food.

From the conception of the earth as the source of vegetation it was but an easy, and an apparently logical, step to think of it as the creatrix of all life, to be personified and deified as the Great Mother, the Earth Goddess.[1] It is possible, too, that the ritual burial of the dead was inspired by some idea of a return to the source of life.[2] Whether in the preliterary era this idea of the earth as the creatrix led men in turn to speculate on its origin, or whether at that stage of mental development the idea itself was found sufficient to account for the beginning of life we cannot tell; as we shall see in our study of the historic cosmogonies, the Earth Goddess herself was invariably regarded as the creature of some transcendent creator or creative principle.[3]

It would seem that the domestication of animals was also a factor in the so-called Neolithic Revolution.[4] Instead of hunting them in their wild state for food, man came to see that it was more profitable to tame certain species and keep them about his habitation so that they might continuously supply him with milk and in time with portage and traction power. Such domestication must have enabled the habits of animals, especially those of mating, to be known better, and we may wonder whether it was from such sources of information, with their comparative significance for his own kind, that man eventually came to understand the principle of biological reproduction. The extant archaeological data do not permit us to know; but, as we shall see from our study of the earliest Egyptian and Sumerian creation texts, such knowledge was already traditional by the time of the first written records so far preserved to us.[5]

It was during the Neolithic period also that the craft of pottery-making was first invented. That the process of fashioning a lump of clay into a vessel, shapely and useful, provided in later times among various peoples an effective image in which to picture the creation of man we shall find some notable evidence.[6] It would seem, however, that the invention of the potter's art as a stimulus to speculation about

---

[1] Cf. James, *The Cult of the Mother Goddess*, pp. 47–8; Eliade, *Traité d'Histoire des Religions*, pp. 211 f.; *Patterns in Comparative Religion*, pp. 239 f.; E. Neumann, *The Great Mother*, pp. 98–9.
[2] Cf. Brandon, *Man and his Destiny*, pp. 9, 14–16, 22–3.
[3] See pp. 26–7, 169.   [4] Cf. Childe, pp. 66, 76–9.
[5] See pp. 22–3, 35, n. 2, 75.
[6] Cf. Childe, pp. 89–90. See pp. 60–1, 77, 89, 123.

the origin of man had been anticipated in a more graphic form by the skill of the Palaeolithic artist, although, as we have seen, it is not possible to determine what influence, if any, it may have had upon the thinking of those earliest ancestors of our race.[1]

Such then appear to be the chief conclusions that we may reasonably draw from a consideration of those aspects of human culture during the preliterary period which would seem to be relevant to the emergence of a sense of creativity. As we have seen, the idea of 'beginning', which must have established itself in the human mind as a prior requisite to any conception of creation, probably derived from experience of the phenomenon of biological birth. Palaeolithic artistic and technical ability were calculated to produce the idea of creativity, together with that of a creator. But there appeared to be no indications that the idea of 'beginning' exemplified in birth, or that of the creative power of the artist, stimulated speculation about the origin of the world, or, to be more exact, of Palaeolithic man's physical environment. Similarly, while the development of agriculture in the Neolithic period may have led to the belief that the earth was the source of life, no evidence was found of curiosity about the beginning of the earth. It has to be recognised, of course, that for this preliterary stage of culture it is difficult to see in what form cosmogonic speculation, if such there had been, might have been preserved to us. However, on *a priori* grounds it would seem reasonable to conclude that the unchanging aspect of the major features of his physical environment would rather have impressed early man with a sense of its permanence. To think otherwise would surely require the experience of some great natural cataclysm that suggested that the earth, like living-beings, was subject to change; and, even so, it would still not explain how the idea arose that the world had a 'beginning'. When we come to study the earliest cosmogonies of which we have documentary evidence, we shall see that they are closely conditioned by the physical features of the areas, namely Egypt and Mesopotamia, in which they originated. The main source

[1] R. Pettazzoni (*Essays on the History of Religions*, p. 31) rejects the suggestion that primitive man's technical ability produced in him the idea of creation, arguing that the first conception of a creator would have been in terms of a magician. However, he neglects to consider how the idea of magical creation originated, if it antedates man's activity as a tool-maker.

of our knowledge of Upper Palaeolithic culture, however, is not these areas but Europe, where geographical conditions were very different and produced no features, so far as we know, comparable to those concerned in Egypt and Mesopotamia. Neolithic culture, from which our general inferences have also been made, is known from its remains over a much wider area, including Egypt and Mesopotamia, and it is possible, as we shall see, that speculation about the beginning of the world may extend in these latter places back into the Neolithic period—but how far back, if at all, we have no means of telling.

We may, accordingly, conclude this introductory survey by observing that the fundamental concepts of cosmogonic speculation were laid far back in the preliterary period; but, since these concepts were essentially related to living beings, it seems likely that interest was limited to biological origins and that true cosmogonic speculation, i.e. speculation concerning the origin of the world or the universe, was probably little developed before the third millennium B.C., when the earliest known cosmogonic texts were composed.

CHAPTER TWO

EGYPT:
COSMOGONIES OF RIVAL SANCTUARIES

Our *a priori* considerations have suggested that man's earliest idea of 'beginning' probably arose from the phenomenon of birth, both of humans and animals, while his artistic and technical ability gave him the dual concepts of creator and creativity. We could find no obvious reasons to lead us to suppose that in the preliterary period of human culture the idea of the beginning of the world, or of his physical environment, should naturally have occurred to man. It is surprising, therefore, that the earliest recorded cosmogonies seem more concerned with accounting for the origin of the world than for that of mankind or of the animals.

The two earliest civilised states, namely in Egypt and Mesopotamia, provide the earliest written evidence of cosmogonic thought. It is impossible to determine which has the older record: the surviving texts in each instance date from about the middle of the third millennium B.C. and probably derive from still earlier traditions. These cosmogonies, although they are thus contemporaneous and come from sister civilisations in the ancient Near East, are, however, very different in their fundamental conceptions. In view of the fact that the Egyptian system involves ideas that may perhaps be considered the more naturally intelligible, it will accordingly be more helpful for our purpose to consider the Egyptian evidence first.

The beginnings of human settlement in the valley and delta of the Nile lie far back in the Neolithic era.[1] At that remote period life there must have been both difficult and hazardous. The annual submergence of the low-lying land by the great river meant that habitation was possible only at places above the level of the inundation, while

[1] Cf. V. G. Childe, *New Light on the Most Ancient East*, chaps. iii-iv; A. Gardiner, *Egypt of the Pharaohs*, pp. 384–399.

large tracts of the valley and delta must have been a permanent swamp, full of water reed and teeming with aquatic life.[1] Only gradually and by immense labour were these swamps drained, and irrigation works constructed to control and conserve the flood waters. Such undertakings in turn extended the area possible for settlement and so allowed the increase of a settled population, occupied in agriculture. These conditions had been substantially achieved by about 3000 B.C., when the country first came under a centralised monarchical government and began to enter into that first vigorous phase of its civilisation known as the Old Kingdom (2740–2270 B.C.).[2]

It is from the Old Kingdom period, with that long period of gradual development behind it, that the earliest Egyptian creation legends come. These legends, in their extant form, are severally the products of three great religious sanctuaries; but, although, as we shall see, each of these compositions was designed to promote the interests of the temple which produced it, they all embody certain common ideas that may be regarded as fundamental to the Egyptian view of the origin of things. Before examining each of these cosmogonies in order to evaluate its specific conceptions, it will, therefore, be useful to consider these common ideas.

The earliest expressions of Egyptian cosmogonic thought are contained in a collection of hieroglyphic texts inscribed on the interior walls of the pyramids of certain of the pharaohs of the Fifth and Sixth Dynasties (2480–2137 B.C.).[3] These *Pyramid Texts* were compiled by the priests of the great temple of Atum-Re at Heliopolis for the mortuary service of the dead kings, to ensure in particular their safe passage from this world to eternal bliss in the next. For this purpose they drew upon much traditional material in the form of myths and legends, hymns, prayers and magical incantations. Among the many devices employed to ensure the dead king's immortality was the solemn declaration that he was of divine origin and existed before death

---

[1] Cf. A. Erman u. H. Ranke, *Aegypten*, pp. 18–19, 263–5.
[2] Gardiner, p. 430, gives as the (conjectural) date of the beginning of the First Dynasty as 3100 ±.
[3] These are the conjectural dates of the fifth and sixth dynasties (Gardiner, 435–6). The *Pyramid Texts* are found in the pyramids of Unis, the last king of the fifth dynasty, and of Teti, Pepi I, Merenre I, Pepi II, the first four kings of the sixth dynasty. On the *Pyramid Texts* generally see H. Bonnet, *Reallexikon*, pp. 620a–623b, S. A. B. Mercer, *The Pyramid Texts*, I, pp. 1 ff.

appeared in the world. Thus the pharaoh Pepi is assured that he was engendered by the god Atum, when "existed not the heaven; existed not the earth; existed not men; before the birth of the gods; before the existence of death".[1] In this passage we have the conception of a primordial state, before the physical universe, its human and divine inhabitants, and death (hypostatised) existed, and when Atum was alone (presumably until he created the king). There is, however, another such declaration, which contains a notable variation of concept. In this the king is proclaimed as "born in Nun, when heaven existed not, and earth existed not, when existed not that which was to be established, when (the) disorder existed not, when (as yet) that fear did not exist that came into being through the eye of Horus".[2] Here we meet a concept that either adds in detail to that primordial state implied in the former passage, or presupposes an even earlier situation. 'Nun' in Egyptian thought was the primaeval waste of waters.[3] An inscription of the time of the pharaoh Osorkon III, recording an inundation of the Nile of catastrophic dimensions, provides a significant insight into this conception of Nun: "Nun came forth from . . . [and covered] this land to its limits. It stretched to the two borders (of the land) as in the first time . . . this land was given to its power as (to) the sea . . .".[4] The image of the primaeval waste of waters, which this great flood had evoked, is paralleled by a passage from an Eighteenth Dynasty (1550–1350 B.C.) version of the *Book of the Dead* in which Atum is represented as threatening, "I shall des-

[1] *Pyr.* 1466b–d (text in Sethe, *P.T.*, II, pp. 302–3: trans. S. A. B. Mercer, *The Pyramid Texts*, I, p. 233; L. Speleers, *Les Textes des Pyramides égyptiennes*, I, p. 94). Cf. Mercer, III, p. 715.

[2] *Pyr.* 1040a–d (text in Sethe, *P.T.* II, pp. 80–1: trans. Mercer, I, p. 181; Speleers, I, p. 71). If it is not taken as a causative form, *śmn.ti* can be interpreted as referring to the two mountain-ranges on the eastern and western sides of the Nile which seemed to support the sky. Cf. *Wb.* IV, p. 135; Mercer, II, pp. 524–5; S. Sauneron et J. Yoyotte in *Sources orientales*, I, p. 46(1). Disorder (*ḫnn.w*) implies an element of violence; since it does not appear to refer to some primaeval strife (see page 57), it probably relates to the legendary conflict of Set and Horus; cf. *Wb.* III, p. 383. On the continuing tradition in Egyptian thought of the concept *n ḫprt* ('when existed not . . .') see H. Grapow in *AeZ*, 67, pp. 34–7.

[3] On Nun generally see Bonnet, *Reallexikon*, pp. 535b–536b; S. A. B. Mercer, *The Religion of Ancient Egypt*, pp. 261–2.

[4] Cf. A. de Buck, *Die Egyptische Voorstellingen betreffende den Oerheuvel*, pp. 16–17, see also pp. 18–22. Cf. Sauneron et Yoyotte, I, p. 22.

troy all that I have made, and this land will return unto Nun, into the floodwaters, as (in) its first state".[1]

We see, then, that the Egyptians envisaged the primordial state ('the first time') as a watery chaos or waste. They designated this water as Nun (*nn(w)*), representing it generally in hieroglyphs as 𓏌𓏌𓏌𓇯𓈗.[2] These signs are significant. 𓏌, which had the phonetic value of *nw*, depicted a bowl for containing liquids; 𓇯 (*pt*) was an ideogram or a determinative sign representing the 'sky'; 𓈗 (*mw*) was an ideogram or a determinative signifying 'water'.[3] Of these signs 𓇯 alone presents a problem, since, as the 'sky', it would appear to oppose the idea of a watery deep such as the concept of Nun would seem to imply. However, since the sign is sometimes found inverted (𓇯), it may be intended to denote the idea, well attested in Egyptian cosmology, that water encircled the universe, above as well as below.[4] In later texts Nun, as meaning the inundation of the Nile, is also written as *nnj*, a word expressing the idea of inertness or stagnancy—possibly we have here a further indication of the concept, namely, that the primaeval waters were motionless and not like the flowing Nile.[5] We may note, too, that the verb used in the Osorkon inscription for the action of Nun, in producing the catastrophic flood there recorded, is *bšj*, which denotes the flowing forth of water from a cavern or well.[6] In this same inscription Nun is given the determinative sign of a divine being, thus indicating that it was both divinised and personified. The fact suggests a further problem: did the Egyptians originally think of the primaeval waters as merely the inert and featureless situation preceding the creation of the world, or did they conceive of it as an entity having creative potentiality, indeed being itself the principle of the demiurge or containing the as-yet unconscious demiurge? The *Pyramid Text*, cited above, in its extravagant declaration that the king was born (*mśj*)[7] in Nun,

[1] In *A.N.E.T.*, p. 9b (trans. J. A. Wilson).
[2] Cf. *Wb.* II, pp. 214–15.
[3] Cf. A. Gardiner, *Egyptian Grammar*, pp. 514(W24), 474(N1).
[4] Cf. *Wb.* II, p. 214, I(a). Cf. J. A. Wilson in *I.A.A.M.*, pp. 45–6; in *Before Philosophy*, pp. 54–5; Mercer, *Pyramid Texts*, IV, pp. 60–5, pl. VI.
[5] Cf. K. Sethe, *Amun und die Acht Urgötter von Hermopolis*, p. 74(145).
[6] Cf. *Wb.* I, p. 474. According to de Buck, *Oerheuvel*, p. 18, "Bšj is een gewone term voor het stijgen van den Nijl gedurende de overstrooming".
[7] On *mśj*, see page 64.

suggests that Nun was regarded as the original creative principle. In other texts of various periods Nun is referred to as the 'Ancient' and the 'Father of the gods', and is specifically described as the father or Atum or Re.[1] These latter titles, however, relate to a problem which we shall be obliged to discuss when we consider what may be described as the first event in the process of creation as imagined by the Egyptians. Before proceeding to that, there are two other ideas basic to Egyptian cosmogonic thought which we must first notice.

Pyramid Text 1040 a-d, as we have seen, contemplates a primaeval waste of waters, called Nun, existent before heaven and earth existed. The verb used here for 'exist' is *kheper* (*ḫpr*), which in the Egyptian language could be used with a subtle variety of meaning. It could mean 'to be born', 'to come into existence' or 'exist', 'to be existent', 'to become', 'to transform oneself', 'to manifest oneself (in some form)'. The substantive *kheperu* denoted either '(mode of) existence', 'manifestation', or 'transformation'. Where it was used in the sense of 'transform' or 'transformation',[2] it logically implied that the subject was already pre-existing. Accordingly, in the context of both *Pyramid Text* 1040 a-d and 1466 b-d, it would seem legitimate to speculate whether, when the heaven and the earth are described as not existing (*n ḫprt*), the underlying conception is that these two fundamental constituents of the universe were already existent in Nun before they took their forms of heaven and earth—the annual spectacle of the inundation would have provided the necessary imagery: the physical features of the Nile valley gradually emerge as the flood-waters recede.

The other idea, which we have to notice in this context, is closely related to the annual phenomenon of the subsidence of the inundation in Egypt. It first occurs in rather obscure form in two passages in the *Pyramid Texts*. In the one the god Atum is addressed: "Greeting to thee, Atum. Greeting to thee, Kheprer (*ḫpr(r)*), 'He who exists of himself'. Thou art high (*ḳ3*) in this thy name of 'Hill' (*ḳ33*)".[3] The

---

[1] Cf. Sethe, *Amun*, pp. 69–70(139), 75(146). See also the myth of the "Deliverance of Mankind from Destruction", in *A.N.E.T.*, p. 11a; *Book of the Dead*, chap. 17; cf. T. G. Allen, *The Egyptian Book of the Dead*, p. 88(52).

[2] Cf. *Wb.* III, pp. 260–66; K. Sethe, *Dramatische Texte zu altaegyptischen Mysterienspielen*, p. 47; Sauneron et Yoyotte, pp. 27–8.

[3] *Pyr.* 1587a–c (text in Sethe *P.T.*, II, p. 344: trans. Mercer, I, p. 246; Speleers, I, p. 99). Cf. Mercer, III, pp. 761–2. On the expression "He who exists of himself" see page 22, n. 3.

other passage also takes the form of an address to Atum: "Atum-Khepre, thou wert high (*ḳ3*) as (the) Hill (*ḳ33*). Thou didst appear as (the) *bn*-bird of the ben-stone in the House of the *bn*-bird in Heliopolis".[1] This strange identification of Atum with a hill is explained by the fact, which we shall have to discuss at some length presently, that several sanctuaries in Egypt claimed to possess or to be founded upon a hill of primaeval significance. Hermonthis, for example, which was the Upper Egyptian equivalent to the famous city of Heliopolis in Lower Egypt, claimed to be considered as the "high ground (*gb*) that grew out of Nun".[2] In other words, it was believed that out of the original waste of waters there first emerged a hillock or high piece of ground, which was consequently a place of unique significance in Egypt and with which various temples sought to identify their sites. So important was this primaeval hill in the process of creation that in our earliest source, as we have seen, Atum himself was actually equated with it.[3]

We see, then, in the earliest records of Egyptian thought that a primordial situation was imagined, in terms of the annual phenomenon of the inundation, as a featureless expanse of water. Inspired further by experience of the Nile's yearly behaviour, when, having submerged all low-lying land, the river gradually returns to its usual level, uncovering in turn the higher parts of the land, it would seem that the Egyptians conceived of the world, at the 'first time', as emerging from Nun and gradually assuming its form. In this process of *kheper* ('becoming'), some eminence would first have showed itself above the waters, thus acquiring the unique status of being the primaeval hill, the first spot of dry land amid the watery abyss. It was at this place that the divine creator, who had himself emerged from Nun, took his stand and began his work.[4]

That ancient Egyptian cosmogony should have been conditioned in this manner by the physical phenomena of the Nile Valley is

---

[1] *Pyr.* 1652a–b (text in Sethe, *P.T.*, II, p. 372: trans. Mercer, I, p. 253; Speleers, I, p. 102). Cf. Mercer, III, pp. 778–80. The *bn*-bird was the sacred bird of Heliopolis, and the ben-stone was an obelisk-like stone in the temple there. Cf. *Wb.* I, pp. 457, 458; Bonnet, *Reallexikon*, p. 100, *sub* 'Benben'.
[2] Cf. Sethe, *Amun*, p. 118(252).   [3] Cf. de Buck, *Oerheuvel*, pp. 23–34.
[4] Cf. de Buck, *Oerheuvel*, pp. 10–13; Bonnet, *Reallexikon*, pp. 847–8, *sub* 'Urhügel'; Sauneron et Yoyotte, pp. 35–6.

understandable; but, in view of our *a priori* considerations, it constitutes a problem. As we saw earlier, to conceive of the beginning of the world, or rather of his physical environment, would demand of man a considerable degree of abstract thinking, unless there was anything in that environment that graphically suggested such an idea. We have found evidence that the phenomena of the Nile's annual inundation provided the Egyptians with a suggestive imagery for conceiving of the creation, or rather, the emergence of the world. But we still have to enquire how such phenomena could alone have supplied the stimulus to such a conception. The inundation, it must be remembered, was an annual spectacle, and it never did cover the high desert lands to the east and west of the Nile Valley.[1] Consequently, it is difficult to see how the inundation itself would have caused the Egyptians to believe that once their familiar landscape of the river valley, and high plateaux that bounded it, had been completely submerged beneath an illimitable waste of water. The stimulus to use such imagery must surely have come from some factor of more practical concern, and it would seem that it was supplied by sacerdotal pretension. As we have already briefly noticed, the priesthoods of several Egyptian temples claimed that their particular sanctuary marked the site of the primaeval hill where the work of creation began. Of these rival claims it appears that the Heliopolitan was the oldest. Whether it was first invented gratuitously by the priests of Heliopolis or formulated to further the primacy of their shrine against differently based claims made for other temples, we do not know. Heliopolis was evidently a predynastic cult-centre of great prestige, since it succeeded in winning the patronage of the pharaohs of the fifth dynasty, although the royal line had not originated there.[2] Consequently it is likely that, in the early dynastic period, the priesthood of Heliopolis would have been concerned to maintain and

[1] The situation would, of course, be different in this respect in the flat lands of the Delta.

[2] Its Egyptian name was 'IWNW, the 'On' of the Bible; its Greek name commemorates, of course, its connection with the cult of the sun. Cf. Bonnet, *Reallexikon*, pp. 543–5, *sub* 'On'; K. Sethe, *Urgeschichte und älteste Religion der Ägypter*, pp. 87–116 (104–138); Gardiner, *Egypt of the Pharaohs*, pp. 84–6, 427. See also S. Schott, *Mythe und Mythenbildung im alten Aegypten*, pp. 10–20; J. Vandier, *La Religion égyptienne*, pp. 24–31. J. Spiegel, *Das Werden der altaegyptischen Hochkultur*, p. 177, seems to overlook the ecclesiastical factor.

extend the prestige of their shrine in the new order of things which came into being with the establishment of a centralised monarchical government. To this end it would have been natural to claim that their temple stood on the first habitable site that was established in the long process of draining the primaeval morass that Egypt once was. Translated into mythic terminology, this would be the spot where their god Atum, the creator of the other gods, had first appeared, and the phenomena of the inundation would supply the natural imagery of the myth.

If the conception of the emergence of the world may have originated thus, it must be noted that the conception itself concerns only the beginning of a process of creation. Accordingly, each of the great cult-centres of Egypt, besides claiming that it was the site of the creation, also propounded a cosmogonic system designed to establish or confirm its prestige. It is to the study of these systems that we must now turn.

The *Pyramid Texts*, despite their Heliopolitan redaction, contain no formal or systematic statement of the Heliopolitan doctrine of the creation. The fact possibly indicates that at the time of their compilation no challenge was being made to Atum's position on such grounds as was to be made by the priesthood of Memphis on behalf of their god Ptah, as we shall see.[1] Consequently in the *Pyramid Texts* there occur only brief references to Atum's creative activity; but they are very significant for their implications, and the crudity of their imagery attests their great antiquity. In a line (1652c) that follows the passage cited above about the primaeval hill (1652a-b),

---

[1] It is significant that in the few *Pyramid Texts* references to Ptah (449a, 560b, 566b, 1482c) no trace of polemic appears; Ptah is represented only as one among the many gods whose help is enlisted on behalf of the deceased king. It is difficult to see how Mercer is justified in assuming that in *Pyr.* 448a-b "Ptah is recognized as the father of the primaeval gods of Hermopolis and Heliopolis at this early period in the development of Memphite theology" (*op. cit.*, II, p. 210); it is significant that he has to add the word Ptah in brackets to his translation of 448a; it is not shown in Sethe's edition of the text, I, p. 232. In 449a Ptah appears to be referred to under the epithet of *nh(hi) nb rnpt*, i.e. 'the Eternal, lord of the years'; however, the identification is contested by M. Sandman-Holmberg (*The God Ptah*, pp. 68–69, 179, 181–2), who thinks that the title applies to Horus. Sethe, *Dramatische Texte*, p. 76, took the title as applying to Ptah, as does also J. Sainte Fare Garnot, *L'Hommage aux Dieux d'après les Textes des Pyramides*, p. 100, cf. p. 300. Cf. Sandman-Holmberg, pp. 23–4; Sethe, *Urgeschichte*, p. 93(112).

Atum's primordial character is also commemorated: "Thou didst spit out (*išš*) that which was as Shu. Thou didst vomit (*tfn*) that which was Tefnut".[1] In this strange statement we have what was evidently a very primitive attempt to describe what was considered to be the first necessary act in the process of creation. Shu was the god of the air. The identity of Tefnut is obscure; this female entity has been identified as the goddess of moisture or as the female counterpart of Shu.[2] There is, however, an alternative account of the production of these two primal beings. In this it is stated that, "Atum became as one who masturbates (*iwš'w*) in Heliopolis. He put his phallus in his hand, to excite desire. The son and the daughter were born, the brother and the sister: Shu and Tefnut" (1248a-d).[3] This crude imagery must be understood in its proper context, and there its significance is very great. It shows that, having conceived of Atum as 'he who exists himself',[4] emergent from the primaeval chaos of Nun, the primitive Heliopolitan thinkers were next faced with the problem of explaining how Atum began his work of creation. In the passages before us we see two attempts to represent Atum as the original and sole cause of the existence of a series of divine beings who personified the main constituents of the world. In the first passage quoted here an attempt has clearly been made to explain the origin of Shu and Tefnut by a piece of naïve etymological reasoning, based respectively on a similarity of sound between the verbs *išš* and *tfn* and the names of the deities. More significant is the other passage. It confirms what we had been led to infer from our *a priori* considerations, namely, that the primitive mind would naturally have thought of the beginning of things in terms of biological birth. Here we have the first literary evidence of that predisposition: given a pre-existent creator, Atum, the early Egyptians instinctively pictured

[1] Text in Sethe, II, p. 373: trans. Mercer, I, p. 253; Speleers, I, p. 102; Wilson in *A.N.E.T.*, p. 3a; Sauneron et Yoyotte, I, p. 46(3), see also *ib.* (5), pp. 47(7), 51; H. Kees, *Lesebuch*, p. 1 (2b). Cf. Garnot, pp. 204–5.

[2] Cf. Wilson, *ibid*, pp. 3a, n. 3, 6b, n. 7; Garnot, pp. 106–8; Bonnet, *Reallexikon*, pp. 770b–774a; S. Morenz, *Aegyptische Religion*, p. 170, n. 13; Sauneron et Yoyotte, I, p. 30.

[3] Text in Sethe, II, pp. 203–4; trans. Mercer, I, p. 206; Speleers, I, p. 82; Kees, *Lesebuch*, p. 1 (2a); Sauneron et Yoyotte, I, p. 46 (4), see also pp. 48–51. Cf. Mercer, III, p. 621.

[4] *Pyr.* 1587b: *ḫpr(r) dš.f*; see also pp. 25–6, 32–3. Cf. Garnot, pp. 192, 193; Bonnet, *Reallexikon*, p. 134, *sub* 'Chepre'.

his first act of creation as the bringing to birth of a primal pair, from whom would stem other beings. Atum's act of masturbation was, therefore, a logical necessity according to their mode of thinking; but it has for us a further significance—it not only shows that the male factor in generation was already understood: it indicates also that the male factor was regarded as decisive.[1]

The Heliopolitan cosmogony, as it finds expression in the *Pyramid Texts*, takes the form of a genealogical system comprising nine gods. The first five are clearly cosmic deities. They include Atum, the creator; Shu (the air) and Tefnut, these being Atum's immediate offspring; Geb (the earth) and Nut (the sky), the children of Shu and Tefnut.[2] The idea of biological generation is, accordingly, still operative, and an effective degree of abstract thinking has already been attained, in that the origin of the world is accounted for in terms of the successive appearance of the divine personifications of its major parts, i.e. Shu = air; Geb = earth; Nut = sky. The four remaining gods of the so-called Ennead of Heliopolis are Osiris and Isis, Set and Nephthys. These deities, however, had no distinctive cosmic associations; they belonged to a different cultic tradition which the Heliopolitan priests desired to incorporate, in a subordinate rôle, in their own theological system.[3]

So far as the evidence of the *Pyramid Texts* goes, it would appear that Heliopolitan cosmogonic thought did not concern itself with the origin of the celestial bodies, of vegetation, the animals or men.[4] As we have yet to see from our study of the Memphite cosmogony, there is reason for believing that the Heliopolitan system in the Old Kingdom period was more subtle or profound than the rather inci-

[1] On Atum's act Bonnet (*Reallexikon*, p. 865a) comments that to the Egyptian it was not an unnatural act, 'sondern ein Zeugungsakt, der durchaus mit seinen Vorstellungen über die Zeugung zusammengeht. Denn er wähnte das Kind in dem Samen des Mannes eingeschlossen; es entsteht nicht im Mutterschoss; er wäckst nur in ihm'. Cf. Kees, *Der Götterglaube im Alten Aegypten*, pp. 219–223.

[2] *Pyr.* 1655 a–b. Cf. Mercer, III, p. 781; B. van de Walle, 'L'Ennéade d'Heliopolis dans les Textes des Pyramides', Excursus II, in Mercer, IV; Bonnet, *Reallexikon*, pp. 521a–524, *sub* 'Neunheit'.

[3] Cf. Schott, pp. 21–2. See also H. Kees, 'Das Eindringen des Osiris in die Pyramidentexten', Excursus XXVII in Mercer, IV.

[4] The creation of animals and men is accounted for in later documents of the Heliopolitan tradition, cf. Sauneron et Yoyotte, I, pp. 51, 75; see also pp. 56–7.

dental reflections of it in the *Pyramid Texts* might lead us to suppose. In later texts various facets of the Heliopolitan system find expression, proving that it was a living, and undoubtedly a developing, tradition. The following extracts from the Papyrus Bremner-Rhind, a fourth-century B.C. document,[1] will serve to illustrate something of its later form, which preserved the crude imagery of earlier times alongside more sophisticated concepts: "The All-Lord said, after he had come into being: I am he who came into being as Khepre. When I had come into being, being (itself) came into being . . . I planned in my own heart, and there came into being a multitude of forms of beings, the forms of children and the forms of their children. I was the one who copulated with my fist, I masturbated with my hand. Then I spewed with my own mouth: I spat out what was Shu, and I sputtered out what was Tefnut. It was my father Nun who brought them up, and my Eye[2] followed after them since the ages when they were distant from me. After I had come into being as the sole god, there were three gods beside me. I came into being in this land, whereas Shu and Tefnut rejoiced in Nun, in which they were. They brought to me my Eye with them. After I had joined together my members, I wept over them. That is how men came into being from the tears which came forth from my Eye . . .[3] I came forth from the roots, and I created all creeping things and whatever lives among them. Then Shu and Tefnut brought forth Geb and Nut. Then Geb and Nut brought forth Osiris, Horus Khenti-en-irti, Seth, Isis, and Nephthys from the one body, one of them after another; and they brought forth their multitudes in this land".

Before we turn our attention to the cosmogony of Memphis, which will raise for us the question of the original nature of Atum, it will be well to notice the problem constituted by the relationship between Atum and Nun in the Heliopolitan tradition. The problem is made more difficult owing to the identification of Re, the sun-god, with Atum in the *Pyramid Texts*: they were originally two separate deities, so that attributes that might properly have characterised the one may

---

[1] Trans. J. A. Wilson in *A.N.E.T.*, p. 6a–b. Cf. Sauneron et Yoyotte, I, pp. 48–51; E. A. W. Budge, *From Fetish to God in Ancient Egypt*, pp. 140–3. The title translated 'The All-Lord', is *nb r dr*, which means 'lord to the limit', cf. Gardiner, *Grammar*, p. 79(100).

[2] The reference is a myth of the 'eye of Re', i.e. the sun, cf. Bonnet, *Reallexikon*, pp. 733b–735b, *sub* 'Sonnenauge'.   [3] See p. 56.

not necessarily be appropriate to the other or even to their combined form.[1]

Atum's identification or essential association with the primaeval hill in the *Pyramid Texts* suggests that it was believed that he had originally emerged from the primaeval waters of Nun. That suggestion is confirmed by passages in later texts. For example, in Chapter XVII of the *Book of the Dead*, which incorporates a tradition going back to the Middle Kingdom (*c.* 2000 B.C.), Atum is represented as declaring: "I am Atum when I was alone in Nun". A little further on in the same passage comes another declaration: "I am the great god who came into being by himself". This is followed by the question "Who is he?" The reply is: " 'The great god who came into being by himself' is water; he is Nun, the father of the gods".[2] In the text of a curious myth about the saving of mankind from destruction, inscribed on the walls of certain royal tombs at Thebes (14–12th cent. B.C.), there are a number of references and allusions which reflect a similar view of the relations of Re(Atum) and Nun. Thus Re is represented as saying to Nun: "O eldest god, in whom I came into being . . ." Nun answers: "My son Re, the god greater than he who made him . . ."[3] The witness of these statements is unequivocal: the Egyptians regarded the creator-god Atum (Re) as himself the creature of the preexisting Nun. This recognition, however, did not prevent them from describing Atum as "he who exists of himself", or from depicting him as saying: "Many were the beings which came forth, from my mouth, before heaven came into being, before earth came into being, before the ground and creeping things had been created in this place. I put some of them in Nun as weary ones, before I could find a place in which I might stand".[4] Indeed in this last passage it

---

[1] Cf. Bonnet, *Reallexikon*, pp. 71a–74b, 626a–627b; Schott, pp. 13–14; A. Erman, *Die Religion der Aegypter*, pp. 18, 21, 27; Kees, *Götterglaube*, pp. 215–6, 230.

[2] Trans. Wilson in *A.N.E.T.*, pp. 3b–4a; cf. Allen, *op. cit.*, p. 87; Sauneron et Yoyotte, I, p. 48 (11). A variant to the question 'Who is he?' in the text, reads 'He is Re'.

[3] Trans. Wilson in *A.N.E.T.*, p. 11a of. A. Erman, *Literature of the Ancient Egyptians*, p. 48.

[4] *Papyrus Bremner-Rhind* (xxvi, 21), trans. Wilson in *A.N.E.T.*, p. 6a. Cf. Sauneron et Yoyotte, I, p. 50. The reference to the 'weary ones', who are 'placed in Nun, probably arises from a play on the words concerned: *nnw*, weary ones', i.e. 'the dead'. See p. 49; cf. p. 63.

would seem that Atum was imagined as already occupied in his work of creation before emerging from Nun. Such an idea naturally leads us on to wonder how the Egyptians accounted for the fact that, after presumably existing in Nun, Atum at length was induced to emerge from it. Possibly the answer to these questions, which a rational interrogation of the Heliopolitan cosmogony inevitably raises, is to be found in the fact that, having envisaged the primordial state as a watery chaos, the Egyptians were often led by a natural disposition to personify it, so that from being the featureless chaos from which the creator-god, self-created, arose, Nun became in turn the father and creator of the demiurge himself.

It would seem that the Heliopolitan theologians, in their desire to establish the precedence of their own temple by identifying it with the primaeval hill, were thus led to envisage a primordial waste of waters from which that hill emerged. But there is reason for thinking that, in so doing, they set aside other primitive ideas about the origin of the world. According to their genealogical system, the priests of Heliopolis represented the earth-god Geb and the sky-goddess Nut as the grandchildren of their tutelary god Atum, thereby, of course, giving him precedence over them. However, certain titles assigned to Geb and Nut, and other references that occur in the *Pyramid Texts*, indicate that these deities were probably once connected with another cosmogonic tradition which the Heliopolitan priesthood re-adapted for their own purposes. Thus Geb is described as the "*r-pʿ(.t)* of the gods", "the lord (*nb*) of the whole land", and as the one "who has power of the Ennead and every (other) god".[1] Atum is, significantly, described as setting Geb over the Ennead (which includes himself).[2] In one place Geb is greeted as "the bull of Nut":[3] the epithet appears to connect him with the sky-goddess in a significant way. Thus Nut is not only called *mwt nṯrw* ('mother of the gods'), but also "she who bears (*mśśt*) Re each day".[4] Here it would seem that we have the vestiges of a very ancient myth, according to which the sun is thought to be born each day from the womb of the sky (goddess), who has

[1] *Pyr.* 1620a–1621b. Cf. Sethe, *Urgeschichte*, pp. 58–62 (71–74). *rpʿ(.t) nṯrw* means 'mouth (or 'spokesman') of the gods'; Schott, pp. 25–6; Bonnet, *Reallexikon*, p. 202a.
[2] *Pyr.* 1617a; cf. Garnot, p. 213.
[3] *Pyr.* 316a; *kȝ nwt* (text, Sethe I, p. 171). Cf. Garnot, pp. 112–13.
[4] *Pyr.* 1419a; 1688b. Cf. Garnot, pp. 114–5.

26

been impregnated by the earth (god). The existence of such a myth in later times is attested by both textual and iconographic evidence.[1] The conception would well accord with our *a priori* inferences that the phenomenon of biological birth would have conditioned primitive speculation about the origin of things. Observing the rise of the sun each day from the eastern horizon, the Egyptians naturally tended to think of it as issuing forth from the body of the sky-goddess, whom

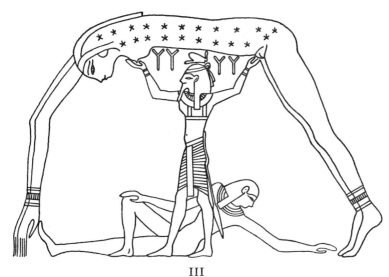

III

A representation, of the New Kingdom period, of Shu, the god of the air, raising Nut, the sky-goddess, from the embrace of the earth-god Geb. The celestial nature of Nut is indicated by the stars on her body; the four Y-shaped symbols depict the four supports of the heaven.

they pictured as bending in an arc over the earth. As it sank into the western horizon, they imagined it returning into the womb of Nut, to be born again on the morrow.[2] In one matter, however, the idea does not accord with our earlier conclusions: the mother-goddess here personifies not the earth but the sky. Indeed, in the comparative study of mythology, Egyptian thought presents an almost unique case by making the earth a male deity and the sky a female one. It is

[1] Cf. Bonnet, *Reallexikon*, pp. 536b–538a. For illustrations see *Bilderatlas zur Religionsgeschichte* (2.-4. Lieferung), Abb. 1, 3, 7, 19.

[2] Cf. *Pyr.* 748a–785a. Cf. Kees, Lesebuch, p. 24(31); Erman, *Religion*, pp. 18, 20. See *Bilderatlas*, Abb. 20. See also fig. IV.

difficult to follow what could have led the Egyptian mind to make this distinction. Possibly it arose from the customary position assumed in sexual intercourse: the earth-god Geb lying beneath his spouse, Nut, the sky-goddess.[1] A further aspect of this ancient myth finds expression in the *Coffin Texts* of the Middle Kingdom (2060–1788 B.C.); for

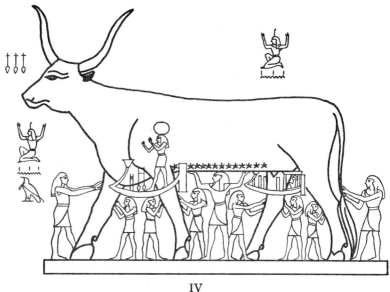

IV

In this scene, from the Tomb of Seti I (1318–1298 B.C.), Nut, the sky-goddess, is represented as a cow, across whose body the sun-god travels in his boat. Shu, the god of the air, is depicted supporting Nut, assisted by other deities.

Shu, the god of the air, is referred to as he who "raised Nut above him, Geb being at his feet".[2] The act finds graphic expression in later Egyptian art: Shu being shown as holding up Nut, whose body over-arches the recumbent Geb—the scene is, of course, symbolical also of the separation of the earth and the sky by the air.[3]

[1] See the representations of the impregnation of Isis by the dead Osiris in *H.G.R.*, I, p. 242.

[2] *C.T.* II, Spell 78a, p. 19 (ed. de Buck). Cf. Sauneron et Yoyotte, I, p. 47(9); Roeder, *Ae.R.T.B.*, III, pp. 378–9.

[3] Cf. *Bilderatlas*, Abb. 1, 2; *H.G.R.*, I, p. 237. On the idea of the separation of natural phenomena as an expression of creation see Morenz, *Aegypt. Rel.* pp. 182–3. See fig. III.

28

It would appear, therefore, that, prior to the compilation of the *Pyramid Texts*, in Egypt speculation about the origin of the world had probably developed already along two different, though perhaps not mutually contradictory, lines. The origin of the sun had been accounted for in biological imagery as the offspring of the earth and the sky. Further back beyond this event it was unlikely that speculation would have gone, since the constant aspect of the earth and sky suggests permanency, not change or a coming into existence. The other line of primitive speculation seems to have found expression in the concept of Nun, the primaeval chaos of waters, as the source of all existence—a concept, which, as we have seen, was suggested by the phenomenon of the river Nile's annual inundation. With another interpretation of this concept, designed to counter that of Heliopolis, we have yet to do; but, before turning our attention to it, we must consider the cosmogony of Memphis.

The foundation of the city of Memphis by the pharaoh Menes traditionally marks the union of the hitherto separate provinces of Upper and Lower Egypt under a common government. A new order was then inaugurated in Egypt which found historic expression in the commencement of the dynastic succession of the pharaohs, Dynasty I dating from about 3100 B.C.[1] Memphis, founded near to the apex of the Delta, was surely intended to be the royal capital of a united kingdom. But its political *raison d'être* was evidently regarded as not in itself sufficient to render the prestige of the new city superior to that of the older centres of the land. Religion was, accordingly, enlisted to reinforce and enhance its claims along two lines, namely, by exalting the local god of Memphis, Ptah, as the creator of the world, and by identifying Memphis as the place at which had been enacted the crucial episode in the legend of the god Osiris, who was associated with both the well-being of the royal house and the fertility of the land.[2]

[1] See p. 15, n. 2.
[2] Cf. Sethe, *Urgeschichte*, pp. 179, 180(217), 181–2(219), 182–4(221–2); *Dramatische Texte*, p. 5; Schott, p. 68; Bonnet, *Reallexikon*, pp. 446b–447b; W. B. Emery, *Archaic Egypt*, p. 122. R. Anthes in *M.A.W.*, pp. 63–4, rejects the idea that Memphite theology contained any anti-Heliopolitan polemic; but he does not deal with the evidence discussed below, and his view seems to be conditioned by his theory of the inverted order of the Heliopolitan genealogy of the gods; cf. *op. cit.*, pp. 35–43; *J.N.E.S.*, xviii, pp. 171–6.

Evidence of this undertaking, which was undoubtedly conducted by the priesthood who served the temple of Ptah at Memphis, has been preserved in a curious manner and by a happy chance. There came into the possession of the British Museum in the early part of last century a large black basalt stone, inscribed on one of its larger sides with an hieroglyphic text—unfortunately at some period in its long history a small portion of the centre was cut out to enable the stone to be used for the grinding of corn, with the result that some of the middle section of the inscription was eroded away. A succession of distinguished Egyptologists has worked on the task of deciphering the text, which is both obscure in its grammatical construction and in places badly damaged.[1] The inscription starts with an explanatory introduction which tells how the pharaoh Shabaka (716–695 B.C.) had found an ancient writing, in a worm-eaten condition, which is described rather cryptically as "unknown from beginning to end".[2] To ensure its preservation, Shabaka ordered its text to be copied, presumably on to the stone now preserved in the British Museum. It is recorded that his majesty "copied it anew, (so that) it is better than its state formerly, in order that his name might endure and his memorial be made to last in the House of his father Ptah-South-of-His-Wall in the course of eternity, . . ."[3] This statement would seem to imply that the work of preservation also included some restoration of the ancient text. To what extent this was so, and, whether in view of the earlier statement about the text's being "unknown from beginning to end", this meant that the scribes of Shabaka also interpreted the meaning of what to them was an obscure archaic text, so that it was 'better than its state formerly', constitutes a problem for our understanding of the document in its present form. The general con-

[1] Cf. Sethe, *Dramatische Texte*, pp. 1–5; H. Junker, *Die Götterlehre von Memphis*, pp. 3–4; J. H. Breasted, *The Dawn of Conscience*, pp. 29–33; Budge, *From Fetish to God*, pp. 261–4. See Plate I.

[2] Sethe, *Dramatische Texte*, p. 20, 1.2, p. 21(f): "Der Sinn dieses Satzes kann entweder sein, dass die Schrift bisher völlig unbekannt gewesen war, was zu der Auffindung passte, oder völlig unverständlich war; oder aber, dass sie nicht mehr ganz vorhanden (falls man *rḫ* 'gekannt werden' in dem modernen Sinne von 'da sein' gebrauchen konnte), oder nicht mehr ganz lesebar war, was beides zu den Lücken des Textes passte. Keinesfalls können die Wörte aber mit Erman so gedeutet werden, dass dem Texte Anfang und Ende fehlte".

[3] Sethe, *Dramatische Texte*, p. 20, 1.2, and p. 21(h)(i).

sensus of authoritative opinion is that the text in its original form probably dated from the earlier part of the Old Kingdom period, i.e. *circa* 2700 B.C.[1] Some independent corroboration of its content is forthcoming from a badly preserved fragment of a papyrus of the late Ptolemaic period, which appears to transmit the contents of a document of the 18th Dynasty concerned with interpreting the cosmogonies of Memphis and Hermopolis.[2]

The portion of the text of the so-called Shabaka Stone that particularly concerns us begins with a commemoration of the union of Upper and Lower Egypt: "Horus stood (as king) over the land. He it is who united this land, named with the great name 'Ta-tenen (*t3-ṯnn*), South-of-his-Wall, Lord of Eternity'. He is this Horus, who appears as king of Upper and Lower Egypt who united the Two Lands in the Wall Nome (i.e. Memphis), in the place where the Two Lands are united".[3] The key to the meaning of these lines lies in the expression 'Ta-tenen'. It was a title of Ptah, the god of Memphis, which may be translated as 'the land that raises itself' or 'the land arising'.[4] In other words, the claim is made here that Horus (the mythical prototype of the king), who united the two parts of Egypt, was Ptah, who in turn is the personification of the whole land which had emerged from the primaeval waters of Nun. Accordingly, the claim of Heliopolis, that it was the primaeval hill, is tacitly set aside by the lordly declaration that Ptah of Memphis is himself the whole land of Egypt which had come forth from Nun, and that he, in the person of the royal Horus, had made it a united realm.

The next significant passage comprises a list of deities who are stated to be manifestations or forms of Ptah:

1. 48   The gods who have (their) form in Ptah:
   49a   Ptah, who is upon the Great Throne . . .;
   50a   Ptah Nun, the Father, who [begot] Atum;

---

[1] Sethe, *Dramatische Texte*, pp. 2–5; Junker, *Die Götterlehre*, pp. 6–16.

[2] W. Ericksen u. S. Schott, *Fragmente memphitischer Theologie in demotischer Schrift*, pp. 10–11.

[3] Sethe, *Dramatische Texte*, p. 32, ll. 13c–14c. Cf. Wilson in *A.N.E.T.*, pp. 4b–5a.

[4] The epithet 'Ta-tenen' is rendered by Sethe as 'das sich (aus dem Urgewässer) erhebende Land', *Urgeschichte*, p. 183(222), see *Dramatische Texte*, pp. 32–5. Cf. Sandman-Holmberg. *The God Ptah*, pp. 19, 31–42; de Buck, *Oerheuvel*, pp. 49–62.

51a Ptah Naunet, the Mother, who bore Atum;
52a Ptah the Great (*wr*), who is the Heart and who is the Tongue of
the Ennead;
49b [Ptah] . . ., [. . . .] who gave birth (*mś*) to the gods;
50b [Ptah] . . ., [. . . .] who gave birth (*mś*) to the gods;
51b [Ptah] . . ., [. . . .];
52b [Ptah] . . ., [Nefer]tem at the nose of Re every day.[1]

The motive behind the composition of this curious catalogue of
equations is surely evident in the fact that it is Atum whose genealogical derivation is stated first. The Heliopolitan tradition of his
emergence from Nun (and from Naunet, the female counterpart of
Nun) is here interpreted in terms of birth, thus implying the in-
feriority or subordination of the creator-god of Heliopolis. This
innuendo is deepened and made more specific by identifying Nun and
his consort as forms (*ḥprw*) of Ptah, the god of Memphis. This claim
in turn makes Ptah logically the creator of all the gods of Egypt, a
claim that is specifically made later in the text (ll. 56, 58). Another
statement in this passage which calls for special comment is that in
l. 52a, where Ptah is described as 'the Great' (*wr*). The epithet is
repeated in a fuller or emphasised form further on in l. 54, where
Ptah is called 'the Great Mighty One' (*wr ʿ3*). As Professor Hermann
Junker has rightly declared, this epithet holds the key to the proper
understanding of the 'theological discourse' that commences with
l. 53.[2] For in the assertion in l. 52a that Ptah is 'the Great One', in
his rôle as the Heart and Tongue of the Ennead, a tacit admission
is in effect being made that this was an epithet of Atum, because, as
l. 53 shows, the Heart and the Tongue were interpreted as the form or
symbol (*ti.t*) of Atum. If this inference is justified, then it would in
turn follow that Atum of Heliopolis connoted a very profound theological concept, or that the Heliopolitan god was identified with a
more transcendent deity. There is evidence that among the Egyptians reference was often made to an anonymous 'Great God'
(*nṯr ʿ3*) or 'Great One' (*wr*), who is 'Lord' (*nb*).[3] Such an identifica-

---

[1] Sethe, *Dramatische Texte*, pp. 46–50; Junker, *Die Göttelehre*, pp. 16–20;
cf. Wilson in *A.N.E.T.*, p. 5a; Sandman-Holmeberg, p. 20. Sethe renders l.
48; *nṯr.w ḥpr.w m Pth* as 'Die Götter, die in Ptah Gestalt haben'. The *m*
could also be translated 'as'.

[2] *Op. cit.*, p. 25. For l. 53 see opposite on p. 33.

[3] Cf. Junker, *Die Götterlehre*, pp. 26–30; *Pyramidenzeit*, pp. 15–18.

tion or ascription calls into question the meaning of Atum's name (*itmw*). It is an enigma: it appears to be connected with some idea of 'completion'—in the *Coffin Texts* Atum is once described as 'the not-yet-Completed One, who will attain (completion)'—an epithet surely suggestive of great metaphysical profundity.[1] Accordingly, the possibility must be borne in mind, when considering the next section of the Memphite document, that we have to do with the statements intended to off-set or denigrate a rival theological system that was based upon more subtle concepts than might be inferred from the rather incidental evidence of the *Pyramid Texts*.

Leaving for later consideration the obscure station in l. 52b,[2] we come next to a section that appears to elaborate the claim made in l. 52a:

ll. 53–4

{ There came into existence something as (in) the Heart } as (in) the
{ There came into existence something as (in) the Tongue } form of Atum

It is the 'Great Mighty One', Ptah, who assigned [life to] all [the god]s

and their *ka's* through { this Heart by which Horus became } as (in)
{ this Tongue by which Thoth became }

Ptah.[3]

The esoteric imagery of these lines is admittedly difficult to interpret with any assurance of certainty. A clue is perhaps afforded by the fact that in Egyptian thought the heart connoted 'knowledge' (*śia*) and the tongue 'command' (*ḥw*).[4] Accordingly, l. 53 may be taken to mean that there came into existence the two essential factors for the subsequent work of creation, namely, the ability to conceive what was to be created (*śia*) and the ability to translate into fact what was conceived (*ḥw*). These powers, moreover, existed in the form or as the symbol (*m tỉ.t*) of Atum.[5] It is possible, therefore, in view of the

[1] *C.T.*, II, spell 141e, p. 174, ed. de Buck. Cf. Bonnet, *Reallexikon*, p. 71b; J. Černý, *Ancient Egyptian Religion*, p. 43; Morenz, *Aegyptische Religion*, p. 24; Junker, *Die Götterlehre*, pp. 32–7; Anthes in *J.N.E.S.*, xviii, pp. 209–10.
[2] See p. 50.
[3] Sethe, *Dramatische Texte*, pp. 50–4; Junker, *Die Götterlehre*, pp. 39–42; cf. Wilson in *A.N.E.T.*, p. 5a; Sauneron et Yoyotte, I, p. 63(22).
[4] Cf. Bonnet, *Reallexikon*, pp. 296b–297a, 318b–319b, 715b.
[5] *tỉ.t*: "das Wort bedeutet überall 'Bild', 'Abbild', 'Zeichen' und nichts anderes", Sethe, p. 51(b). "*Tj.t* ist überdies doch durchweg etwas Sichtbares, Greifbares, und es ist von vornherein bedenklich, einen Gedanken als *tj.t* zu bezeichnen.", Junker, *Die Götterlehre*, p. 41.

conscious reference that exists in this Memphite document to the theology of Heliopolis, that Atum's creative acts may also have been thought to involve the operation of 'knowledge' and 'command', despite the crude imagery employed to explain the creation of Shu and Tefnut in the *Pyramid Texts*. However that may be, the passage goes on to claim that Ptah, as 'the Great Mighty One', created the other gods by the exercise of these powers. In turn these powers are severally identified, as manifestations or emanations of Ptah, with two important gods of the Egyptian pantheon, namely Horus and Thoth.[1]

The next section of the text provides as great, if not a greater, problem of interpretation, and expert opinion is divided about its basic meaning. It can be legitimately translated, so that it reads as a continuation of the preceding lines, to the effect that Ptah operates as the heart and tongue in all living beings—gods, men and beasts. With equal reason the passage may be interpreted as a kind of commentary on the essential functions of the heart and tongue in every living creature. To the present writer this latter line of interpretation seems in the end to be the more probable, owing to the absence of any explicit mention of, or reference to, Ptah in the lines concerned. Indeed the passage has all the appearance of an interpolation into the true theme of the doctrine expounded here, and, as such, it may well represent an interpretative gloss inserted by those scribes of Shabaka, who in copying out the worm-eaten original sought thus to explain the obscure statements about the heart and tongue in the preceding verses. Interpreted in this manner, the passage may accordingly be rendered as follows:

(l. 54) Now, the heart and the tongue have power over all (the other) members, on account of the fact that the one is in every body, (and)

---

[1] Cf. Junker, *Die Götterlehre*, pp. 43–7. Junker (p. 45) thinks that l. 54 may be interpreted in two ways (a) that Horus and Thoth are respectively the heart and tongue (b) that the two gods come forth from the heart and tongue as thought and command. He prefers to render the pertinent words as 'hervorgekommen war (Horus; Thoth) als Ptah'. Sethe translates 'dieses Herz (Zunge) . . . in dem Horus (Thoth) geworden ist zu Ptah'. Wilson has 'through this heart (tongue), by which Horus (Thoth) became Ptah'. Sauneron and Yoyotte give 'par ce coeur (cette langue) de qui le dieu Horus (Thot) est issu, en Ptah'. The original words concerned are: 'this heart (tongue) [space] *ḫpr n* (Horus: Thoth) *im.f m ptḥ*. Cf. P. Boylan, *Thoth*, pp. 110–115.

The Shabaka Stone, now in the British Museum, on which is recorded the creation of the world by Ptah. At a later date the monument was used as a nether millstone for grinding corn: hence the damage to the centre of the inscription. (See pp. 30-1.)

PLATE I

Ptah, the Creator God of Memphis. A bronze statuette dating from about 600 B.C. (Manchester Museum, on loan from Reading Museum.)

PLATE II

the other is in every mouth of all the gods, of all men, all cattle, all reptiles, and (all else) that lives—the one conceiving, (and) the other decreeing that which is willed.[1]

If our interpretation of the foregoing passage is correct, then we return to the theme proper of the Memphite teaching in the next lines (55–6), where Ptah once more clearly holds the stage:

ll. 55–6 His (Ptah's) Ennead is before him as teeth and lips, (being) the semen and the hands of Atum. The Ennead of Atum indeed came into being through the semen and the fingers of Atum. But the Ennead (of Ptah) is the teeth and lips in this mouth, which pronounced the name of all things, from whom came forth Shu and Tefnut who created (*msj*) the Ennead.[2]

Once more the Memphite theologians draw a comparison between their own god and Atum of Heliopolis, designed to assert the superiority of Ptah. It is impossible to follow the logic of the comparison in all its parts. For example, while Ptah's Ennead is equated as teeth and lips with the semen and hands of Atum, Atum's Ennead is the product of his (Atum's) semen and hands (fingers). Next, Ptah's Ennead is represented as part of his mouth by which the creation was effected, presumably by the utterance of the (magical) name of each entity that was brought into being. It is, moreover, strange that in this account of Ptah's creative utterance no reference is made to the 'knowledge' and 'command', hypostatised as Horus and Thoth, which were the subject of attention in ll. 53–4. Then, it is, by implication, the Ennead of Ptah that produces the Ennead of Atum, through Shu

[1] This rendering follows Junker, *Die Götterlehre*, pp. 48–54, accepting the force of his argument against Sethe's trans. (p. 55). Sethe gets his meaning by interpreting *wn.t.f* as referring to Ptah (in which he is followed by Kees, *Lesebuch*, p. 10 (4), and Wilson, *A.N.E.T.*, p. 5a). Sauneron and Yoyotte (p. 63) is in line with Junker's interpretation.

[2] Sethe, *Dramatische Texte*, pp. 57–9; Junker, *Die Götterlehre*, pp. 55–8; cf. Wilson, *ibid*; Sauneron et Yoyotte, *ibid*. Sethe connects the words *msj-n pśd.t* ('created the Ennead') with the next line. The other three translations, to which reference is made here, take the words as logically connected with the preceding line and as referring immediately to the creative work of Ptah's Ennead (cf. Junker, p. 58). The present writer can see no reason why the words do not refer to Shu and Tefnut, especially since in their case *im.f* has been inserted to make clear that the agent of their creation is the Ennead of Ptah. It should be noted that the word *mtw.t* ('semen') used in the context of this passage probably represents our earliest evidence of man's knowledge of the function of this substance in the process of procreation.

35

and Tefnut. Accordingly, it may be asked, what comprises the Ennead of Ptah, seeing that it is equated with the semen and hands of Atum which produced the Ennead of Atum? In view of the antiquity of the text and the uncertainty of our knowledge of its grammar, it would clearly be unwise to press such questions or to try to fabricate a logically coherent exposition of the Memphite claim. What seems to be tolerably certain is that Ptah's act of creation by pronouncing the name of each thing is presented as attesting his superiority to Atum in his creative action. But it must be noted that this superiority is not being based, as would seem proper to us, on moral grounds. There is no condemnation implied here of Atum's creative act of masturbation—indeed, to the contrary, the teeth and lips which constitute the organ of Ptah's creative utterance are actually equated with the semen and hands of Atum.[1] Therefore it would seem that, as in ll. 53–4, Ptah is depicted as creating through 'knowledge' and 'command', which are symbols of Atum, so here he subsumes Atum's creative act in the prior activity of uttering the name of that which is to be created—for knowledge of the name connotes the power to conceive that which is named.

The following verse seems to be another interpolated commentary similar to that in l. 54; it serves to illustrate Egyptian psychology in this connection:

The eyes see, the ears hear, the nose breathes. They inform the heart. It is that which causes all knowledge to come forth; it is the tongue that repeats what the heart has thought.[2]

A return to the theme of the original document seems to be made in the ll. 56–7:

So were all the gods created and his (Ptah's) Ennead completed. Every utterance of the god (*md.w.ntr*) truly came into being through that which was conceived by the Heart and commanded by the Tongue.—Thus were also the ka's (*k3w*) created and the *hemsut* (*ḥmwś.wt*) determined, which produce all nourishment and food through this utterance (*md.t*), which the Heart conceived and the Tongue commanded [and justice was given to him] who does what is loved, [and injustice was given to him] who does

[1] Cf. Junker, *Götterlehre*, p. 56: see n. 1, p. 23 above. In process of time the creative hand of Atum was personified as a goddess; cf. Sauneron et Yoyotte, I, p. 82 (n. 48).

[2] Junker, *Götterlehre*, pp. 58–9; cf. Wilson, *ibid*; Sauneron et Yoyotte, *ibid*. See Sethe, *Dramatische Texte*, pp. 59–60 and pp. 34–5 above.

what is hated—So life is given to the peaceful, and death is given to the transgressor [through this utterance which the Heart conceived and the Tongue commanded].[1]

According to this passage, a further stage in the process of creation is envisaged. The theme of divine creation, as the transformation into concrete reality of that which Ptah had conceived in his mind (heart), is now extended to account for the existence of the essential bases of life (according to Egyptian ideas) of both gods and men and to the establishment of an ethical order and its consequences.

It is time for us now to look at this idea of creation by divine word more closely, especially since it has an apparent significance for the study of the later Hebrew account of creation by divine *fiat* in *Genesis* i. In terms of Egyptian thought the idea may derive from two different, though not necessarily contradictory, sources. As is well known, belief in and the practice of magic constituted a factor of immense importance in almost all departments of Egyptian life, and particularly in those connected with religion.[2] To know the right magical formula appropriate to each contingency, either in this world or the next, and duly to pronounce it would bring one safely through all perils and achieve a blessed destiny. One of the greatest claims to respect that a man could make was that he was one 'whose mouth knows', i.e. the correct spell or incantation.[3] And what was practised by men was practised even more effectively by the gods. Indeed magic itself, '*Hike*', was personified, and there actually exists a hymn in which Hike proclaims itself as 'the son of the supreme creator': "I am he who gave life to the Ennead (of Atum); I am the one 'he wills, so he does', the Father of the gods, with the high status proper to a god, as the Creator commanded, a venerable god, who speaks with his mouth . . ."[4] This text is indeed of crucial importance for us,

[1] Junker, *Götterlehre*, pp. 59–61; cf. Wilson, *A.N.E.T.*, p. 5b; Sauneron et Yoyotte, I, p. 64. Sethe, *Dramatische Texte*, p. 60, translates l. 56 as: 'Und so wurden alle Götter erschaffen, Atum und seine Götterneunheit', rendering thus *tm* as '*Itmw*, i.e. Atum. *tm* is given no divine determinative. *tm* here makes better sense as the verb 'to be complete'; cf. *Wb.* V, p. 303.
[2] Cf. Bonnet, *Reallexikon*, pp. 301a–302b ('Hike'), 875a–880b; A. H. Gardiner in *E.R.E.*, VIII, pp. 262a–269a.
[3] Cf. Sethe, *Urkunden des Alten Reichs*, I, 123, l. 13: *rḫ r.f.* Cf. J. H. Breasted, *Development of Religion and Thought in Ancient Egypt*, p. 169.
[4] From a text on a coffin of the Herakleopolitan period (2240–2060 B.C.) found at Assiût, in Kees, *Lesebuch*, p. 2(4).

because it not only attests the idea that creation was effected by magical utterance, but it also shows that Heliopolitan tradition taught that Atum had created in this way. The other possible source of inspiration of the concept of so potent a word of command in the Memphite document is that of the royal decree. It may be recalled that Ptah is identified as the unifier of the land with the royal god, Horus, and Horus is also equated with his heart.[1] Perhaps no distinct line of demarcation should be drawn between these two sources of derivation, since for the Egyptian the decree of the divine pharaoh would be charged with an authority and power little different from that of *hike*. But, whatever the magical content of the concept, we must be careful not to overlook the innate nobility of the concept. In this ancient Memphite text the acts of creation are not achieved only by the pronouncement of a magical formula. The utterance of the tongue of Ptah is preceded by the conceiving of his heart—in other words, the divine creator is not imagined as a magician reciting his spells; he is seen as one who first conceived in his mind that which should be created to form the world, and then brought it into being by pronouncing the necessary command for it to be.[2]

The creation of the *ka's* and the *hemsut*, to which reference is made in ll. 56–7, requires explanation. Both the terms, *ka* and *hemsut*, are fundamental to Egyptian psychology, but, probably because of it, they are very difficult to define in a manner intelligible to our notions. Briefly, it might be said that in their psychology or anthropology the Egyptians endeavoured to express their conviction that the individual's being consisted of other elements or factors apart from his body.[3] These elements or factors are non-corporeal; yet they cannot safely be described as non-material or spiritual in the generally accepted understanding of these terms. They are distinguished by a variety of names: among them the *ka* seems to have the widest connotation, and it possibly came into more general use. It was essentially connected with the idea of some vital principle or force upon which the existence of individual person absolutely

[1] See pp. 31, 33.

[2] Cf. Sethe, *Dramatische Texte*, pp. 60–1(b), 64(c); Junker, *Götterlehre*, pp. 71–5; Morenz, *Aegyptische Religion*, pp. 173–4; Wilson in *I.A.A.M.*, pp. 55–61, in *Before Philosophy*, pp. 65–70. For a Sumerian parallel see pp. 86–7.

[3] Cf. Brandon, *Man and his Destiny in the Great Religions*, pp. 39–45.

depended. It is often referred to as a kind of double which protected and nourished the individual's life. It was an entity possessed by gods as well as men. Indeed the sun-god Re is described as having either seven or fourteen *ka's*, which he mediates to his divine son, the pharaoh. When grouped in this manner, the *ka's* severally seem to represent various vital qualities which the Egyptians evidently regarded as essential to an effective and prosperous life.[1] The *hemsut* is an even more esoteric concept, and it seems to have formed a kind of female parallel to the *ka*, and, like it, to have been concerned with protection and well-being.[2] We may reasonably conclude, therefore, that the Memphite theologians, as they mapped out the process of creation, gave this degree of priority to the appearance of the *ka's* and the *hemsut*, since, according to their notions, these entities constituted the essential foundations of the life of human beings.

The next part of the passage under consideration clearly deals with an ethical issue. The translation given here has included the additions suggested by certain scholars to make the meaning of the lines concerned intelligible:[3] as the text stands, it seems that certain words must be missing—possibly their absence is due to lacunae in the damaged original from which the inscription was made. The appearance of such a topic as the divine establishment of a moral order and its consequences is notable, and it well accords with other evidence that witnesses to the early emergence of a moral sense among the ancient Egyptians.[4] The terminology employed is also notable, although it raises an interesting, but insoluble, problem. The statement that "life is given to the peaceful, and death is given to the transgressor" involves the use of two terms of great interest in a most significant context. Life (`nḫ) is decreed as the reward for virtue, and death (*mwt*) for evil. Are these terms to be understood in the sense

[1] Cf. Bonnet, *Reallexikon*, pp. 357–62 ('ka'); H. Kees, *Totenglauben und Jenseitsvorstellungen der alten Aegypter*, pp. 43–53; U. Schweitzer, *Das Wesen des Ka im Diesseits und Jenseits der alten Aegypter*, *passim*; H. Frankfort, *Kingship and the Gods*, pp. 61–78; J. Sainte Fair Garnot, 'L'Anthropologie de l'Égypte ancienne', in *Anthropologie religieuse*, pp. 17–20; Brandon, pp. 40–2.

[2] Cf. Sethe, *Dramatische Texte*, pp. 62–4; Bonnet, *Reallexikon*, pp. 286a–b.

[3] Cf. Sethe, *Dramatische Texte*, pp. 64–5.

[4] Cf. Bonnet, *Reallexikon*, pp. 430–434a ('Maat'); J. H. Breasted, *The Dawn of Conscience*, pp. 36–42, 128 ff.; Brandon, pp. 50 ff.; Bleeker in *R.H.P.R.*, 42 (1962), pp. 193–200.

that the evil-doer in this world is to be put to death? It could mean this; but, if so, a weak sort of comparison is made, in that, while vice brings death, the virtuous receives no other reward than that he goes on living. A more effective contrast is made, if the terms are taken to have a *post-mortem* reference. Then 'life' would mean 'eternal life' or 'new life', and death would be tantamount to annihilation.[1] If the passage is to be interpreted in this manner, it would constitute a most notable reinforcement to the evidence that seems to indicate that already in the Old Kingdom period belief was firmly established that the quality of a person's life in this world would decisively affect his *post-mortem* condition.[2] But it would be notable also in another way: it would mean that it was believed at this time that the evil person died a kind of second death or was annihilated, not tormented only in the next world.[3] Further, the passage raises an interesting question about the origin of death. As we have seen, the *Pyramid Texts* envisage a primordial age before death existed.[4] It would be interesting to know what the Memphite theologians understood here by death. It can scarcely be that they meant that death only came to the unjust, thereby implying that the righteous were immortal—we shall find this problem occurring again in Hebrew thought. If, on the other hand, we are to assume that death here is a kind of second death or annihilation in the next world, we are left with another problem—if the Memphite thinkers taught that this second death was thus decreed by Ptah as a punishment, how did they interpret physical death in this world?[5] Our modern logic causes us perhaps to ask questions here which would never have occurred to an ancient Egyptian. It must suffice, therefore, that we note the truly

---

[1] *ꜥnḫ* has a wide connotation: it was used of life after death, although with expression *ꜥnḫ m wḥm* was a more precise designation for 'to live again', Cf. *Wb.* I, p. 193.

[2] Cf. Brandon, *ibid.*, 'A Problem of the Osirian Judgment of the Dead', in *Numen*, V, pp. 110–127; J. Yoyotte in *Sources Orientales*, IV, pp. 21–36.

[3] Cf. E. Horning 'Die "Verurteilen" des aegyptischen Totengerichts'. On the idea of a 'second death' see J. Zandee, *Death as an Enemy*, pp. 186–8; Brandon, *Man and his Destiny*, p. 67, n. 5.

[4] See p. 16.

[5] Cf. C. E. Sander-Hansen, *Der Begriff des Todes bei den Aegyptern*, pp. 8–9, 28–9; Brandon, "The Personification of Death in Some Ancient Religions", in *B.J.R.L.*, vol. 43, pp. 318–322; *Man and his Destiny*, pp. 35, 66–7.

significant fact that already in Egyptian cosmogonic speculation the establishment of a moral order was envisaged and moral conduct seen as decisively affecting personal destiny.

The content of the next two verses (57–8) can be fairly interpreted as a continuation of the original Memphite theme: alternatively, it may be reasonably regarded as another interpolated commentary after the manner of the two that we have already noted, and which may come from those scribes of Shabaka who made their copy of the ancient worm-eaten writing 'better than its state formerly'. Whatever its origin, the passage is valuable in showing that it was thought proper to ascribe all human abilities and achievements to divine creation:

Thus were made all the works and all the arts, the activity of the hands, the going of the legs and the movement of all (other) limbs, according to this command, which the heart conceived and the tongue brought forth, which constitutes the essence of all things.[1]

The original theme of the document appears again in the next lines (58–9):

(So) it happened that Ptah was named, 'He who created all and caused the gods to be(*s̆pr*)'. He is verily Ta-tenen, who created (*ms̆j*) the gods. All things came forth from him; as food and nourishment, as offerings to the gods, as every good thing. So it was found and recognised that his power was greater than that of the (other) gods. Thus was Ptah satisfied, after he had made all things and every divine utterance.[2]

This comprehensive statement, so clearly presenting Ptah as the creator supreme of all, would seem to form an adequate conclusion to the Memphite thesis that Ptah is the source of all that exists, whether divine or human, including Atum, the venerable god of Heliopolis.

[1] Sethe, *Dramatische Texte*, pp. 65–6; Junker, *Götterlehre*, pp. 62–3; Cf. Sauneron et Yoyotte, I, p. 64; Wilson in *A.N.E.T.*, p. 5b.

[2] Junker, *Götterlehre*, pp. 63–5. Cf. Wilson, *ibid.*; Sauneron et Yoyotte, *ibid.* Sethe, *Dramatische Texte*, p. 66, translates the beginning of the passage as 'Es geschah, dass gesagt wurde "der den Atum machte (d.i. erzeugte), der die (anderen) Götter entstehen liess" von Ptah'. Sethe takes *tm*, as in l. 56 (see p. 37, n. 1) to mean Atum: again the text shows no determinative sign for a god. See Junker's discussion of the point (*ibid*). The expression *ḥtp ptḥ* ('Ptah was satisfied'), after his work of creation, is significant both in its meaning for Egyptian religious thought and for its anticipation of the divine contentment after creation in the Priestly creation legend in *Genesis* ii. 2–3.

The cosmogonic passage that follows accordingly constitutes a kind of anticlimax, which may be explained by again assuming the presence of another interpretative interpolation or glossary.[1] The passage, however, has a considerable interest for us, because it provides an apparent account of the origin of religion as the Egyptians saw it:

(ll. 59–61) He created the gods, he made the cities, he founded nomes, he set the gods in their cult-places, he established their offerings, he founded their shrines, he made their forms (*twt*) to satisfy their hearts. So the gods entered into their bodies (*ḏ.t*), (made) of (*m*) all kinds of wood, all kinds of mineral, all kinds of clay, and of every other thing which grows on him (i.e. Ptah Ta-tenen), in which they manifest themselves. So all the gods gathered themselves to him, even their *ka's*, satisfied and united with the Lord of the Two Lands.[2]

Thus the cosmogonic section of the Shabaka Stone ends. In the absence of a systematic presentation of the Heliopolitan cosmogony in the *Pyramid Texts* or in any other contemporary document, the Memphite inscription constitutes the most comprehensive statement that has come down to us of the earliest Egyptian attempts to account for the origin of things. For, as we have seen, by virtue of its intention to off-set the claims of Heliopolis, it incidentally provides us with invaluable information about the earlier doctrine that the world had been created by Atum. Whether the Memphite theologians are to be credited with a nobler conception of the method of divine creation than that of their Heliopolitan rivals or whether they were merely trying to ascribe a priority of action to Ptah by depicting his creative acts as the fiats of his mental conceptions, is an issue which we have already discussed. Here, however, we may go on to note that this Memphite cosmogony is distinguished also for the extension of its range of consideration beyond that of the creation of earth and

---

[1] Cf. Junker, *Götterlehre*, pp. 65–6, who thinks that in this passage there is a reversion to an archaic concept of Ptah as the 'lebenspendende Erde'. Cf. Sethe, *Dramatische Texte*, p. 68(a); Sandman-Holmberg, p. 23.

[2] Junker, *Götterlehre*, pp. 65–8. Cf. Wilson, *ibid*; Sauneron et Yoyotte, *ibid*. See also Sethe, *Dramatische Texte*, pp. 68–70, who renders the last part of the last line cited here as: 'Ḥtpj Ḫnmj war Herr der beiden Länder'. Sethe (p. 71c) maintains *ḥtp.j* and *ḥmn.j* are 'appellativische Namen des Ptah'; however, see Junker's case (pp. 67–8) for taking the words as an irregular form of the 3rd person plural masculine of the pseudo-participle.

heaven, to which apparently the Heliopolitan system was limited.[1] Mention is made of the creation of the basic principles of life and the establishment of a moral order. The origin of the other gods is stressed, and, whether it were in the original text or not, considerable attention is given to describing how the ritual service of the gods was instituted. But there is a curious silence about mankind: its existence is only implied in the provision made for food and the consequences of infringement of the moral order. Nothing specific is said of the creation of human beings, or for what purpose they existed. The absence of any reference to mankind in connection with the institution of the cultus is particularly significant, as we shall see by way of contrast with the Mesopotamian thought on the subject. Perhaps this almost total concern with the presentation of the creation of the gods by Ptah, and the arrangements which he made for their service, is to be explained by the obvious apologetical nature of the Memphite teaching *vis-à-vis* the doctrine of Heliopolis.

It would appear that in Upper Egypt, probably before the union of the two lands, there also existed a distinctive cosmogony centred on the city of Hermopolis, which at that time possibly enjoyed some temporary political prominence.[2] In later times the city became the cult-centre of Thoth, the god of wisdom, who held a place of considerable importance in Egyptian religious thought. But Hermopolis was associated from a remote period with a mysterious company of eight divine beings: so close indeed was the association that the city's Egyptian name was Chmunu (*ḫmn(w)*), meaning 'Eight', which is perpetuated in its modern name of el Aschmūnên.[3] Although numerous significant references are made to this Ogdoad throughout all periods of Egyptian history, there exists no formal statement of belief about them; however, the doctrine of creation with which they were connected can be effectively pieced together from many sources. Thus in a magical papyrus of the New Kingdom period (1580–1085 B.C.) the following incantation, despite its esoteric terminology, reveals some

[1] This is, of course, only an inference: the Heliopolitan system may have included the creation of mankind; see p. 57.

[2] Cf. Sethe, *Amun und die Acht Urgötter von Hermopolis*, pp. 41–(40);2 Spiegel, *Hochkultur*, pp. 185–9.

[3] Cf. G. Roeder, *Hermopolis*; pp. 24–5(26); Sethe, *Amun*, pp. 36–7(65–7); Bonnet, *Reallexikon*, pp. 293b–294b.

of the essential features of the Hermopolitan cosmogony: "O Egg of the water, source of the earth, product (eggshell) of the Eight, great in heaven and great in the underworld, dweller in the thicket, chief of the Isle of the lake of the Two Knives, I came forth with thee from the water; I came forth with thee from thy nest (thicket)".[1] Here we meet for the first time with an idea that occurs in the mythologies of some other peoples in later ages: it is that of the cosmic egg from which the demiurge or some other primaeval being emerged. The idea, though quaint to our minds, is one that would naturally occur to primitive thinkers, seeking for some first cause of creation. In conceiving of such a cosmic egg, the Egyptians seem already to have been puzzled by the question that has been asked so many times since then: who laid the first egg? The rather confused form of address, as well as the complex imagery, of the passage before us obscures its statement on this point. The incantation seems really to be addressed to the god Thoth, who was imagined in the form of an ibis bird—hence the reference to its habitation or nest in the reed-thicket, hence also the implication that this primaeval egg may have been originally associated with Thoth[2]. However, as we have noted, Thoth's associa-

[1] *Pap. mag. Harris*, Recto Col. VI, 10–12, in Kees, *Lesebuch*, p. 2(5); Sauneron et Yoyotte, I, pp. 60–1(18). The 'Isle of the lake of the Two Knives' was located at Hermopolis, cf. Roeder, *Hermopolis*, pp. 36–7; Sethe, *Amun*, pp. 79–80.

[2] Reference to the bird which laid the egg occurs in a *Coffin Text* (*C.T.*, III, spell 223, p. 208 (ed. de Buck). The bird and the egg are located at Hermopolis in the later *Book of the Dead*, cap. 59; "It is I who occupy that seat in the midst of Hermopolis. I watched over the egg of the Great Honker", trans. T. G. Allen, *op. cit.*, p. 135; see also cap. 56a. Geb seems in some way to have been connected with this egg according to cap. 54a of the *Book of the Dead*: since this deity is denoted in hieroglyphs by the figure of a goose, it has been thought that in an early form of the myth the primaeval egg was produced by the earth-god Geb. Morenz (*Aegypt. Rel.*, pp. 188–9) wonders whether Thoth was responsible for bringing the idea of the egg to Hermopolis, "wo sie (the idea) sich u. a. mit der dort heimischen Weltentstehungslehre um die acht Urgötter assoziieren konnte und wohin man später überhaupt auf jede Weise den Ursprung von Welt und Leben verlegte". According to a later transformation of legend, Thoth himself was thought to have originated from an egg (cf. Roeder, *Hermopolis*, pp. 165(c), 186(b). Cf. Bonnet, *Reallexikon*, pp. 162a–163b; Roeder, *Hermopolis*, pp. 37a, 186(44); Sauneron et Yoyotte, I, pp. 60 (17a–b), 61–2. For further identifications of the producer of the egg see pp. 53, 55, 64, n. 2. It should be noted that the word for egg in Egyptian (*śwḥ.t*) is feminine and is used to denote the seat of germinating life in the maternal womb; cf. *Wb.* IV, p. 73.

tion with Hermopolis was not so ancient as that of the Eight, and it appears that the text, despite its primary concern with Thoth, incorporates a tradition that connects the Eight with the cosmic egg, which is also significantly connected with the primordial waters. These intimations of the existence of some legend that associated Hermopolis with a cosmic egg produced by the mysterious Eight can be expanded by other instructive references of the later pharaonic period. Thus an inscription of king Nacht-nebôf of the thirtieth dynasty (378–341 B.C.) refers to the Eight as "the gods of the primaeval age of the hill", or as "the Great Ones of the primaeval age".[1] Next we may notice a statement contained in the tomb-inscription of a priest, Petosiris, who lived about 320 B.C.: "(Chmunu) the place at which Re arose in the beginning, when the earth was surrounded by the primaeval deep, the birth-place of all the gods who came into being since the time of Re, for all things took their origin in him".[2] To the evidence of this statement we may add that, bearing on the same theme, from two other sources. The first occurs in a salutation to the sun-god, dating from the New Kingdom period:

Thou art ascended on high, (coming forth) from the secret egg, as the child of the Eight![3]

Then from an inscription of the late sixth century B.C.:

... thy habitation, at the beginning, was the hillock of Hermopolis. Thou didst touch the earth in the Isle of the Two Knives. Thou didst raise thyself from the waters, out of the secret egg, with Amunet in attendance.[4]

From these scattered references we may, accordingly, make out the lineaments of a cosmogony which differs notably from those of Heliopolis and Memphis. It would appear that Hermopolis also claimed to be the site of the primaeval hill. Here the cosmic egg was produced by the eight mysterious beings, whose identity we have yet to investigate. This egg contained Re, the sun-god, who was to be the creator of the world.

We must now turn to consider the natures of the eight primordial

---

[1] Roeder, *Hermopolis*, p. 173 (12(b)). Cf. Sethe, *Amun*, pp. 47–8 (90–2).
[2] Cf. Sauneron et Yoyotte, I, p. 61(21); Kees, *Lesebuch*, p. 2(6).
[3] Ostracon in the Museum at Cairo, cf. Sauneron et Yoyotte, I, p. 61(19a).
[4] Sauneron et Yoyotte, I, p. 61(19b), cf. p. 80, n. 28.

beings of Hermopolis as they can be deduced from various sources.[1] This Ogdoad appears to have comprised four pairs of male and female counterparts, the latter arrangement clearly denoting a primitive mode of thought. The first pair consisted of Nun and Naunet, the female partner representing the heaven under the earth, conceived as arching itself over the watery deep.[2] The conception of a primaeval expanse of water, as we now know, was an old and well established tradition in Egypt. Some indication of its particular Hermopolitan form appears to be preserved in an inscription at Medinet Habu. There Nun is described as "the old god, who first existed (ḫpr), who created the earth as the first existent, who causes the Nile (mw) to arise": Naunet is "she who makes the Nile (mw), who creates the grain and causes the corn to arise".[3] The next pair, Huh and Hauhet, are difficult to interpret. Their names have the determinative sign for "water", but ḥḥ is also the word for eternity, in the sense of millions of years. Consequently, these beings seem to connote some idea of 'unending'—perhaps with reference to the unceasing and ever-expanding movement of water, or to the infinite nature of the primordial deep.[4] The third pair, Kuk and Kauket, appear to be personifications of the darkness which covered the primaeval waters before the creation of light, i.e. the emergence of the sun-god. They are also pictured in the guise of night as being the underlying cause of the daily rising and setting of the sun, and they represent that profound darkness in which the underworld of the dead is enfolded.[5] Amun and Amaunet constitute the fourth pair of the Ogdoad,[6] and they also constitute or rather Amun does, one of the most fascinating problems of ancient Egyptian religion. The name 'Amun' seems to be derived from a root imn meaning 'hidden'.[7] How such a condition or quality, personified as a member of the primaeval company of Hermopolis, should be interpreted is a problem. It would seem to con-

[1] Cf. Sethe, *Amun*, pp. 61–78 (120–154); Bonnet, *Reallexikon*, pp. 5a–6b ('Achtheit'); Roeder, *Hermopolis*, pp. 171–3 (11–12).

[2] Cf. Sethe, *Amun*, pp. 64(127), 74(145). See above p. 17.

[3] Sethe, *Amun*, p. 75(146).

[4] Cf. Sethe, *Amun*, pp. 64–5(128), 76(148).

[5] Cf. Sethe, *Amun*, pp. 65(129), 76(149).

[6] Cf. Sethe, *Amun*, pp. 66–8(131–135). The names of the fourth pair are sometimes given as Nia and Niat, which derive from a root meaning 'nothing' and appear to connote 'air'.

[7] Sethe, *Amun*, pp. 87–90(179–186). Cf. Bonnet, *Reallexikon*, pp. 31a–37a.

note some primordial function or activity which was hidden or invisible in its operation. A clue to its identification is possibly provided by the fact that Amun was later venerated as a god of air or breath.[1] As air in motion or wind, Amun as a member of the primaeval Eight might accordingly have represented some function of moving air that was essential to the process of creation. If Nun, the primaeval waters, was conceived as originally motionless, as we have seen, then motion had to be imparted to it before creation could begin. It would, therefore, seem reasonable to suppose that, if Amun did personify wind, he was conceived as such moving across Nun in the beginning to stir it into activity—to cause such eddies and convolutions in it, that from its depths the primaeval hill began to emerge.[2]

This company of eight primordial beings at Hermopolis appears, therefore, to represent a group of what might be regarded as elements or forces necessarily antecedent to the beginning of creation. With the exception of the last pair, they constitute what might naturally be imagined to have been the chief features of the primaeval chaos that preceded the creation of the world or cosmos. Nun would thus have been conceived as an infinite waste of waters, covered about with utter darkness. To the ancient Egyptian, thinking in terms of his own environmental experience, this conception of a motionless primaeval deep, invested in eternal night, would have presented the problem of explaining how the first land came to emerge from it. In other words, how was change to be introduced into that which was static? This, as we have seen, was the apparent function of the fourth pair. In the valley of the Nile, wind sets stagnant water into motion: hence motion must have been imparted in this manner to the motionless Nun to start that process of change, of which the first consequence was the emergence of the primaeval hill.

This primaeval hill may in the Hermopolitan cosmogony have had another connection with the Eight. In art these primaeval beings are

[1] Cf. Sethe, *Amun*, p. 52–3(101), 77–8(151–4), 90–108(187–230); Kees, *Götterglaube*, pp. 350–1, 352.

[2] Cf. Sethe, *Amun*, p 77(151). Sethe sees in Amun's creative activity an anticipatory parallel to that of the 'spirit of God' (רוּחַ אֱלֹהִים) in *Genesis* i. 1–2. Cf. Sethe, *ib.*, pp. 110–122(255–260); Morenz, *Aegypt. Rel.*, p. 186. See pp. 52–4, 147–8.

shown in a curious manner. For whereas the creator-gods of Heliopolis and Memphis are depicted in human form, the male members of this Ogdoad are given frogs' heads, and the female members the heads of serpents.[1] The significance of these forms may be explained by what the Greek historian Diodorus Siculus tells of Egyptian beliefs about the origin of life which were current when he visited the country in 59 B.C. He writes: "it is manifest that, when the world was first taking shape, the land of Egypt could better than any other have been the place where mankind came into being because of the well-tempered nature of its soil (τῆς γῆς εὐκράτου καθεστώσης); for even at the present time, while the soil of no other country generates any such things, in it alone certain living creatures may be seen coming into being in a marvellous fashion . . . During the inundations of Egypt the generation of forms of animal life can clearly be seen taking place in the pools which remain the longest; for, whenever the river has begun to recede and the sun has thoroughly dried the surface of the slime, living animals, they say, take shape, some of them fully formed, but some only half so and still actually united with the very earth".[2] Such a belief, which Diodorus met in his day, is likely to have been a long established tradition in Egypt. It may, accordingly, be reasonable to suppose that when the Egyptians represented the eight primaeval beings of Hermopolis in the forms of amphibian animals, as frogs and snakes, they imagined them as the first forms of life generated from the mud of the primaeval hill after its emergence from the waters. Although such a conception would in fact contradict that of the Eight as personifications of aspects of the primaeval chaos, this would constitute no serious difficulty for Egyptian mythology, as we have already sufficiently seen in other connections. On the other hand, the idea would well account for the fact that the Eight were evidently connected with the production of the cosmic egg at Hermopolis, out of which the sun-god came.

In later ages in Egypt it would seem that men came to look back on that 'first time' of the Eight as the Golden Age. Thus it is recorded: "The divine ones (ḏd.w) created the sun. Order was established in their time and truth (mȝꜥt) came forth from heaven in their days. It

[1] See *H.G.R.*, I, p. 248; Roeder, *Ae.R.T.B.*, I, p. 216, Abb. 33.
[2] *Diod. Sic.*, I, 10, 3 (Loeb Classical Library, ed. and tr. C. H. Oldfather, vol. i, pp. 34–7).

48

united itself with those who were on earth. The land was in abundance; bodies were full; there was no year of hunger in the Two Lands. Walls did not fall; thorns did not pierce in the time of the Primaeval Gods (*ntr.w p3w.t*)".[1] Another text tells: ". . . there was no unrighteousness in the land, no crocodile seized, no snake bit in the time of the First Gods".[2] After they had completed their work of creation, so it was believed, these eight primordial beings apparently died and returned to the underworld, where they continued to serve the world above by causing the Nile to flow and the sun to rise each day.[3]

Hermopolis must indeed have claimed to be the place *par excellence* in Egypt to which the pious should make pilgrimage. The priest Petosiris, a citizen of Hermopolis, in recording the work of restoration which he accomplished there on the temple buildings, provides an interesting commentary on the religious antiquities of the place: "I reserved a zone about the Great Pool, in order to prevent its being desecrated by the common people; for it is the place where Re was born in the 'First Time', when the earth was still engulfed in Nun. It is indeed the birth-place of all the gods who came into existence at the beginning; it is truly the site where every being was born . . ., for part of the (cosmic) Egg was buried in this place, and here were found all beings who came forth from the Egg".[4] It would seem that in a large park adjacent to the temple was a lake or pool, known by the curious appellation of *mr ds wi* ('the Sea of the Two Knives')—it was apparently large enough to permit the passage of a boat carrying the cult-image of Re, the sun-god, at festivals. In this lake was an island, called the 'Isle of Flames', which also marked the site of the primaeval hill—here was undoubtedly located the place where the sun-god was believed to have appeared for the first time.[5] From the fact that Petosiris refers to the preservation in the temple at Her-

---

[1] Sethe, *Amun*, Taf. IV (Theb. T. 90k), p. 63(125).

[2] Sethe, *Amun*, Taf. IV (Theb. T. 95k), p. 63(125).

[3] Cf. Sethe, *Amun*, pp. 53(102), also 44(87), 75(146–7). Their mortuary cult was celebrated to the west of Thebes, at Medinet Habu.

[4] Sauneron et Yoyotte, I, p. 61(21); cf. Roeder, *Hermopolis*, p. 186(c).

[5] Cf. Roeder, *Hermopolis*, pp. 36–7: 'Auf der Flammen-Insel stand eine Nilakazie (*šnd*), der heilige Baum des Hasen-Gaues (i.e. Hermopolis). In ihm mag man sich das Nest für das Ei gedacht haben, aus dem der Sonnengott entstand' (*ib.* p. 37(40)). Cf. de Buck, *Oerheuvel*, pp. 40–2.

mopolis of relics of the primordial egg, it would be reasonable to suppose that the Isle of Flames was shown to pilgrims as the site of the epiphany of the sun-god on his emergence from the primordial egg. It appears, however, that the sacred lake at Hermopolis was itself the location of another myth concerning the first appearance of the sun-god, who was also regarded as the creator of the world. In this myth the male members of the Eight seem to have been specially involved. The myth was apparently centred on a kind of primaeval lotus which arose out of the depths of Nun; on bursting into bloom, it revealed in its calix a beauteous child—the infant sun-god. No formal statement of the myth has been found, and it has to be reconstructed from various references and allusions of diverse origin. That it expressed a very ancient idea about the beginning of things is evident from the fact that in the *Pyramid Texts* the appearance of the resurrected king is likened to that of "Nefertem as the flower of the lotus at the nose of Re, when he comes forth from the horizon each day".[1] As we have already seen, in the Shabaka Stone inscription Ptah is significantly equated with "[Nefer]tem at the nose of Re every day".[2] This curious, but certainly poetical, idea, connecting the daily appearance of Re with the lotus-flower, is possibly to be explained as an imaginative comparison inspired by the fact that the flower of the lotus opens and closes each day with the rising and setting of the sun. Our earliest evidence of the association of this solar myth of the lotus with Hermopolis comes from an inscription on a statue dating from about the fourth century B.C.[3] It takes the form of an invocation of the sun-god, to heal a sick man, as "he who came forth from the lotus on the high mount and illumines the Two Lands with his eyes . . . Save this sick man, as thou didst save thyself from the four enemies who came against thee to the north of Hermopolis".[4] For fuller indications of the myth we must turn to

[1] *Pyr.* 266a (text in Sethe, I, p. 144; cf. Speleers, I, p. 22; Mercer, I, p. 76). Cf. Mercer, II, pp. 123–4.

[2] See p. 32. Nefertem seems to have been a personification of perfume, and, as such, was associated with the lotus. According to Morenz (S. Morenz u. J. Schubert, *Der Gott auf der Blume*, p. 22), 'Nefertem ist, streng genommen, nur der Duftgott. Der Urlotos aber ist nicht an ihm gebunden', cf. *ib.*, pp. 17–22. Cf. Bonnet, *Reallexikon*, pp. 508b–510b.

[3] Cf. E. Jelinková-Reymond, *Les Inscriptions de la statue guérisseuse de Djed-Her-le-Sauveur*, pp. 1–2.

[4] Jelinková-Reymond, pp. 42–3.

Scene from an Akkadian cylinder seal, showing the sun-god journeying in an animated boat, its prow having the form of a man who punts it. The scene is reminiscent of Enki's voyaging; see p. 73.

This scene, from an Akkadian cylinder-seal, appears to represent Ea (Enki) and Marduk. Ea is shown on the right enthroned in the Apsû, which is depicted by the encircling wavy lines. Marduk appears twice on the left, with the attributes of a sun-god. In the first position it would seem that he is represented as standing between the two halves of Ti'âmat, brandishing his weapon; in the second, he is shown ascending a mountain to salute Ea (see p. 100).

PLATE III

Scene, from an Akkadian cylinder-seal, of two deities fighting a seven-headed dragon. (See pp. 99, 120, 154.)

PLATE IV

certain liturgical texts of the Ptolemaic period (third-first cent. B.C.) which are concerned with the ritual offering to the sun-god of a jewelled replica of a lotus. (Rubric for offering the lotus): "Receive this god (who is) at the heart of his piece of water, which spouted from your body (O ye Eight!). The great lotus, come forth from the Great Pool, which inaugurated the light, in the First Time . . . You behold its light, you breathe its perfume, your nostrils are filled with it. It is your son, who produced himself as an infant, illuminating the land with his two eyes . . . I bring to you the lotus, come from the marsh-land, the eye of Re in person in his marsh-land, he who summed in himself the Ancestors; who created the Former Gods and made all that exists in this land . . . Opening his two eyes, he illumined the Two Lands, he separated night from day. The gods came forth from his mouth and mankind from his eyes. All things took their birth from him, the child (who shines) in the lotus and whose rays cause all beings to live".[1]

From this complex and esoteric imagery certain ideas may be discerned which are evidently connected with a myth about the epiphany of the sun-god at Hermopolis. The Eight appear in some way connected with the generation of a lotus, with which the sun-god is identified, from the sacred lake at Hermopolis.[2] The sun-god in turn is regarded as the creator of all beings, divine and human. That such a myth could be located at Hermopolis, where legend placed the primordial egg, from which the sun-god was born, need not astonish us by the illogicality of concept involved, for there is abundant evidence elsewhere, some of which we have seen, attesting the ability of the ancient Egyptians to hold together in their religious thinking ideas that are mutually contradictory.

This myth of the primaeval lotus must not, however, be despised because of the strangeness of its imagery; for it has a considerable

---

[1] Sauneron et Yoyotte, I, pp. 58-9(16b).

[2] Cf. Sauneron et Yoyotte, I, pp. 58-9 (15, 16a); Ericksen u. Schott, *Fragmente memphitischer Theologie*, pp. 56-60; Roeder, *Hermopolis*, p. 190(50). Morenz (*op. cit.*, pp. 75-6), thinks that the idea of the primaeval lotus originated at Herakleopolis and was in due course solarised, owing to the prestige of the sun-god. To him, 'Diese Kosmogonie ist einfach: Aus einer Urmaterie—Wasser oder Land—sposst eine Pflanze auf . . . Der Ursprung ist ein *Lebendiges*, Tier oder Pflanze, das am Anfang steht' (p. 73). Cf. Morenz, *Aegypt. Rel.*, pp. 188-9.

significance for our understanding of Egyptian cosmogonic speculation. Quite clearly the phenomenon of the lotus, which springs from the mud beneath the waters, and whose flowers respond to the daily movements of the sun, provided a pregnant image of the beginning of things. Its utilisation reveals two aspects of the mind of the ancient Egyptian. On the one hand, it attests his preoccupation with the problem of the origin of life. Environmental experience caused him to regard water as the source of fecundity: if life had first emerged from the primaeval deep of Nun, in what form had it appeared? Frogs and other amphibious creatures, seemingly generated from the Nile mud, suggested the eight primaeval beings of Hermopolis. An egg, deposited mysteriously on the first piece of land that had emerged from Nun, provided him with an image in terms of which to think of the first appearance of the sun-god. Then, the lotus, rising from the dark depths of the waters and rooted in the mud, touched his imagination as a symbol of emergent life—a symbol, moreover, curiously appropriate to the rhythm of the sun's daily movement. The adoption of this lotus symbol into cosmogonic speculation surely attests the essentially poetical strain in Egyptian thinking, and it should serve to remind us that the Egyptians sometimes used imagery which could be a subtle blend of elements, at once symbolic and poetic.

The elevation of Thebes in the New Kingdom period to be the political capital of the land, and the establishment of Amun, its patron deity, as the state god *par excellence*, had its repercussions in the sphere of cosmogony. As in earlier centuries, Heliopolis, Hermopolis and Memphis had each sought to increase its prestige by claiming that it was the focal point of creation and that its own divine patron was the creator of the world, so now Thebes began to advance similar claims. Being a late comer in the field, it was obliged to take account of the cosmogonies of its predecessors, and, if possible, incorporate them in its own system; for the disposition of the Egyptian was always to conserve, not to reject, the traditions of the past. This process was greatly assisted by the nature of Amun himself, for, as we have seen, in the Hermopolitan Ogdoad he seems to have personified the invisible and dynamic quality of wind. Accordingly, a cosmogony was developed at Thebes of a synthetical character, designed to represent Amun as the supreme embodiment of all the earlier creator deities. The following passages, taken from a papyrus dating from the time of Ramses II (*c.* 1301–1234 B.C.), contain a characteristic statement of this Theban doctrine.[1] In the first passage the intention to make Thebes the site of primaeval acts of creation is manifest: "Thebes (*wst*) is the pattern (*mtr*) to all other cities. The water and the land were in her at the First Time. Then came the sand to set the bounds to the fields and to create her foundation upon the hill. Thus the earth came into being. Then men came into being, in order to found every city in her true name. They were each denominated 'city' (as Thebes), and they were under the oversight of Thebes, the Eye of Re".[2] Amun is described as: "He it is who began with (the beginning of) existence, Amun, who came at the first into being, so that his form is not known. There is no other god who existed before him. There was no other god with him who might have told what was his form. He had no mother, to whom might have been ascribed his name. He had no father, who generated him and (so) could have said: 'it is I!' He formed his own egg, the mighty one of secret birth, who created his own beauty, the divine god who formed himself. All (other) gods came into being after he had himself made a beginning of being".[3] Another passage makes clear the primacy and the all-inclusive nature of Amun: "The Ogdoad (of Hermopolis) was the first of thy forms until thou didst complete those (other forms), for thou art the Unique One. Thy body is wholly hidden among the Great Ones. Thou art hidden as Amun at the head of the gods. Thou changest thy form into Ta-tanen (of Memphis), in order to bring forth the primaeval gods in thy first being as the Primaeval God. Exalted is thy beauty (phallus) as 'the steer of his mother' (Ka-mutef). Thou didst remove thyself as the dweller of heaven, in that thou abidest there as Re . . ."[4] Further aspects of this process of syncretism are found in a text inscribed on a temple at Karnak, dating from the time of Ptolemy VII (145–116 B.C.): "He created Ta-tenen, he made the Eight, he fabricated his own body as that of a holy child, who came forth from a lotus, in the

[1] Cf. Roeder, *Ae.R.T.B.*, I, pp. 276–282.

[2] *Leiden Papyrus* I 350 (Hymn 10), trans. Roeder, *op. cit.*, p. 287; Wilson in *A.N.E.T.*, p. 8a.

[3] Hymn 100, in Roeder, *op. cit.*, p. 295; Wilson, *A.N.E.T.*, p. 368b.

[4] Hymn 80, in Roeder, *op. cit.*, p. 293; Sauneron et Yoyotte, I, p. 68(c).

midst of Nun. He illumines the lands by his eyes. He made men, he created the gods. He organised the company of the Ennead; he instituted the members of the Ogdoad as his divine fathers and prophets (priests), with Shu as prophet-pastophoros, and Tefnut as Spouse of the God . . ." And a significant passage on Amun's work as the creator of the world: "The land was (still) in the depths of Nun. (Amun) stood thereon, and all the torpor which held it vanished, when he placed himself upon its face".[1]

The syncretistic tendency in Egyptian religion, motivated as it was both by an instinctive conservatism and sacerdotal ambition, tended to promote a henotheism, if not a true monotheism. The priesthoods of each great shrine proclaimed their own tutelar deity as the true form of a supreme universal god who manifested himself under other forms in other places. A classic expression of this theology occurs in the Leyden Papyrus I 350, from which a passage was quoted above: "Three are the gods in all: Amun, Re and Ptah, and there is no other beside them. 'He who conceals his name' is Amun, he is Re as to his face, and his body is Ptah. Their cities upon earth abide for ever: Thebes, Heliopolis and Memphis, unto eternity".[2] As we have already seen in the case of Amun, this syncretistic process had its repercussions in terms of cosmogonic speculation. An equally illuminating example, obviously emanating from Memphis, is found in a badly preserved Ptolemaic papyrus which probably records the text of an earlier (18th dynasty) document.[3] The relevant passages (as restored by the editors of the papyrus) reveal a most thorough-going eclecticism:

[Ptah found himself in the Primaeval Waters . . .
He sought a place for] his foot.
[The god sought a place for his foot in] the Primaeval Waters
because he had grown old. [. . .
He found], that a place was in [this land
There] came [he] forth from the Primaeval Waters. [. . .
He came to Heliopolis.
· · · · · · ·
· · · · · · ·

---

[1] Sauneron et Yoyotte, I, pp. 70–1(a, b).

[2] Hymn 300, in Roeder, *op. cit.*, p. 296; Wilson, *A.N.E.T.*, p. 369a.

[3] *Pap. demot. Berlin* 13603. Cf. Ericksen u. Schott, *Fragmente memphitischer Theologie*, pp. 10–11. See p. 31.

[There] said (he) 'Land' as the name of Memphis,
. . . .
He desired (himself) [gods,
in order . . . (and) to cause light to exist
and there came into existence the Eight.]
He [gave] four of them a snake's head.
[four of them the head of a frog,
and he gave them names:
Nun and Naunet, Heh and] Hehet,
Kek [and Keket, Niu and Nit.
. . .]
. . .
[. .
So they came into being in the Waters]
'Amun and Amaunet', as he named them another time.
. . .
They were united with those (the Eight),
to complete ten names.[1]

The text then goes on to tell how these (now) ten primordial beings carry out Ptah's wish and the sun-god (*pȝ 'Itm wr*) comes into existence.[2] Afterwards the Eight (*sic*) are settled by Ptah at Hermopolis, where on the great lake the lotus is produced in the form of the solar symbol.[3] This solar symbol (the scarab beetle) then transforms into a boy, from the tears of whose eyes mankind are formed.[4] Further on in the text Ptah is proclaimed as the creator of the Nile and of the corn (barley and emmer), whose growth depends on its fructifying stream.[5]

As we have made our survey of the creation legends associated with the four great cult-centres of ancient Egypt, it has become increasingly evident that interest in each instance has been concentrated on showing that the particular centre concerned should have precedence as being the place where the first acts of creation were accomplished. Now, it is undoubtedly due to the ecclesiastical motives involved that all these cosmogonies deal only with a distinctive pattern of such first acts, i.e. with the emergence of the first land from the primaeval waters, together with the divine creator(s), the creation

---

[1] Ericksen u. Schott, pp. 78–80, cf. p. 13.   [2] *Ibid.*, p. 80.
[3] *Ibid.*, pp. 80–1.   [4] *Ibid.*, p. 81.   [5] *Ibid.*, p. 84.

of the chief cosmic entities, namely, heaven and earth, and the sun.[1] This pattern may be slightly expanded at various places to include the origin of the moral order or the institution of the cultus or the provision made for food. The most remarkable omission from this cosmogonic pattern is the creation of mankind, whether in the sense of a number of human beings or of an original human couple as the progenitors of mankind. The fact that the existence of men is tacitly assumed in the Memphite system, as we have noticed, may indicate that, in terms of the priestly interests that produced these cosmogonies, the origin of mankind was irrelevant.

It is a meagre harvest that may be gathered from Egyptian literature concerning the origin and status of man in a world that was divinely created. We have already met, in the passage from the Ptolemaic papyrus extolling Ptah as the creator, an allusion to what appears to have been an ancient tradition about the origin of mankind.[2] It is based upon an extremely naïve piece of etymological reasoning, namely, that men (*rmt*) were first born of the tears (*n3 rmi.t*) of the sun-god, Re.[3] A nobler tradition of the origin of man and of his place in the scheme of divine providence is found in so-called *Instruction for King Meri-ka-re*, which undoubtedly dates from the second half of the third millennium B.C.[4] "Well directed are men, the cattle of the god. He (God) made heaven and earth according to their desire,

---

[1] In a recent article (*Ae.Z.*, Bd. 87, 1962, pp. 41–54), E.A.E. Jelinková has shown that in the Ptolemaic temple at Edfu two primaeval beings (the 'Shebtiu') were venerated as creator gods. Their first creative act was to provide a perch on the primaeval waters for a divine falcon; this act preceded the appearance of the primaeval hill. Dr. Jelinková believes that the myth is older than its record at Edfu, and she suggests that it had a pre-Memphite origin. These Edfu texts are generally very obscure and will require much further study before their significance may be confidently defined. See *J.E.A.*, 48 (1962), pp. 81–8.

[2] See p. 55; cf. p. 51.

[3] Other instances of this idea are to be found in various texts translated in *A.N.E.T.*, pp. 6b, 8a, 11a, 366b. Cf. Morenz, *Aegypt. Rel.*, p. 192.

[4] Cf. Erman, *Literature*, p. 75; Wilson in *A.N.E.T.*, p. 414b; Breasted, *Dawn of Conscience*, pp. 154–160. Reference might also be made here to the remarkable statement concerning divine providence found in a *Coffin Text* of the Middle Kingdom. The 'All-Lord' is represented as saying that he had created men as equals, that he was not responsible for human evil-doing, and that he had encouraged their service of the local gods: see Wilson in *A.N.E.T.*, pp. 7b–8a. Cf. Brandon, *Man and his Destiny*, p. 65, n.1.

and he repelled the water-monster.[1] He made the breath of life (for) their nostrils. They who have issued from his body are his images. He arises in heaven according to their desire. He made for them plants, animals, fowl, and fish to feed them. He slew his enemies and injured (even) his (own) children because they thought of making rebellion.[2] He makes the light of the day according to their desire, and he sails by in order to see them.[3] He has erected a shrine around them, and when they weep he hears. He made for them rulers (even) in the egg, a supporter to support the back of the disabled. He made for them magic as weapons to ward off what might happen or dreams by night as well as day. He has slain the treacherous of heart among them, as a man beats his son for his brother's sake. For the god knows every name".[4]

The simple, clear, but fundamentally noble, picture given in this passage of the divine providence for men is a refreshing change from the involved and esoteric imagery of the theological systems which we have reviewed. Its impression is the greater, too, since the document in which it is contained takes the form of advice given by an old king to his son during a period of political and social upheaval in Egypt. However, it would be unwise to conclude from the comparison that there was a definite hiatus in Egyptian life between religious doctrine and the practical philosophy of life. This *Instruction* itself witnesses to a firmly established belief in a *post-mortem* judgment by which the individual's eternal future will be determined,[5]

[1] This appears to be the only reference in Egyptian tradition that the creation was opposed by some hostile force. As we have seen, the primaeval water was regarded as static and not as a monster as was the Ti'âmat of the Babylonian cosmogony. In Egyptian mythology a huge serpent Apophis, probably a personification of darkness, was thought to oppose the sun-god on his nightly journey through the underworld (cf. Bonnet, *Reallexikon*, pp. 51b–53a). There is some late evidence of a belief in a 'Erdschopfer-Schlange', with which Amun was related (cf. Sethe, *Amun*, pp. 26–7 (38–40), 56–7(110)). Cf. R. T. Rundle Clark, *Myth and Symbol in Anc. Egypt*, pp. 50–1, 239–245.

[2] The reference here is to an ancient myth concerning a revolt of mankind against Re and the measures which the deity had finally to take to prevent the complete destruction of the human race. Cf. Erman, *Literature*, pp. 47–9; Wilson in *A.N.E.T.*, pp. 10b–11b; Brandon, *Man and his Destiny*, pp. 65–6.

[3] The sun-god, Re, was imagined as sailing each day in a boat through the heavens. See fig. IV.

[4] Trans. Wilson in *A.N.E.T.*, p. 417b. Cf. Erman, *Literature*, p. 83; Kees, *Lesebuch*, p. 44(73).

[5] Cf. Wilson, *ib.*, p. 415b; Brandon, p. 52.

and the very passage which we have been considering clearly shows the influence of the traditional solar theology. What we may perhaps more reasonably infer is that the outlook of the Egyptian was essentially religious, and that he believed himself to be the creature of a good God. Yet, when he sought in turn to explain the origin of that God, he was inevitably led on to imagine a primordial situation which could only be conceived in abstract or symbolical terms, and these were necessarily conditioned by his own experience of life as he knew it in the valley of the Nile. In Egypt, moreover, where only once, and then unsuccessfully, an attempt was made forcibly to unify religious belief and practice,[1] such speculation about the origins of things could not be a purely academic exercise. Those most capable of undertaking it were priests serving at some great sanctuary. This meant, as we have well seen, the development of a kind of competitive cosmogony: it also meant that, owing to the innate conservatism of the Egyptian, especially in matters of religion, a truly radical cosmogonic system could never be worked out which would present one deity only as the creator of the universe. Consequently, apart from the primitive form of the Heliopolitan cosmogony, the others are the essentially syncretistic systems which we have studied—systems compounded of both naïve and subtle imagery, and many mutually contradictory concepts.

Before leaving this subject of the creation of man and of the ordering of divine providence for him, we must notice two other very notable expressions of Egyptian belief in connection with it. The one occurs in the celebrated hymn which that remarkable pharaoh, Amen-hotep IV (Akhnaton), very probably himself composed in honour of the Aton, the form of the sun-god, whose worship he sought to make supreme in Egypt.[2] The passage concerned not only commemorates most vividly the divine action that brings into being each individual life; it reveals a belief, that divine providence is equally extended to all peoples, which was to remain unique for many long centuries in the ancient world. The Aton is being addressed:

---

[1] On the reformation of Amenhotep IV (Akhnaton), see Bonnet, *Reallexikon*, pp. 59b–71a ('Aton'); Roeder, *Ae.R.T.B.*, IV, pp. 23–112; Gardiner, *Egypt of the Pharaohs*, chap. ix; Brandon in *History Today*, xii (1962).

[2] See preceding note.

Creator of seed in women,
Thou who makest fluid into man,
Who maintainest the son in the womb of his mother,
Who soothest him with that which stills his weeping,
Thou nurse (even) in the womb,
Who givest breath to sustain all that he has made!
When he descends from the womb to *breathe*
On the day when he is born,
Thou openest his mouth completely,
Thou suppliest his necessities.
When the chick in the egg speaks within the shell,
Thou givest him breath within it to maintain him.
When thou hast made him his fulfilment within the egg, to break it,
He comes forth from the egg to speak at his completed (time);
He walks upon his legs when he comes forth from it.
. . . . . .

. . . . . .
The countries of Syria and Nubia, the *land* of Egypt,
Thou settest every man in his place,
Thou suppliest their necessities:
Everyone has his food, and his time of life is reckoned.
Their tongues are separate in speech,
And their natures as well;
Their skins are distinguished,
As thou distinguishest the foreign peoples.
Thou makest a Nile in the underworld,
Thou bringest it forth as thou desirest
To maintain the people (of Egypt)
According as thou hast made them for thyself,
. . . . .

. . . . .
All distant foreign countries, thou makest their life (also),
For thou has set a Nile in heaven,
That it may descend for them and make waves upon the mountains,
Like the great green sea,
To water their fields in their towns.
How effective they are, thy plans, O lord of eternity!
The Nile in heaven, it is for the foreign peoples
And for the beasts of every desert that go upon (their) feet;
(While the true) Nile comes from the underworld for Egypt.[1]

The other form in which the creation of man was depicted is of a
more mythical kind; it represents an old and well-established tradi-

[1] Trans. J. A. Wilson in *A.N.E.T.*, pp. 370a–371b. For other trans. see
Erman, *Literature*, pp. 289–291; Kees, *Lesebuch*, pp. 7–8.

tion. It is most graphically presented in a bas-relief commemorating the divine birth of king Amen-hotep III (1405–1370 B.C.) on a temple at Luxor.[1] Beneath a scene which depicts the conception of the infant pharaoh through the intercourse of the god Amun with the queen Mut-em-uia, another scene is clearly intended to show the consequence of the act, namely, the formation of the child prior to its birth. The ram-headed god Khnum is represented seated before a potter's wheel, on which he is fashioning the figures of two infants—the king and his *ka*. On the other side sits the goddess Hathor, who holds the *ankh*, the symbol of life, to the two children, evidently to animate them as their forms are completed by Khnum.[2] Another scene records the actual birth of the royal infant and his *ka*. This fashioning of the child, obviously in or for the womb, before birth, by a divine potter, was an idea not limited to royalty; it was invoked to illustrate the creation of every human person. Khnum was an ancient fertility god, associated with Elephantine;[3] the concept of him as a creator evidently goes back to the Old Kingdom, for in the *Pyramid Texts* the pharaoh is called the son of Khnum.[4] Of what substance Khnum was thought to mould his creatures is not revealed. The potter's wheel naturally suggests clay—according to the *Instruction of Amen-em-opet* (c. 7th–6th cent. B.C.) "man is clay and straw".[5] One is prompted to enquire also whether the appearance of the *ka* as well on the potter's wheel in the Luxor relief means that this mysterious entity was considered as being of the same material as the (body of?) individual then being formed. Khnum himself was never one of the great gods of Egypt, but in the Roman period (1st–2nd cent. A.D.) he was identified with Re and worshipped at Esna in Upper Egypt under the twofold aspect of the creator of the world and the divine potter who fashions living beings. In the inscriptions on the temple there Khnum is saluted:

---

[1] See *H.G.R.*, I, p. 257; A. M. Blackman, *Luxor and its Temples*, pp. 162–170. See fig. V.

[2] For another scene in which the goddess Hekt takes the place of Hathor, see Roeder, *Ae.R.T.B.*, II, Abb. 41.

[3] Cf. Bonnet, *Reallexikon*, pp. 135b–140a.

[4] *Pyr.* 1238a.

[5] *A.N.E.T.*, 424b (xxiv. 13). According to Sauneron, *Esna*, I, pp. 99–100, Khnum creates each organ of the body—he even "organisa une course du sang dans les os" (p. 100(a)).

Thou art the master of the wheel, who is pleased to model on the wheel,
the god beneficent, who orders the land,
who places in contact the seeds of the earth, . . .
Thou art the All-Mighty . . . and thou hast made men on the wheel,
thou has created (the gods),
thou hast modelled (both) the small and the great cattle,
thou hast formed *every thing* on thy wheel, each day,
in thy name of Khnum, the potter.[1]

As the ancient Egyptian contemplated his world, the black land of
the Nile valley and the deserts stretching eastward and westward,

V

The Egyptian conception of the creation of man. In this bas-relief from
Luxor, the ram-headed god Khnum creates the infant king, Amenhotep III,
and his *ka*, on his potter's wheel. The goddess Hathor animates them by
touching them with the *ankh*, the symbol of life.

[1] Sauneron et Yoyotte, I, p. 73(30). Cf. Kees, *Lesebuch*, pp. 19–20(25).
See Sauneron, *Esna*, I, pp. 69, 77, 79, 99–100, 113–14. On column B (time
of Domitian) the goddess Neith appears as the creatrix: "père des pères,
mère des mères, la mère du dieu qui créa les Huit Dieux, qui fit Rê, le
dieu qui n'a pas d'égal, à la suite de la Majesté de laquelle vinrent les premiers
des Antérieurs, et qui inaugura toute chose à l'origine", p. 65. On Neith see
Bonnet, *Reallexikon, sub nom.*

he believed, despite their apparent permanence, that once they had a beginning. When did he think that unique event had occurred? According to the texts, he called it the 'First Time' (*sp tpy*). The expression is an interesting one, because the essential meaning of *sp* is that of 'occasion', 'when something happened'; logically it implies the first event in a series.[1] It would clearly be unwise to press these distinctions, and to conclude that the Egyptians accordingly envisaged the original creation as the first event in a succession of acts of creation. The theological importance that was attached to showing that a specific deity was the first agent in the 'First Time', as we have seen, attests the fact that there was a unique quality about the *sp tpy*: we have also seen that it was regarded as a kind of 'Golden Age', thus implying rather a period than an occasion. However, it must be recognised that the Egyptians evidently regarded the daily rising of the sun not as an event essentially predetermined when the sun-god was created. The emergence of the sun each day above the eastern horizon was hailed as the victory of Re over the serpent Apophis which dwelt in the darkness of the underworld and unceasingly sought to prevent the sun-god's emergence therefrom to enlighten the world above.[2] Then, the annual phenomenon of the inundation was a recurrent reminder of the beginning of things—indeed in a sense the emergence of the flooded land, as the Nile returned to its bed each year, was a recreation of the world; moreover, there was always the threat, as the inscription of Osorkon III witnesses, that an abnormal inundation might renew the primaeval chaos of Nun.[3] Nevertheless, whatever may have been the degree of real anxiety felt by the Egyptian as he saw the sun set each evening or the flood-waters of the Nile arise each year, it is significant that in no New Year festival was an account of the creation ritually recited, as it was in Babylon when it was believed that the great god Marduk renewed the destiny of the state for the coming year.[4]

---

[1] Cf. *Wb.* III, pp. 436–8; Morenz, *Aegypt. Rel.*, pp. 174–6: 'Denn indem die Anfänglichkeit auf ein Geschehen eingeschränkt wird, bleibt Existenz ohne Geschehen vor der Schöpfung möglich. Es ist also das nicht nur ungeordnete, sondern auch träge Chaos denkbar' (p. 175).

[2] Cf. Morenz, p. 176; see n. 1., p. 57.

[3] See above p. 16. Cf. Sauneron et Yoyotte, I, pp. 77–8.

[4] According to Sauneron, *Esna*, I, p. 88, in a ritual concerning the creative activity of the goddess Neith reference was made to the birth of Apophis

This reference to Babylonian practice serves also to remind us of another notable feature of Egyptian cosmogonic thought. As we shall see when we come to study the Babylonian tradition, in this sister civilisation men thought primarily of the creation as the achievement of an awful struggle against the forces of primaeval chaos. In Egypt, however, such a conflict *motif* does not appear.[1] The primaeval deep of Nun may indeed fairly be regarded as chaos, in that it is boundless, featureless and enveloped in darkness. But, instead of being personified as a dragon of disorder that must be overcome before order can be established and creation begin, Nun is pictured as motionless and inert—motion has to be imparted to it before the process of creation can start. Further, in Egyptian thought Nun is generally regarded as a benevolent being; never as a fierce hostile monster as Ti'âmat, the Babylonian personification of primaeval chaos.[2] Undoubtedly the Egyptian concept here is framed in terms of the languid waters of the Nile's inundation, and it knows nothing of the turbulence of mighty rivers when in full spate.

The anticipatory reference which we have made to Babylonian cosmogony also suggests, by way of comparison, another notable feature of the Egyptian creation tradition. The material, of which heaven and earth are fashioned, is not taken out of the substance of Nun, as Marduk took the material for the Mesopotamian heaven and earth from the body of Ti'âmat.[3] Instead, either the original creator or creators dwell in Nun, apparently in an inert and unconscious manner, and from which they at length emerge to begin the work of creation, or Nun itself possesses the potentiality of producing creative emanations from itself.[4] Moreover, as we have seen, the favourite words employed in the cosmogonies to describe the origin of primaeval beings or deities are kheper (*ḫpr*) and *mśj*. The first term, as we noted, can be used with a variety of nuance to denote 'becoming' or 'coming into existence'—it is in fact a term of an amazing metaphysical content to have been employed at so early a stage in

as the principle of disorder; the text is very late (time of Trajan). At Esna also, at the festival on the 1st of Phamenoth the chief events of the creation were ritually commemorated, p. 117. Cf. Ph. Derchain in *R.H.R.*, CLXI (1962), pp. 188–95.

[1] As we shall see below, Sumerian cosmogony was like the Egyptian in this respect.   [2] See above pp. 17–18, 25 and pp. 97, 99–100 below.
     [3] See p. 100.   [4] Cf. Morenz, pp. 181, 184–5, 186–190.

Egyptian culture. *mšj* means essentially 'birth' in the sense of 'bringing forth' or 'producing',[1] and its use clearly witnesses to a concept of beginning which derives, as we have seen, from a very primitive tradition. The verb *irj* ('to do' or 'make')[2] seems to have been less frequently employed, at least in the earlier texts.

To form a proper estimate of the Egyptian *Weltanschauung*, we must bear in mind the fact that the cosmogonies with which we have been dealing are concerned only with accounting for the origin of certain great deities and the chief cosmic phenomena. They tell nothing, or almost nothing, of another group of deities who were associated with a myth of the profoundest concern to all Egyptians. This is the company of the Osirian gods, who, as we have noted, were very artificially included in the Heliopolitan Ennead as the great-grandchildren of Atum. The myth of Osiris, which told of his death at the hands of the evil Set and his subsequent resurrection and vindication, came to form the *rationale* of the Egyptian mortuary cultus and its influence permeated the whole of Egyptian life. By virtue of ritual assimilation to Osiris in death, every devotee believed that he would he raised to a new *post-mortem* life as the divine hero had been. Moreover, he believed that he, like Osiris, would have to face a judgment after death, and he trusted that he also would be declared *maa kheru* ('true of voice') by the awful judges.[3] This Osirian faith helped to make sense of life and death for the average Egyptian: as Osiris had suffered and yet had ultimately triumphed, so he trusted would he through Osiris. Death, therefore, seems to have formed no problem such as to cause him to question the divine providence. As we have seen, in his cosmogonic speculation the Egyptian never tried to account for the origin of death—he seems ever to have regarded it as caused by the intervention of some hostile force, as Osiris had been struck down by his enemy Set; and, as Osiris had ultimately triumphed, so he hoped would he.[4]

---

[1] *Wb.* II, pp. 137–8.

[2] *Wb.* I, pp. 108–9; *ir tȝ* ('der Weltschöpfer') is cited. On a palette of the nineteenth dynasty Ptah is described as he 'who created (*iri*) things that be and made that which exists, the Lord of Mankind, he who made (*iri*) the gods', Sandman-Holmberg, *The God Ptah*, p. 34, 10(32).

[3] Cf. Brandon, *Man and his Destiny*, pp. 35–9, 50–7.

[4] Cf. Brandon, in *B.J.R.L.*, 43(1961), pp. 318–322, 333–5; *Man and his Destiny*, pp. 66–7.

The legend of Osiris' death and resurrection, which sanctioned the funerary ritual, was not, however, only a parable or symbolic tale; quite clearly the Egyptians regarded it as the record of something that had actually happened in Egypt long ago. The *Turin Papyrus* and Manetho assign Osiris an early place in the succession of the gods who were believed first to have ruled in Egypt,[1] and the long circumstantial account which the Greek writer Diodorus Siculus gives of the exploits of Osiris were evidently derived from traditions which were current in the land when he visited it in the first century B.C.[2] Such traditions, fanciful though they admittedly are, have their significance for us; for they witness to the fact that the Egyptians must have endeavoured to work out a scheme of history from the creation in the 'First Time' to the beginning of the dynastic period. Manetho, a priest of Heliopolis who wrote a history of his people about the time of Ptolemy II (283–245 B.C.), apparently gave it four consequent divisions: the period of the gods, of the demi-gods, of the spirits of the dead, of the mortal kings who ruled down to the time of the invasion of Darius, the king of the Persians.[3] Although no evidence exists in the native sources, it would accordingly seem probable that in Egyptian tradition the story of the creation was not limited to explaining the origin of the world and of the gods: very probably legends existed, such as those concerning the Osirian gods, which accounted for the origins of many institutions and customs, both social and religious, after the manner of the so-called Primaeval History of the Yahwist writer in the book called *Genesis*.[4]

However that may be, the evidence that we have of ancient Egyptian cosmogonic speculation places it in a unique category in the history of human thought as one of the two earliest attempts by man to abstract himself from immersion in present experience, and to conceive of the world as having had a beginning, and to make a sustained intellectual effort to account for it.

[1] Cf. T. E. Peet, *C.A.H.*, I, p. 250; Manetho (Loeb Class. Lib., ed. W. G. Waddell), pp. 3–5.
[2] *Diod. Sic.*, I, 11, 13.4–15.6, 17.1–23.1.
[3] ed. Waddell, pp. 3 ff.
[4] See pp. 140 ff. On Osiris as creator cf. Reallexikon, 571.

CHAPTER THREE

MESOPOTAMIA: CREATION BY DIVINE INVENTION OR BY CONQUEST OF PRIMORDIAL CHAOS

OUR study of Egyptian cosmogonic thought has shown how profound can be the influence of geographical environment in suggesting and moulding speculation about the beginning of things. Accordingly, in turning now to consider the creation legends of ancient Mesopotamia, we may naturally expect that there too the factor of the physical environment must have played a decisive part. Moreover, since lower Mesopotamia, where the earliest civilised states were established, was dominated by the two great rivers, Euphrates and Tigris, thus paralleling the situation of Egypt in relation to the Nile, we might also reasonably expect that similarity of environment would find expression in a similarity of concept about the origin of the world. As we shall see, there is some similarity; but there are also some striking differences. Hitherto it would seem that scholars have been more impressed by the differences, which are also so very apparent between other aspects of Mesopotamian and Egyptian culture, and they have tended to explain them by emphasising the differences of physical environment between the two lands.[1] Thus, while admitting the significance of the fact that these two earliest centres of civilised living were established in the area of great rivers, they go on to point out the differing characteristics of the Nile and the great Mesopotamian rivers. The Nile, it is stressed, is generally an orderly river and its annual inundation is a gradual process; on the other hand, the Tigris and Euphrates are turbulent, and, when in spate, can cause sudden and widespread destruction. To the Mesopotamians, therefore, it is argued, water was a fierce, incalculable and

[1] E.g. T. Jacobsen in *I.A.A.M.*, pp. 125–8, in *Before Philosophy*, pp. 137–40; H. Frankfort, *The Birth of Civilization in the Near East*, pp. 51–2. Cf. Brandon, *Man and his Destiny in the Great Religions*, pp. 70–1, 103–5.

destructive monster, and, as evidence of this, the great Babylonian Creation Epic, the so-called *Enuma elish*, can be cited in apparent confirmation. The thesis is a serious one, and we shall have to consider it carefully when we come to discuss the significance of the *Enuma elish*. But first we must notice the equally important fact that in the earliest examples of Mesopotamian cosmogonic thought, while water is indeed a primordial factor in the process of creation, it is not envisaged as a fierce and destructive element.

Every study of Mesopotamian culture and civilisation quickly runs into the problem of the racial origins of the earliest inhabitants of lower Mesopotamia, and we cannot avoid the issue in seeking to evaluate Mesopotamian cosmogony. The area around the northern end of the Persian Gulf, where the earliest civilised centres were established, was known as Sumer, and its inhabitants are accordingly denominated Sumerians. Although there is no decisive physiological evidence to prove that they were racially different from their Semite neighbours of Akkad, which lay to the north, these Sumerians had a language that was fundamentally different from the Akkadian tongue, which belonged essentially to the Semitic group of languages.[1] Whether the Sumerians were indigenous to the area of the Tigris-Euphrates delta or were migrants from elsewhere has been much debated, without definitive demonstration either way, although it would seem that opinion rather inclines in favour of their being migrants.[2] However that may be, there is general agreement that the foundations of Mesopotamian culture were laid by the Sumerians. This is particularly to be seen in the matter of religion: the Sumerian pantheon continued to be accepted and venerated by the Babylonians and the Assyrians, with their respective local or national deities worked into the system, the Sumerian tongue remained traditional for liturgical recitation, and Sumerian ritual practice constituted the accepted pattern of worship. This foundational quality of Sumerian thought and practice accordingly invests the Sumerian cosmogonic legends with a peculiar significance, and it renders any important deviation from its general tradition the more notable.

---

[1] Cf. Frankfort, p. 50, n. 1; G. R. Driver, *Semitic Writing*, pp. 1–3, 5, 7–8.
[2] Cf. V. G. Childe, *New Light on the Most Ancient East*, pp. 104, 114–15; Frankfort, pp. 47, 48 and n. 1; S. N. Kramer, *From the Tablets of Sumer*, pp. 238–48. See also A. Parrot, *Archéologie mésopotamienne*, pp. 138–40.

That there was a general tradition of Sumerian cosmogony might at first sight appear questionable; for, when we survey the exceeding variety of legends dealing with the origin of things that have been recovered, invariably in a fragmentary condition, from the clay tablets of Sumer, it would seem that there was no common pattern in the Sumerian thought on this subject. However, on closer consideration there does appear to be reason for thinking that water was regarded as the primordial substance out of which the world emerged or was created. Professor S. N. Kramer, whose devoted work of decipherment and interpretation is steadily revealing the rich content of Sumerian mythology, has pointed out that the name of the comparatively obscure goddess Nammu is written in a list of Sumerian gods with the ideogram for 'sea' and given the epithet *ama-tu-an-ki*, "the mother who gave birth to heaven and earth"; in another text she is described as "the mother, the ancestress, who gave birth to all the gods".[1] This evidence is important, but its significance is confused by the apparent contradiction implicit in a number of other factors. For example, it is understandable that the early inhabitants of Sumer should have been impressed by the sea, which they saw extending away in a vast arc from the shores of what is now the Persian Gulf. However, their cities were not actually built on these shores, but on the plain lying a little inland that was intersected by the Euphrates and its various branches.[2] It would seem, accordingly, that the Sumerians would have been more closely associated with the spectacle of water in the form of a river than as the sea. That the Euphrates was recognised as a creative entity is attested by an incantation, probably connected with some purificatory ritual and apparently of Babylonian origin, in which the river is addressed as: 'thou river, (thou) creator of all things!'[3] However, from what follows in this text and from the general witness of other evidence, it is certain

[1] *Sumerian Mythology*, pp. 39, 114, n.41. Cf. C.-F. Jean, *La Religion sumérienne*, pp. 134, 220, n. 2, 5. T. Jacobsen in *J.N.E.S.*, 5 (1946), p. 139, disputes the identification of Nammu with the sea: "Nammu is ... the 'watery deep' of the Mesopotamian marshes extending below the surface of the earth, as the water-bearing strata."

[2] Cf. L. Delaporte, *La Mésopotamie*, pp. 11–13; S. H. Langdon in *C.A.H.*, I, pp. 356–60, and Map 9, p. 400. For the exception constituted by Eridu see p. 72. See H. W. F. Saggs, *The Greatness that was Babylon*, pp. 14–15.

[3] In L. W. King, *The Seven Tablets of Creation*, I, p. 129. Cf. A. Heidel, *The Babylonian Genesis*, pp. 74–5.

that neither the Euphrates nor the Tigris, vital though they were to Mesopotamian economy, were identified as the primordial creatrix, the embodiment of the original source of the life-giving waters. We are perhaps helped in understanding the nature of this primordial creatrix by a statement that occurs in what appears to be a commentary on the ritual of the Babylonian New Year festival. The passage concerned deals with Ti'âmat, who appears in the *Enuma elish* as the personification of the deep of the salt waters and with whom we shall be much involved when we come to consider the great Babylonian Epic of the Creation. What concerns us now is the statement in this commentary, *apropos* Ti'âmat, that "the Tigris are her two right eyes, the Euphrates her two left eyes".[1] If Ti'âmat personifies the sea, as would seem probable, then the statement has a great significance for us: for it would appear that the concept envisages the sea as the primaeval creatrix, extending inland right and left along the rivers Tigris and Euphrates—an orientation of view implying a point of observation looking northwards from the head of the Persian Gulf.

If we may thus reasonably conclude that behind the later figure of Ti'âmat lies an original Sumerian conception of the sea as the primordial creatrix, under the name of Nammu, we are next faced with the question how the Sumerians came to imagine that the sea produced the heaven and the earth. Now, the fact that the present coast-line at the head of the Persian Gulf lies far to the south of its position in the fourth millennium B.C. means in effect that the land has gradually replaced the sea in this area, probably as a result of the accumulation of alluvial deposits brought down by the rivers. The fact suggests an explanation of the origin of the Sumerian idea of creation, namely, that the Sumerians believed that the land was formed out of the sea from their own observation of the phenomenon.[2] It may, however, be questioned whether there would actually have been ocular evidence of the process, since it must always have been gradual. Possibly folk-memories of an earlier coast-line, reinforced by observation of the silting up of canals, tidal phenomena in the maritime marshland, and the formation of sand-banks all conspired to

---

[1] In E. Ebeling, *Tod und Leben nach den Vorstellungen der Babylonier*, I, p. 35.
[2] Cf. Jacobsen in *I.A.A.M.*, pp. 171–2, in *Before Philosophy*, pp. 185–7.

suggest that the sea could produce land. A late ritual text (sixth cent. B.C.) in Sumerian and Akkadian, which probably preserves a much older tradition, provides interesting evidence in this connection. It purports to describe the creative activity of Marduk, the great god of Babylon, and in the course of so doing it paints a vivid picture of the way in which a Mesopotamian imagined the primordial state and what he thought might have been the first act in the process of divine creation:

1. A holy house, a house of the gods in a holy place, had not been made;
2. A reed had not come forth, a tree had not been created;
3. A brick had not been laid, a brick mold had not been built;
4. A house had not been made, a city had not been built;
5. A city had not been made, a living creature had not been placed (therein);
    . . . . .
10. All the lands were sea;
    . . . . .
17. Marduk created a reed frame on the face of the waters;
18. He created dirt and poured (it) out by the reed frame.
19. In order to settle the gods in the dwelling of (their) hearts' delight,
20. He created mankind.
    . . . . .
31. Lord Marduk piled up a dam at the edge of the sea;
32. [. . . .] a swamp he made into dry land.
33. [. . . .] he caused to be;
34. [He crea]ted [the reed(?)], he created the tree;
35. [. . . .] in the place he created;
36. [Bricks he laid, the br]ick mold he built;
37. [The house he built], the city he built;
38. [The city he made], living creatures he placed (therein);
    . . . .[1]

The first essential of creation, as we see here, was envisaged in terms of the practice of the marsh-dwellers of the Euphrates-Tigris delta —a reed platform forms a foundation about which the mud will pile to form a kind of *pied-à-terre* and ultimately a place for settlement.[2]

As we have seen, the sea, personified as Nammu, was regarded as

[1] Trans. A. Heidel, *The Babylonian Genesis*, pp. 62–3. Cf. King, I, pp. 130–7; P. Garelli et M. Leibovici in *Sources orientales*, I, pp. 145–7.
[2] Cf. L. Woolley, "From Reed Hut to Brick Palace", in *History Today*, V (1955), pp. 156–7.

the primaeval creatrix who brought forth heaven and earth. Now, according to Sumerian cosmology, heaven (*an*) and earth (*ki*) were thought of as two essentially related and complementary entities— indeed there is some indication that *an-ki* was conceived as having been originally an interlocked whole which was personified respectively as a male (*an*) and a female entity (*ki*). From the union of this primaeval pair it would appear that it was believed that the god of the air, Enlil, had been born.[1] According to an early Sumerian text, Enlil separated the interlocked heaven and earth, a primordial act that affords an interesting parallel to the rôle of the Egyptian air-god Shu, who, as we have seen, was represented in Egyptian mythology as having separated the earth-god and the sky-goddess, whom he continued to hold apart.[2]

Our attempt, to trace a coherent cosmogonic scheme in the diverse myths of ancient Sumer concerning various aspects of creation, now encounters a peculiar difficulty. The god who appears most often in the extant texts in the rôle of a creator is Enki, who was essentially the god of the waters. In one place he is actually described as the son of Nammu, the primordial sea.[3] However, his connection with the waters is a more complicated one than that of the filial relationship represented here. The name En-ki signifies 'the lord of the earth', and there must have been some original justification for it; but in the historic Sumerian pantheon the god Enlil was clearly regarded as the lord of the earth, and Enki's relation to the earth finds expression in terms of his sovereignty over the subterranean area from which the springs and rivers have their source.[4] This sovereignty is represented in a curious way. Enki is called the 'king of the *abzu*', and his

---

[1] Cf. Kramer, *Sumerian Mythology*, pp. 39–41, *Tablets of Sumer*, p. 72. "il paraît légitime d'estimer que *en-lil* équivalait, à peu près, à 'seigneur de l'*atmosphère*' où était le vent, l'ouragan", Jean, p. 36. Cf. E. Dhorme, *Les religions de Babylonie et d'Assyrie*, p. 27.

[2] Cf. Kramer, *Sumerian Mythology*, p. 52, see also pp. 40–1, *Tablets of Sumer*, p. 77, see pp. 27–8 for the Egyptian parallel, and pp. 168–9 for a similar concept in Hittite mythology and in Hesiod.

[3] Cf. Kramer, *Sumerian Mythology*, p. 70.

[4] Cf. Jean, p. 45: "En-ki signifie 'seigneur de *la terre*', par opposition au ciel AN, ou 'seigneur du territoire' au centre duquel il est honoré; ou bien encore 'seigneur du sol' et du sous-sol, y compris les nappes *d'eau douce*, que l'on voyait sourdre en certains lieux. L'étymologie autorise, sans les imposer, ces trois conceptions". On Enlil as the 'lord of the earth' see *op. cit.*, 36–7; Dhorme, *Les religions* pp. 27, 48–9.

temple in the city of Eridu was said to have been founded on this *abzu*.[1] The idea of the *abzu* or *apsû* derives from Sumerian cosmology, which distinguished between the waters that are salt, i.e. the sea, and the sweet waters. The reservoir of the latter was conceived as situated beneath the earth, an idea which obviously derived from observation of the sources of springs and rivers and from the digging of wells. Mythologically the *abzu* was personified as a male being, as the sea was as a female.[2] The later *Enuma elish*, as we shall see, incorporates a myth which tells how from the union of these personifications of the sweet and bitter waters the gods were born, and how in process of time Ea (i.e. Enki) killed Apsû and "on Apsû he established his dwelling place".[3] What lies behind this mythological imagery is uncertain; but the fact that Eridu, obviously a very ancient place of settlement, was founded on the shore of a fresh-water lagoon, may be significant—Enki, the god of the marsh-lands, was there established on the *abzu*, and the building of his temple there would give him lordship over this form of the primordial deep.[4]

Enki, who was thus essentially associated with the sweet waters and the marshes of the Euphrates delta, was pre-eminently the creator god of the Sumerians, although he was never represented as the demiurge. In a Sumerian hymn commemorating the foundation of E'ongurra, as the temple of Enki at Eridu was named, a lively picture is given of the manner in which this primordial act was imagined:

> When to all who were born destiny was decreed,
> When mankind in a year of abundance, which An created,
> As grass had through the earth broken,
> Then built the lord of the Abzu, king Enki,
> Enki, the lord, who decides the destinies,

[1] Cf. Jean, pp. 45–6; A. Falkenstein u. W. von Soden, *Sumerische Hymnen und Gebete*, p. 133.

[2] Cf. Dhorme, *Les religions*, p. 32; P. Jensen in *Reallexikon der Assyriologie*, I, pp. 122–24 (*apsû–Apsû*); G. Furlani, *Miti babilonese e assiri*, pp. 75–6.

[3] See p. 96.

[4] Cf. B. Meissner, *Babylonien und Assyrien*, I, pp. 12–13, 105; E. Burrows, in *The Labyrinth*, p. 49; T. Fish in *B.J.R.L.*, 30, p. 7. Excavation has shown that "Eridu était non au bord de la mer (ceci contre l'indication d'un texte de Dungi) mais sur une lagune de l'Euphrate, soumise à la marée", Parrot, p. 271. Cf. G. Widéngren in *Numen*, VII (1960), p. 6.

His house complete of silver and lapis lazuli.
. . . . .
Of silver has he built the house; it is decked with lapislazuli,
Thickly with gold overlaid;
In Eridu had he the house built on the bank (of the lagoon).[1]

The Sumerians apparently thought of Enki as having arrived by sea in their land at the dawn of time. His coming is vividly pictured in some verses that commemorate the antiquity of the carob-tree:

When the heaven was removed from the earth,
When the earth was separated from the heaven,
When mankind was sown,
When the heaven-god was installed in heaven,
When Enlil was installed on the earth,
And the goddess Ereshkigal had received the nether-world as her portion,
At the time when he navigated, where he navigated,
At the time when the Father sailed to the world,
At the time when Enki sailed to the world . . .

His ship is imagined as a living thing:

> For the Master, the prow of the boat
> Unceasingly, as a wolf, devoured the water;
> For Enki, the stern of the boat
> Violently, as a lion, beat the water.

The land, to which the god came, was apparently barren except for the primaeval carob-tree:

At this time but one tree grew; it was the tree unique;
The carob-tree was the tree unique.
Planted on the sacred banks of the Euphrates,
It drank of the Euphrates,
And the south wind beat upon its trunk, it moved itself in its foliage.[2]

Another text of unknown provenance is notable for its association of Enki with a kind of golden age, and also for its exceedingly strange sequel which seems to contain a variety of *motifs*. The myth set forth in this text appears to be aetiological in character; but there seems to be some confusion of theme, and the purpose of the myth as a whole cannot be discerned, nor is there any indication as to what

---

[1] Falkenstein u. von Soden, p. 133. Cf. M. Lambert in *Sources orientales*, I, pp. 96–7.
[2] Lambert in *Sources orientales*, I, pp. 98–9. See Plate III.

use the text was put.[1] However, the very fact of its existence attests its original significance as an expression of Sumerian interest in the origin of things. The myth starts with a description of the paradisal nature of the land of Dilmun, a place which features in several Mesopotamian legends and which scholars have sought to locate variously in and about the Persian Gulf:[2]

> The land Dilmun is pure, the land Dilmun is clean;
> The land Dilmun is clean, the land Dilmun is most bright.
> . . . . .
> In Dilmun the raven utters no cries,
> The *ittidu*-bird utters not the cry of the *ittidu*-bird,[3]
> The lion kills not,
> The wolf snatches not the lamb,
> Unknown is the kid-devouring *wild dog*,
> . . . . .
> [Unknown] is the . . . widow,
> . . . . .
> The sick-eyed says not 'I am sick-eyed',
> The sick-headed (says) not 'I am sick-headed',
> Its old woman (says) not 'I am an old woman',
> Its old man (says) not 'I am an old man'.

However, although there is no violence, sickness, old-age, or death in Dilmun, it lacks fresh sparkling water. Consequently, Enki's spouse, Ninsikilla, appeals to him as the lord of the sweet waters to provide for this paradise. Enki bids the sun-god to supply Dilmun with the needed water:[4]

> He brings up the water into her large . . .,
> Makes her city drink from the waters of abundance,
> Makes Dilmun (drink from it) the waters of ab(undance),

[1] The extracts given below are translated by S. N. Kramer in *A.N.E.T.*, pp. 38–40, see also p. 37. For further studies of the text and translations see Kramer, *Tablets of Sumer*, pp. 169–175; *Sumerian Mythology*, pp. 54–9; Lambert in *Sources orientales*, I, pp. 103–112; Jacobsen in *I.A.A.M.*, pp. 157–160, in *Before Philosophy*, pp. 170–4.

[2] On the nature and location of Dilmun see S. N. Kramer in *B.A.S.O.R.*, 96, pp. 18–28; P. B. Cornwall in *op. cit.*, 103(1946), pp. 3–11.

[3] According to Kramer, the *ittidu*-bird was probably one of ill-omen, whose cry foretold death and desolation.

[4] It is certainly surprising to find Utu, the sun-god, as the provider of water (rain?) here. Cf. Jean, pp. 59–61. In the text, which is damaged at this place, the moon-god Nanna seems also to have been connected with the matter.

74

Her well of bitter water, verily it is become a well of sweet water
Her *furrowed* fields (and) farms *bore* her grain,
Her city, verily it is become the *bank-quay* house of the land
Dilmun, (verily it is become) the bank-(quay) house (of the land).

The obscure episode that follows starts with Enki impregnating the goddess Ninhursag, 'the mother of the land',[1] who bears the goddess Nimmu painlessly after a pregnancy of nine days. Enki then impregnates Nimmu, who gives birth after a similar marvellous pregnancy. The process continues until Enki prepares to impregnate his great-granddaughter, Uttu. Ninhursag now intervenes to counsel the maid to withhold her favours until Enki presents her with a gift of cucumbers, apples and grapes—possibly an attempt is being made here to account for the origin of these fruits, the production of which Enki makes possible by filling the dikes with water. The narrative then goes on to relate a strange happening, but one that clearly had a great significance for those who composed the myth and those for whom it was composed. Having provided the fruits,

> Enki took his joy of Uttu,
> He embraced her, lay in her lap,
> He . . . s the thighs, he touches the . . .,
> He embraced her, lay in her lap,
> With the young one he cohabited, he kissed her.
> Enki poured the semen into the womb,
> She took the semen into the womb, the semen of Enki.

But a pregnancy does not follow; instead Ninhursag uses the semen of Enki to produce eight, apparently new, plants. Strange though this relation is to our minds, it can be recognised as a piece of primitive aetiology, ascribing to the water-god the origin of other plants familiar to the Sumerian agriculturalist. The sequel, however, is even stranger. Enki discovers the plants, and, in order apparently to determine their fates by knowing their 'hearts', he eats them. For this act it would seem that Ninhursag puts upon him a fatal curse ("Until he is dead I shall not look upon him with the 'eye of life' "). Enki sickens, and the other gods,[2] fearing his death and its likely

[1] In this text Ninhursag appears to be identified with the goddess Nintu; other evidence suggests that they were two distinct deities, cf. Jean, pp. 16–17, 42–3.
[2] The myth makes no attempt to relate the other gods to the apparent primordial situation in Dilmun.

75

consequences, finally succeed in persuading Ninhursag to relent and restore the dying god. What follows appears to be another piece of aetiology whereby the mother-goddess produces in turn, personified as deities, a cure or remedy for each of the ills from which Enki suffers:

> Ninhursag seats Enki *by* her vulva:
> 'My brother, what hurts thee?'
> 'My . . . hurts me'.
> 'Abu I have caused to be born for thee'.
> 'My brother, what hurts thee?
> 'My *jaw* hurts me'.
> 'Nintulla I have caused to be born for thee'.

The dialogue describes the birth of eight of these healing deities. The extant form of the myth ends with the decreeing of the fates of the new-born deities; an essential act, according to Mesopotamian thought, as we shall see, that has to be performed for every entity, animate or inanimate.

It would seem that it was also to Enki that Mesopotamian tradition most consistently ascribed the creation of mankind; other gods, as we shall see, were sometimes associated with this primordial act, but the extant texts clearly attest that it was Enki who was primarily regarded as the creator of man. To Professor Kramer we again owe the discovery and decipherment of the most important Sumerian text in this connection, which he considers to reflect the ideas that were current to Sumer on the subject during the third millennium B.C.[1] The myth, which is recorded here, is essentially aetiological in character, in that it provides reasons both for the creation of the human race and for the many ills that afflict it. At its beginning the narrative clearly expresses the fundamental premiss of the Mesopotamian *Weltanschauung*, namely, that human beings exist only to serve the gods, who caused them to be created for this very purpose. Accordingly, the scene opens with Nammu, the personification of the primordial sea, urging her son Enki, who is the Sumerian god of wisdom as well as the water-god, to relieve the gods from the toil of providing their bread:

[1] *Sumerian Mythology*, pp. 68–72. Cf. Jacobsen in *I.A.A.M.*, pp. 161–5, in *Before Philosophy*, pp. 175–9; Brandon, pp. 82–3.

O my son, rise from thy bed, from thy . . . work what is wise,
Fashion *servants* of the gods, may they produce their . . .

Enki accedes to his mother's request, and he gives directions for the
making of the new creatures:

O my mother, the *creature* whose name thou hast uttered, it exists,
Bind upon it the . . . of the gods;
Mix the heart of the clay that is over the abyss,[1]
The good and princely *fashioners* will *thicken* the clay,
Thou, do thou bring the *limbs* into existence;
Ninmah (the earth-mother goddess) will work above thee,
. . . (goddesses of birth) will stand by thee at thy fashioning;
O my mother, decree thou its (the new born's) fate,
Ninmah will bind upon it the . . . of the gods,
. . . as man . . .

According to this passage, it would seem that Enki was regarded as
the god who designed the nature of man and arranged for the practical execution of his design by other deities. The idea that clay is the
basic substance of which mankind is fashioned is significant. As we
have seen, the same idea was held in Egypt, where it naturally
followed from the image of Khnum as the divine potter. Possibly the
technique of pottery-making inspires the Sumerian myth here;
however, it may also be asked whether the concept may not perhaps
also have arisen from the conviction that man is essentially a product
of the earth—that he is made of it, he is nourished by it, and eventually he returns to it.

However that may be, the text, which we are considering, now
takes a new turn. After the creation of these new servants, Enki calls
the gods to a feast, during which Enki and Ninmah are led to challenge each other's ingenuity in finding some use for freak human
beings that they severally create:

The . . . she (Ninmah) made into a woman who cannot give birth.
Enki upon seeing the woman who cannot give birth,
Decreed her fate, destined her to be stationed in the 'woman house'.

---

[1] "('Above the *apsu*', means below the earth but above the watery deep
which lies under the earth and is more or less identical with the goddess
Nammu herself). This clay was to be severed from Nammu as one severs a
human infant from its mother", Jacobsen, *I.A.A.M.*, p. 162.

The . . . she (Ninmah) made into one who has no male organ, who has no
  female organ.
Enki, upon seeing him who has no male organ, who has no female organ,
To stand before the king, decreed as his fate.

Here it would appear that we have an attempt to explain the origin
and purpose of the barren woman and one who is sexless or an
eunuch. Such deviations from the normal must have puzzled the
Sumerians, and they sought thus to find an answer. It is to be noted,
however, that in the tale there is no echo of complaint or criticism
that the gods should, in their play, have made such freaks; the
emphasis is rather on the ingenuity of Enki, who finds a social use
for these malformed beings. But after Ninmah had tried Enki with
six such freaks and Enki had successfully dealt with each and 'given
them bread to eat', Ninmah has to face the challenge of what Enki
then makes:

> Of him whom thy hand has fashioned, I have decreed the fate,
> Have given him bread to eat;
> Do thou decree the fate of him whom my hand has fashioned,
> Do thou give him bread to eat.

Enki appears to have produced a creature that was stiff-jointed, weak
and ailing; with the challenge that it constitutes Ninmah can do
nothing, and she curses Enki—perhaps for the reason that what he
had done could not be undone, and mankind must include those who
are hopelessly malformed and diseased.

Although in this myth his character appears somewhat ambivalent,
Enki was generally regarded as pre-eminently the patron of mankind.[1]
His benevolence is graphically commemorated in another text which
depicts him moving about the earth as a culture hero, arranging for
the basic necessities of the city-state and its supporting agriculture
according to the Mesopotamian fashion. Thus Enki is represented as
visiting Ur, which was probably the leading city of Sumer at the time
of the composition of the text:[2]

To Ur he came,
Enki, king of the abyss, decrees the fate:
"O city, well-supplied, washed by much water, firm standing ox,

[1] Cf. Dhorme, *Les religions*, pp. 35–6.
[2] For translation and commentary see Kramer, *Sumerian Mythology*, pp.
59–62.

Shrine of abundance of the land, knees opened, green like the 'mountain',
. . . . .
Thy perfected decrees he has directed,
The great mountain, Enlil, in the universe has uttered thy exalted name;[1]
O thou city whose fates have been decreed by Enki,
O thou shrine Ur, neck to heaven mayest thou rise".

Enki is then depicted as going to Meluhha, the 'black mountain', which is perhaps to be identified with the coastal areas of east Africa, and there blessing the inhabitants and their resources—a remarkable instance of universal benevolence on the part of a Sumerian god. After this, Enki turns his attention to the Tigris and Euphrates and arranges that their waters should be wholesome and contain much fish. His providential care is next concerned with the sea, i.e. the Persian Gulf, and the winds. Then provision is made for the essentials of agriculture:

The plow and the yoke he directed,
The great prince Enki caused the . . . ox to . . .;
To the pure *crops* he *roared*,
In the steadfast field he made the grain grow;
The lord, the jewel and ornament of the plain,
The . . . farmer of Enlil,
Enkimdu, him of the canals and ditches,
Enki placed in their charge.
The lord called to the steadfast field, he caused it to produce much grain,
Enki made it bring forth its small and large beans . . .,
The . . . grains he heaped up for the granary,
Enki added granary to granary,
With Enlil he increases the abundance of the land
. . . . .

The poem continues to detail the fruits of Enki's providence, among which notably are the two essential implements of Mesopotamian economy, namely, the pick-axe and the brick mould.

From another myth, which describes, with many amusing details, an encounter between Enki and the great goddess Inanna, we learn that the Sumerians attributed to Enki more than a hundred laws or rules (*me's*) which were held to constitute the basic pattern of civilisation. These *me's*, so far as they can be identified, afford an interesting insight into the Sumerian mind by revealing the variety of entities,

[1] On this epithet for Enlil see Dhorme, *Les religions*, p. 27.

institutions, qualities and evils that were considered essential factors of civilised life; the following indicate something of the range and nature of these *me's*, which incidentally were regarded as of divine origin: godship; kingship; truth; descent into the nether world; sexual intercourse; prostitution; enmity; the destruction of cities; falsehood; art of woodworking; weariness; the troubled heart; musical instruments.[1]

Enki's pre-eminence as a creator and culture hero is curious, since he ranks but third in the Mesopotamian pantheon, and, while An is a rather shadowy figure, Enlil, who has the second place, was a mighty god of great prestige.[2] From what we learned of the importance of the factor of sacerdotal rivalry in our study of Egyptian cosmogonies, we might expect that the serious rivalry that existed between the Sumerian city-states would have been reflected also in the form of cosmogonic claim and counter-claim. We shall indeed encounter a notable instance of this when we come to consider the Babylonian *Enuma elish*; but there is scarcely any evidence of its existence in Sumerian mythology, and the example which we are now to consider primarily shows that in Sumer cosmogony could not have been exploited for propagandist purposes as it clearly was in Egypt.

Eridu, the cult centre of Enki, must certainly have been one of the most ancient, if not the most ancient city of Sumer.[3] However, in the text with which we are next concerned it is evidently implied that Nippur, the city of Enlil, is older than Eridu and that Enki had been obliged to seek Enlil's blessing on the sanctuary that he had established on the abyss (*abzu*).[4] The narrative begins by describing how Enki had built his temple at Eridu and how splendidly he had adorned it; in the process of doing this Enki is depicted as raising Eridu from the abyss and causing it to float on the water like a high mountain—possibly some reminiscence is here preserved of the original establishment of human habitation at this place in the mari-

---

[1] Kramer, *Sumerian Mythology*, pp. 64–8; *Tablets of Sumer*, pp. 91–6.

[2] Cf. Dhorme, *Les religions*, p. 28.

[3] According to the Sumerian King List (cf. *A.N.E.T.*, p. 264b), kingship first came down from heaven at Eridu. Cf. Childe, pp. 11, 13. Parrot, pp. 270–1; Saggs, pp. 15–18.

[4] For translation and commentary see Kramer, *Sumerian Mythology*, pp. 62–3.

time marshland about the Persian Gulf. Having completed his temple, Enki then makes his way by boat to Nippur for Enlil's confirmation and blessing on his deed. The water-god's emergence from the abyss is graphically described:

> When Enki rises, the fish . . . rise,
> The abyss stands in wonder,
> In the sea joy enters,
> Fear comes over the deep,
> Terror holds the exalted river,
> The Euphrates, the South Wind *lifts it in waves.*

Arrived at Nippur, Enki prepares a banquet for the gods, including Enlil, who is termed 'his father'. The food and good fellowship of the meal put the gods into a happy disposition, and Enlil is ready to give the required blessing, which is evidently designed to make clear the relationship between the two deities and their respective states:[1]

Enlil says to the Anunnaki:

> Ye great gods who are standing about,
> My son has built a house, the king Enki;
> Eridu, like a mountain, he has raised up from the earth,
> In a good place he has built it.
> Eridu, the clean place, where none may enter,
> The house built of silver, adorned with lapis lazuli,
> The house directed by the seven 'lyre-songs', given over
>   to incantation,
> *With pure songs . . .,*
> The abyss, the shrine of the goodness of Enki, befitting
>   the divine decrees,
> Eridu, the pure house having been built,
> O Enki, praise!

Several Sumerian myths depict Enlil as the creator of various things: he is never represented as the demiurge, although, as we have seen, the separation of heaven and earth was ascribed to him. In one text, which is particularly notable for its fuller explanation of the purpose of the creation of mankind, Enlil is associated with Enki in bringing down to earth the cattle-god (Lahar) and the grain-goddess (Ashnan).[2]

[1] "La finale, voyage d'Enki à Nippur, montre la réele suprématie d'Enlil, même sur un dieu comme Enki", M. Lambert in *R.A.*, lv(1961), p. 186.

[2] For translation and commentary see Kramer, *Sumerian Mythology*, pp. 72–3, see also pp. 53–4, *Tablets of Sumer*, pp. 144–6. Cf. Lambert in *Sources orientales*, I, pp. 100–102.

The story opens with a description of the gods (the Annunaki), after their creation by An, living ignorant of the basic principles of a civilised economy:

> They (the Annunaki) knew not the eating of bread,
> Knew not the dressing of garments,
> Ate plants with their mouth like sheep,
> Drank water from the ditch.

From this state of primitive ignorance, which probably reflects the Sumerian idea of life before civilisation,[1] the gods are rescued by the creation of the personifications of cattle and grain and by the creation of mankind to manage the production of these two basic entities of a civilised economy.

To Enlil, as well as to Enki, was attributed the invention of the necessary pickaxe, the various uses of which are carefully detailed, thus affording a valuable glimpse of Sumerian economy:[2]

> The pickax and the basket built cities,
> The steadfast house the pickax builds, the steadfast
>   house the pickax establishes,
> The steadfast house it causes to prosper.
>
> The house which rebels against the king,
> The house which is not submissive to its king,
> The pickax makes it submissive to its king.
>
> Of the bad . . . plants it crushes the head,
> Plucks at the roots, tears at the crown,
> The pickax *spares* the . . . plants;
> The pickax, its fate decreed by father Enlil,
> The pickax is exalted.

The creative activity of Enlil was not, however, as was apparently Enki's, confined to the production of what was needed for life on the earth and for the service of the gods. In another myth, which is equally significant for its anthropomorphising of divine activity as it is for its implicit revelation of human behaviour, Enlil is represented

[1] See the view of mankind before civilisation as exemplified in Enkidu in the *Epic of Gilgamesh*, Tab. I, col. ii, ll. 34–col. iv. l. 47. Cf. Brandon, p. 90; Fish in *B.J.R.L.*, 30, p. 12. See also pp. 111–12.

[2] For translation and commentary see Kramer, *Sumerian Mythology*, pp. 51–3.

as the procreator of the deities who personified the moon and the underworld.[1] The myth would appear to have been a product of Nippur, the cult-centre of Enlil, which is grandiloquently described as the 'bond of heaven and earth'. Although it is implied that the city of Nippur was thus already in existence, no reference is made to mankind and a kind of primaeval situation is conceived in that Enlil is represented as the 'young man of Nippur' and his divine consort Ninlil as 'its young maid'. The myth describes their fateful meeting in a Sumerian prototype of Arcadia:

> In the pure stream, the woman bathes, in the pure stream,
> Ninlil walks along the bank of the stream Nunbirdu,
> The bright-eyed, the lord, the bright-eyed,
> The 'great mountain', father Enlil, the bright-eyed, saw her,
> The shepherd . . . who decrees the fates, the bright-eyed, saw her.
>
> The lord speaks to her of intercourse (?), she is unwilling,
> Enlil speaks to her of intercourse (?), she is unwilling;
> "My vagina is too small, it knows not to copulate,
> My lips are too small, they know not to kiss" . . .

Enlil, however, has his way with the virgin goddess, and he begets on her the moon-god, Sin. The myth goes on to relate how Enlil, metamorphosing himself variously on three other occasions, impregnates Ninlil, thereby begetting more sons who are destined to be deities of the underworld.

That Enlil was regarded as the sovereign god of Sumer an abundance of evidence attests, as it does also the religious primacy of his sacred city of Nippur.[2] But, if this supremacy had been generally recognised from the beginning of Sumerian culture, it would be difficult to account for Enki's traditional rôle as a creator, for in historical times he certainly ranked behind Enlil in power and prestige. The problem seemingly implicit here may be only apparent to us after our study of the significance of creatorship in ancient Egypt and from our acquaintance with Judaeo-Christian teaching which holds creativity as an essential part of the monotheistic concept of deity. However, as we have already had reason to suspect, it would

---

[1] The text is translated and explained by Kramer in his *Tablets of Sumer*, pp. 79–82, and earlier in his *Sumerian Mythology*, pp. 43–7. See also Jacobsen in *I.A.A.M.*, pp. 152–6, in *Before Philosophy*, pp. 165–170.

[2] Cf. Jean, pp. 36–41; Dhorme, *Les religions*, pp. 26–31, 48–50.

appear that such a view was not held in Sumer. Acts of creation could be attributed to various deities; indeed in one text, actually excavated at Nippur itself, the creation of mankind is in one single line, without qualification or differentiation, attributed to Anu, Enlil, Enki and Ninhursag.[1] It must, however, be recognised that the tradition of Enki as the creator *par excellence* was strong and enduring; for example, it is found at Babylon in a cuneiform text of a temple ritual as it is also in the *Enuma elish*; and, as we shall see, it was still current there in the third century B.C. The ritual text just mentioned is particularly notable for us here because it further attests the association of Enki's creative activity with his dual rôle of water-god and the god of wisdom; herein Enki is presented both as a creator of the physical environment and of the personified principles of the basic arts and crafts:[2]

When Anu created the heaven,
(And) Nudimmud[3] created the *apsû*, his dwelling-place,
Ea (i.e. Enki) pinched off clay in the *apsû*;[4]
He created Kulla[5] for the restoration of [the temples],
He created the reed-brake and the forest for the work of [their] construction;
He created Nin-ildu, Nin-sinuig, and A-ra-zu[6] as the executants of the work of [their construc]tion;
He created mountains and seas, for every [. . . .];
He created Gushkin-banda, Nin-a-gal, Nin-zadim,
  Nin-kur-ra[7] for [their] works;

[1] Cf. Lambert in *Sources orientales*, I, pp. 102–3.

[2] Cf. F. Thureau-Dangin, *Rituels accadiens*, p. 47; A. Ungnad, *Die Religion der Babylonier und Assyrer*, pp. 54–5; Heidel, pp. 65–6; P. Garelli et M. Leibovici in *Sources orientales*, I, pp. 147–8.

[3] "le nom sous lequel apparaît Éa dans les premières lignes de l'*Enuma elish* est celui de Nu-dim-mud qui signifie 'procréateur de l'homme' ", Dhorme, *Les religions*, p. 35. It may be noted that the name Ea, by which Enki was also known, signifies '*maison de l'eau*', Jean, p. 48.

[4] *É-a ina apsi iq-ru-ṣa ṭi-ṭa* (-*am*): "Éa prit dans l'Abîme une poignée d'argile", Thureau-Dangin, *ib.*; "Kniff Ea im Ozean Lehm ab:", Ungnad, p. 54; "Ea nipped off clay in the *Apsû*;", Heidel, p. 65. The act is significant for its reference to the potter's art and may be compared with that of *Job* xxxiii. 6: מֵחֹמֶר קֹרַצְתִּי גַם־אָנִי.

[5] The brick-god.

[6] These are respectively the deities concerned with the work of carpenters and smiths, and apparently with prayer.

[7] Respectively the divine patrons of goldsmiths, smiths, engravers, and stonecutters.

(He created) the abundant produce (of the mountains and the seas) for
  offerings [. . . .];[1]
He created Ashnan, Laḫar, Siris, Ningizzida, Nin-sar, A[. . . .]
To provide in abundance the appointed [revenues];
He created Umun-mu-ta-am-ku, Umun-mu-ta-am-nag[2] to present
  [their] offerings;
He created Azag-su(g), the high priest of the great gods, to perform [their]
  rites and ob[servances];
He created the king for the maintenance [. . .];
He [created] men to do [. . . .]
[. . . .] Anu, Enlil and Ea [. . . .].

That the Sumerians were interested in the origin of things, and
speculated much about them, is obvious from the comparative
abundance of texts dealing with the subject among the rather sparse
remains of their literature that have been recovered by archaeological
research. What inspired this interest is less certain. As we have seen
from our study of the Egyptian material, cosmogonic speculation in
the sister civilisation of the Nile valley was wholly motivated by
theological, or perhaps rather by ecclesiastical, interest. We have
noted some signs of the operation of such a motive in Sumerian cosmogony, but it clearly does not predominate. In later Mesopotamian
records we shall see some evidence of the employment of cosmogonic
texts for ritual purposes, and even to assist dentistry;[3] but generally
there is an absence of any obvious indication of purpose in these
texts. Professor Kramer, to whom the study of Sumerian mythology
owes so much, is of the opinion that the texts were essentially literary
compositions, being the products of the *Edubba*, i.e. the 'house of
tablets', the scribal academy.[4] But, even as such, these cosmogonic
texts must have had some purpose beyond that of attesting literary
ability: what that purpose was may be defined as aetiological—the
desire to explain the cause or origin of a thing. The *trait* is well known
and wide-spread; what is remarkable about its Sumerian expressions
is that it was not apparently strongly organised or rationally dis-
ciplined—no attempt was made to present a logically consistent
aetiology whereby the origin of things could be systematically traced

---

[1] Deities associated severally with grain, cattle, wine and vegetation (last
two named).

[2] Designations of Marduk's cook and cupbearer.

[3] See p. 90.

[4] In *The Bible and the Ancient Near East* (ed. G. E. Wright), p. 254.

back to a first cause or an original act of creation. In Sumer there was a kind of innate conviction that water was the source of all things; but this conviction was never consolidated into a definitive belief, and, as we have seen, various origins could be assigned to the constituent parts of the universe, to human institutions and the bases of human economy.

Another characteristic of the Sumerian cosmogonies, which makes them the more remarkable by way of contrast with a notable later development, is the absence of any disposition to think that creation had been achieved by conflict—that the forces of chaos had sought to oppose the formation of a cosmos. There do indeed survive three fragmentary texts which tell of the overthrow of a dragon named Kur respectively by Enki, Ninurta and Inanna.[1] But, although this monster was in some way associated with the primaeval waters in the exploits of the first two of these deities, no clear cosmogonic theme is developed in the myths concerned; it is possible, as we shall see, that the monster Kur may have provided a prototype of the celebrated Ti'âmat of the *Enuma elish*. In general, however, it would appear that the Sumerians imagined the beginnings of things as set in a kind of idyllic scene where the gods perform their acts of creation quietly, without labour, and unhindered.[2]

The Sumerian creation legends do, however, contain a feature that is both notable in itself and for its continuance in later Mesopotamian thought. It is that of decreeing the destiny of a thing. As has been apparent in many of the examples cited, it was not deemed enough to tell only of the creation or invention of some entity; its destiny had also to be decreed, just as did the destinies of cities or human beings. The concept is an important one for understanding the Mesopotamian view of life, and we shall have to return to its consideration later; it will suffice now to note that, used in what might be termed a cosmogonic context, the decreeing of a destiny implies on the part of the one who

[1] Cf. Kramer, *Sumerian Mythology*, pp. 76–83; *Tablets of Sumer*, pp. 196–200.

[2] A number of Sumerian cylinder seals show representations of heroes struggling with animals (lions, stags, or bulls); some later Akkadian and Assyrian specimens illustrate deities combating dragons. For the Sumerian examples see D. J. Wiseman, *Cylinder Seals of Western Asia*, pp. 16, 17, 19, 26; H. Frankfort, *The Art and Architecture of the Ancient Orient*, Pl. 40a, b; *Cylinder Seals*, Pl. X-XIV; Kramer, *Tablets of Sumer*, p. 140(68).

does it the ability both to conceive of the purpose of the object and to determine and authorise its continuing fulfilment, as, for example, in the case of a plant or an implement, where clearly it is the prototype that is involved and sets the pattern for the future.

It would appear that in the minds of the Sumerians the creation, or rather perhaps the process of creation, was not seen as an event that had happened in a kind of 'age of the gods', a mythical, far-off time that was quite unconnected with human history. As a tablet, recovered from the site of Nippur, shows, though unfortunately in a fragmentary manner owing to its damaged condition, the development of human affairs was traced out in its consequent stages from the very creation of mankind, the institution of kingship and the founding of six cities, apparently as cult centres, being specially commemorated:

After Anu, Enlil, Enki, and Ninhursag
Had fashioned the black-headed (people),
Vegetation luxuriated from the earth,
Animals, four-legged (creatures) of the plain, were brought artfully into
  existence.
                 ‹a break of about thirty seven lines›
After the . . . of kingship had been lowered from heaven,
After the exalted [*tiara*] (and) the throne of kingship had been lowered
  from heaven,
He [per]fected the [rites (and) the ex]alted
[(divine) ordinances] . . .,
Founded the [five]ci[ties] in . . . p[ure places],
Cal[led] their names, [appor]tioned them *as* [*cu*]*lticenters*.[1]

The course of human affairs is then interrupted by a flood of water, sent by the gods, in order to destroy mankind. From the common fate one man, Ziusudra, and apparently some animals, escaped in a great boat which Ziusudra would seem to have constructed on the advice of the god Enki.[2] The idea of this universal cataclysm was evidently a well established feature of Sumerian folk-lore; it constitutes an obviously traditional point of division in the Sumerian King List,[3] and in process of time it was incorporated into the *Epic of Gilgamesh*, where it plays an effective part in defining the Meso-

---

[1] Translated by S. N. Kramer in *A.N.E.T.*, p. 43a, cf. pp. 42b–43a.
[2] *A.N.E.T.*, p. 44.   [3] Cf. *A.N.E.T.*, p. 265b.

potamian philosophy of life.[1] The Nippur tablet does not tell how the earth was re-populated after the Flood; but it has been suggested by Dr. A. Heidel that the fourth (Assyrian) fragment of the so-called *Atraḥasis Epic*, which tells of the plagues and the flood with which Enlil afflicted mankind, preserves a tradition of an act of re-population, performed by the mother-goddess Mami:[2]

[Mama reci]ted the incantation; when she completed [her] incantation,
[. . .] she drew upon her clay.
[Fourteen pie]ces she pinched off; seven pieces she placed on the right,
[Seven pie]ces she placed on the left; between them she placed a brick.
[E]a was kneeling on the *matting*; he opened its navel;
[. . . he c]alled the wise wives.
(Of the) [seven] and seven mother-wombs, seven brought forth males,
[Seven] brought forth females.
The Mother-Womb, the creatress of destiny,
In pairs she completed them,
In pairs she completed (them) before her.[3]

Accordingly, we see that the Sumerians looked back to a remote past that divided itself curiously into two parts. An antediluvian age, extending from the Creation, was marked by the institution of kingship and the founding of certain cities: in the King List this period lasted for 241,000 years, and was made up of the prodigious reigns of a few kings. After the Flood, 'kingship was lowered (again) from heaven': but the reigns of the recorded kings, though starting at an impossibly high figure, gradually reduce until they reach the more credible number of thirty-six years. This post-diluvian period constituted a kind of Sumerian heroic age, for among its rulers are mentioned several heroes famous in legend.[4]

The mention of the goddess Mami will serve to introduce us to another creation text which, besides being of Babylonian origin and dating from the time of the First Dynasty there (1894–1595 B.C.), contains a *motif* that we have not met hitherto in our study of the

[1] *Epic of Gilgamesh*, Tab. XI, cf. *A.N.E.T.*, pp. 93–95. Cf. Brandon, p. 93.

[2] *The Gilgamesh Epic and Old Testament Parallels*, p. 107.

[3] Trans. E. A. Speiser in *A.N.E.T.*, p. 100 a-b. Cf. Heidel, *Gilgamesh Epic*, pp. 115-16.

[4] Cf. *A.N.E.T.*, pp. 265b–266a. See also E. A. Speiser in *The Idea of History in the Ancient Near East*, p. 50; Brandon, *Time and Mankind*, pp. 45–7.

Sumerian cosmogonies: it is the idea of creation by means of sub-stitutionary sacrifice. The account of the creation of man in this text appears to have constituted a rather lengthy introduction to an incan-tation designed to facilitate childbirth:[1]

. . . .
The goddess they called, [. . .], [the *mot*]*her*,
The most helpful of the gods, the wise Mami:
"Thou art the Mother-womb,
The one who creates mankind.
Create, then, Lullu[2] and let him bear the yoke!
The yoke he shall bear, . . . [. . .];
The *burden* of creation man shall bear!"
Nintu opened her mouth,
Saying to the great gods:
"With me is the *doing* of all that is suitable;
With his . . . let Lulu appear!
He who shall *serve* all the gods,
Let him *be formed* out of clay, be *animated* with blood!"[3]
Enki opened his mouth,
Saying to the great gods:
"In the month of the *restoration* of *confidence*,[4]
Cleansing of the land, judgment of its people,
Let them slay one god,
And let the gods be purified in the *judgment*.
With his flesh and his blood
Let Ninhursag mix clay.
God and man
Shall . . . *benefit* jointly by the clay!"[5]
Unto eternity [. . .] we shall hear."
                           (reverse of tablet)
[. . .] her breast,
[. . .] the beard,

[1] Trans. Speiser in *A.N.E.T.*, pp. 99b–100a. Cf. Ebeling, pp. 172–5; Heidel, *The Babylonian Genesis*, pp. 66–7; Ungnad, p. 55.
[2] *lu-ul-la-a*: 'Name des Urmenschen' (Ebeling); "the savage, the first man' (Speiser). See p. 104, n. 3.
[3] "soll in den Ton eingedrückt werden, mit Blut(?) sei er belebt!", Ebe-ling, p. 173.
[4] "Am Neulichtstag ist Ersatz (?) Leben (?) und Stärke", Ebeling, *ib.*; "In the month of substitution (?) and help", Heidel, p. 67.
[5] "Gott und Mensch
   sollen daraus hervorgehen, vereingt im Ton!", Ebeling, *ib.*;
   "God and man
   . . . united (?) in the clay", Heidel, *ib.*

[. . .] the cheek of the man.
[. . .] and the raising
[. . .] of both eyes, the wife and her husband.
[Fourteen mother]-wombs were assembled
[Before] Nintu.
[At the ti]me of the new moon
[To the House] of Fates they called the *votaries*.
[. . .] Ea came and
[*Kneel*]*ed down*, opening the womb.
[. . .] . . . and happy was his countenance.
[. . . bent]the knees [. . .],
[. . .] made an opening,
She brought forth her issue,
Praying.
Fashion a clay brick into a core,
Make . . . stone in the midst of [. . .],
Let the vexed rejoice in the house of the one in travail!
As the Bearing One gives birth,
May the mo[ther of the ch]ild bring forth by herself![1]

The rest of the text is too damaged to permit of its translation; but it is evident from what has been preserved that it was already the custom of Babylon to use the principle of what might be termed the ritual perpetuation of the past in the practice of magic.[2] Here, in order to accomplish the safe delivery of a child, appeal is in effect made to the past, to what was believed to be the original act of the bringing forth of human beings by the mother-goddess, Mami.[3] It would seem that the efficacy of this appeal to the fateful primordial act was reinforced by practical action, namely, the making of some clay emblem, recalling the fashioning of the first beings from clay. This use of a cosmogonic text in the practice of ritual magic is confirmed by other examples, the most notable of which is an incantation for the cure of toothache that takes the form of explaining the origin of the worm that was thought to prey upon the teeth, causing their decay.[4] Such a use, too, is found underlying the composition of the great Babylonian Epic of the Creation, the *Enuma elish*, to which we must now turn; herein also we shall find a most notable occurrence of the *motif* of creation by means of substitutionary sacrifice.

[1] Cf. Ebeling, p. 174d.
[2] Cf. Brandon, "The Ritual Perpetuation of the Past", in *Numen*, VII (Leiden, 1959).
[3] On Mami see Meissner, II, p. 11.   [4] Cf. *A.N.E.T.*, pp. 100b–101a.

The *Enuma elish*[1] is justly famous both for its being the epic tale of the creation of the world by Marduk, the patron god of the great city of Babylon which in popular thought epitomises the civilisation of ancient Mesopotamia, and for its own dramatic quality. The original Babylonian form of the poem is generally thought to date from the period of the First Babylonian Dynasty (1894–1595 B.C.).[2] That it was composed from earlier traditions is obvious, if only in view of the curious part played therein by the god Ea (Enki); and there would seem to be much reason for concluding that, in his rôle of creator of heaven and earth, Marduk has usurped the achievement of Enlil—indeed, as we shall abundantly see, the poem is very much concerned with the exaltation of Marduk over the other (and older) gods of the Mesopotamian pantheon, a concern which may well reflect the political hegemony obtained by Babylon at the beginning of the second millennium B.C.[3] How this apparent political interest was actually served by the composition would seem to be explained by the fact that it was ritually recited during the *akîtu* or New Year festival at Babylon.[4] This recitation occurred twice during the course of the eleven days of ceremonies that constituted the festival. Of one of the occasions we have a fairly precise description in an account of the *akîtu* ritual. The rubric describes the actions of the high-priest (the *urigallu*) on the evening of the fourth day of the month Nisan, which was also the fourth day of the festival: "after the 'little' meal at the close of day, the *urigallu* of the *É-ku-a* will recite before Bêl (i.e. Marduk), with raised hand, the *Enuma elish* from beginning to end. While he recites the *Enuma elish* before Bêl with raised hand, the front of the tiara of Anu and the throne of Enlil shall remain

[1] The title *Enuma elish* is derived from the beginning of the opening line: "When on high . . ."

[2] See the introductions of Heidel, pp. 1–17; Speiser in *A.N.E.T.*, p. 60; Garelli et Leibovici in *Sources orientales*, I, pp. 117–27; G. Furlani, *Miti balilonesi e assiri*, pp. 3–38; King, *The Seven Tablets of Creation*, pp. xxv–cxxiii.

[3] Cf. Dhorme, *Les religions*, pp. 139–144; Meissner, II, pp. 15–17, 160–3; H. Frankfort (*Cylinder Seals*, p. 98), rejects the idea, that Marduk was an obscure local deity until Babylon became the capital, on the ground that Akkadian seals show a sun-god in situations resembling in detail Marduk's performances in the *Enuma elish*. See also S. A. Pallis, *The Babylonian Akîtu Festival*, pp. 186–9; Saggs, pp. 338–40.

[4] On the *akîtu* festival see Pallis, *The Babylonian Akîtu Festival*, pp. 11–54; Jean, pp. 168–73.

covered".[1] Owing to the fragmentary condition of this *rituale*, no rubric is found for the second recitation; however, in another fragmentary source we have a brief enigmatic reference to it: "*Enuma elish* which is recited before Bêl, which they chant in the month of Nisan, (it is) because he is held prisoner".[2] These passages, however, really raise more difficulties than they solve. That the *Enuma elish* should have been liturgically recited at a New Year festival is intelligible, since there would be a natural analogy of *motif* in the idea of the creation of the world and the beginning of a new year with all its potentiality for good or ill. But it would be reasonable to expect that the recitation should be clearly related to the ritual. However, this is not so in regard to the first instance of the recitation: nothing in the ceremonies performed on the fourth or the fifth day of the festival provides a ritual occasion for the recitation of the *Enuma elish*.[3] The reference to the other occasion upon which it was recited is wholly problematical, and it has been the source of the considerable controversy that has been waged by scholars about the nature of the *akîtu* festival and whether the ritual death and resurrection of Marduk were then enacted.[4] Although the passage concerned clearly indicates a situation in which Marduk was envisaged as a prisoner (in the underworld?), as we shall see, the whole tenor of the *Enuma elish* absolutely contradicts any suggestion that Marduk could be weakened or defeated. The impossibility of relating the recitation of the *Enuma elish* in these two passages to any ritual occasions in the course of the New Year festival does not mean that the ritual had no connection with the story of Marduk's creation of the world. The casting of the destinies for the coming year was an important feature of the festival, and, as we shall see, the authority to determine the destinies is one of the main themes of the *Enuma elish*. Moreover, in another text

[1] Thureau-Dangin, *Rituels accadiens*, p. 136. Cf. C. J. Gadd in *Myth and Ritual*, pp. 50–2; H. Frankfort, *Kingship and the Gods*, p. 319.

[2] Cf. Pallis, p. 229.

[3] Cf. Pallis, pp. 297–8. Gadd, *op. cit.*, p. 62, suggests that the *Enuma elish* was recited on the second occasion as "part of the means employed to release him (Marduk) from that captivity". The suggestion is in line with the thesis of the so-called 'Myth and Ritual' school, but it only emphasises the inexplicable occasion of the first recital.

[4] Cf. S. H. Hooke, *Babylonian and Assyrian Religion*, pp. 58–60, in *Myth, Ritual and Kingship*, pp. 1–11; Frankfort, *Kingship and the Gods*, pp. 318–25; E. O. James, *Myth and Ritual in the Ancient Near East*, pp. 55–8.

which seems to take the form of a speculative commentary on the ritual of some festival, possibly that of the New Year, we have a reference to the ritual bisection of a dove as a symbolic substitute for the primaeval monster Ti'âmat.[1]

This involved and rather inclusive discussion of the connection between the *Enuma elish* and the *akîtu* festival has been necessary, since our understanding of this Babylonian account of the Creation must depend in part upon its liturgical purpose or use. To this end, it will also be helpful to note here Dr. S. A. Pallis's conclusion to his important study of the Babylonian *akîtu* festival: "Hence I do not hesitate to hazard the hypothesis that Enuma eliš was originally simply a cult text, . . ., belonging to the primitive agricultural drama of Babylon, which was originally performed at the *akîtu* festival. The creation and ordering of the universe, 'the determination of its destiny', was originally inseparably associated with the drama of the seasons and the phallos drama. But at the same time we must strongly emphasize that in the form in which we now know Enuma eliš, it is no cult text. The epic is a text influenced by the urban culture, which now appears as a cult legend of a similar character to, e.g., the *Homeric Hymn* to *Demeter*. It is a poetic production which has become detached from the cult, but in the sense that the poet has drawn upon the old cultural traditions. This is the very reason why the creation epic is of such interest to us; it is reminiscent of an earlier stratum of culture, in which each detail as well as the whole had a different meaning".[2] The liturgical significance of the *Enuma elish* is possibly somewhat underestimated in this summary of Dr. Pallis, and perhaps too much emphasis is put upon its being a literary product; however, as we shall see as we now turn to the study of its text, the *Enuma elish* certainly incorporates many earlier traditions, which also show evidence of tendentious editing in the interest of Babylon's god.

The poem begins impressively with a picture of the primordial state before the emergence of the gods, through whom ultimately the creation of the world would be achieved. This picture does not differ significantly from that contained or implied in the earlier Sumerian

[1] Cf. Ebeling, p. 36: "Die Taube, die man wirft, ist Tiamât. Man wirft (sie) und schlagt (sie): in zwei Hälften".

[2] *Op. cit.*, p. 299. "L'*Enūma eliš* è una creazione eminentemente letteraria, una vera epopea, e va riguardato quindi anche dal punto di vista dell' arte", Furlani, p. 24.

93

cosmogonies, except that the primordial deep of waters is here distinctly personified as two beings:

> When on high the heaven had not been named,
> Firm ground below had not been called by name,
> Naught but primordial Apsu, their begetter,
> (And) Mummu-Tiamat, she who bore them all,
> Their waters commingling as a single body;
> No reed hut had been matted, no marsh land had appeared,
> When no gods whatever had been brought into being,
> Uncalled by name, their destinies undetermined—
> Then it was that the gods were formed within them.[1]

Mummu-Ti'âmat, Mother-Ti'âmat,[2] is the personification of the salt-waters of the sea, and it would seem that behind this Babylonian concept must lie the Sumerian figure of Nammu, the personification of the sea and the original creatrix, whom we have already met in the earlier cosmogonies. With Apsû, the personification of the sweet waters, we are also already acquainted. What appears to be a new idea is the commingling of these two forms of water. The idea could be derived from the spectacle of the passage of the Euphrates and Tigris into the sea;[3] it does not seem to have had any prototype in Sumerian thought, although in some ways it both explains and contradicts Enki's relations with Nammu, the sea, and with the Apsû.

From the union of Ti'âmat and Apsû two pairs of beings are successively born. They are named respectively Lahmu and Lahamu, and Anshar and Kishar: their natures and functions, so far as our knowledge at present extends, seem inexplicable, although the names of the latter pair mean in Sumerian 'totality of the higher (heavenly) elements' and 'totality of the lower (earthly) elements.'[4] Anshar and Kishar become the parents of Anu, and so we reach the appearance of the high-god of the traditional Mesopotamian pantheon. Anu is described as the equal of his father, and in turn he himself becomes

---

[1] Tablet I, ll. 1–9. The translation given throughout here is by E. A. Speiser in *A.N.E.T.*, pp. 60b–61a (square brackets for restorations omitted).

[2] "Mummu. L'accezione esatta di questa parola ci è ancora ignota, e la sua interpretazione è una vera *crux interpretum*", Furlani, p. 76. Furlani is inclined also to see the word as "un epiteto di Ti'āmat, ummu = 'madre' ". Saggs, p. 410, suggests that theologically it means something like 'Creative Life-Force'.

[3] Cf. Jacobsen in *I.A.A.M.*, pp. 171–2.

[4] Cf. Garelli et Leibovici in *Sources orientales*, I, p. 121; Furlani, p. 77.

the father of Nudimmud, i.e. Enki. The emphasis which is then laid upon the superiority of Enki would suggest that this part of the *Enuma elish* must be derived from the tradition of some cult-centre of Enki, probably Eridu, where this deity was exalted above all the other gods—there is indeed other evidence of a close association between Eridu and Babylon and their respective deities:[1]

> Anu begot his image Nudimmud.
> This Nudimmud was of his fathers the master;
> Of broad wisdom, understanding, mighty in strength,
> Mightier by far than his grandfather, Anshar.
> He had no rivals among the gods,
> > his brothers.[2]

A curious episode then follows which would seem also to be drawn from Eridu tradition. Their divine progeny now begin to disturb and affront Ti'âmat and Apsû by their unseemly behaviour. Apsû wants to destroy them, but Ti'âmat opposes his design. The maternal solicitude shown by Ti'âmat here invests her with a very different character from that in which she appears in the sequel of the poem:

> As soon as Tiamat heard this,
> She was wroth and called out to her husband,
> She cried out aggrieved, as she raged all alone,
> Injecting woe into her mood;
> "What? Should we destroy that which we have built?
> Their ways indeed are most troublesome, but let us
> > attend kindly!"[3]

Apsû, however, persists with his plan to destroy the younger gods, who are terrified when they learn of it—all, except Ea (Enki), who is

---

[1] Cf. Dhorme, *Choix de Textes religieux assyro-babyloniens*, pp. 82–9 (see p. 84); *Les religions*, pp. 141–2, 168–9.

[2] Tab. I, ll. 16–20, in *A.N.E.T.*, p. 61a. On the name 'Nudimmud' given to Ea here, see n. 3, p. 84. Furlani, p. 78, proposes a somewhat different interpretation: "Nudimmud è un nome sumero di Ea e significa 'procreatore dell' increato', cioè di quello che non esisteva, è dunque un titolo che esalta la sua facoltà fattrice, produttrice".

[3] Tab. I, ll. 41–6, in *A.N.E.T.*, p. 61b. The idea of the insubordination, leading to revolt, of a generation of younger gods against their elders and progenitors, is found in Greek mythology, as we shall see, and it is reflected perhaps in the story of Noah and his sons in Genesis ix. 21 ff. Cf. Brandon, *Time and Mankind*, pp. 80–1, and below pp. 172–3. Furlani comments, p. 78, "Senza lo schiamazzo diurno e notturno di alcuni ragazzacci nessuna umanità!"

roused to employ his wisdom in counter-action. As the god of magic, Ea causes Apsû to fall into a deep sleep, and in that condition he slays him.[1] The episode clearly derives from the myth of the foundation of Ea's temple at Eridu, as the continuation of the narrative makes plain, the personified Apsû being metamorphosed into a place:

> After Ea had vanquished and trodden down his foes,
> Had secured his triumph over his enemies,
> In his sacred chamber in profound peace had rested,
> He named it "Apsu", for shrines he assigned (it).
> In the same place his cult-hut he founded.
> Ea and Damkina, his wife, dwelled (there) in splendour.[2]

This account of Ea's triumphant establishment in his sanctuary at Eridu is now used as a means of introducing Marduk, who, though represented as the offspring of the union of Ea and Damkina after the subduing of the Apsû, nevertheless appears as full grown and supremely powerful as, in Greek mythology, Pallas Athene sprang from the head of Zeus:

> In the chamber of fates, the abode of destinies,
> A god was engendered, most able and wisest of gods.
> In the heart of Apsu was Marduk created,
> In the heart of holy Apsu was Marduk created.
> He who begot him was Ea, his father;
> She who bore him was Damkina, his mother.
> The breasts of goddesses he did suck.[3]

The attempt to describe this paragon of the gods is notable both for its imaginative endeavour and for the fact that resort is made to the reduplication of features in the attempt to create a figure of supernatural proportions, a device well known in later Indian iconography:

> Alluring was his figure, sparkling the lift of his eyes.
> Lordly was his gait, commanding from of old.

[1] Tab. I, ll. 47–72.

[2] Tab. I, ll. 73–8, in *A.N.E.T.*, pp. 61b–62a. Furlani, pp. 79–80, rightly comments on the change of Ea's character implied here. He thinks that 'l'eroe Ea' is an *ad hoc* creation here in order to exalt Ea's son, Marduk.

[3] Tab. I, ll. 79–85, in *A.N.E.T.*, p. 62a. l. 85: "Gli fece succhiare mammelle di dee", Furlani, p. 41; cf. Heidel, p. 26, n. 34. To be nourished at the breasts of a goddess was a prerogative of the Egyptian pharaohs. Jacobsen in *I.A.A.M.*, pp. 175, 180, suggests that in the myth of this marvellous birth and the subsequent defeat of Ti'âmat, Enlil has been substituted by Marduk. See p. 102.

When Ea saw him, the father who begot him,
He exulted and glowed, his heart filled with gladness.
. . . . .
Perfect were his members beyond comprehension,
Unsuited for understanding, difficult to perceive.
Four were his eyes, four were his ears;
When he moved his lips, fire blazed forth.
Large were all four hearing organs,
And the eyes, in like number, scanned all things.
He was the loftiest of the gods, surpassing was his stature;
His members were enormous, he was exceeding tall.[1]

The slaying of Apsû was not, however, to go unavenged, and the
narrative relates how Ti'âmat was roused by the deed from her
former benignity to seek the destruction of those who had now added
to their earlier insolence the crime of killing their progenitor, who
was also her spouse. She prepares for the conflict by creating, as
auxiliaries, a brood of monsters, the description of which affords an
interesting insight into the horrific side of the Mesopotamian imagination. Further, she appoints from among the gods who sided with her,
one, Kingu, to be both the commander of her forces and her own
consort, and to him she gives also the 'Tablets of Fate', the possession of which was to be an important factor in the sequel of the
tale.[2]

The preparations of Ti'âmat become known to the gods, and they
are appalled by them. Anshar prevails upon both Ea and Anu in turn
to confront or to endeavour to appease the awful Ti'âmat; they each
seem to have fled on beholding the monstrous creatrix.[3] Appeal is
then made to Marduk, who readily accepts the invitation to become
the champion of the gods; but he lays down one condition:

If I indeed, as your avenger,
Am to vanquish Tiamat and to save your lives,
Set up the Assembly, proclaim supreme my destiny!
When jointly in Ubshukinna you have sat down rejoicing,
Let my word, instead of you, determine the fates.

[1] Tab. I, ll. 87–100, in *A.N.E.T.*, p. 62a. For a representation of Marduk,
showing possibly his two faces, see A. Jeremias, *Das Alte Testament im Lichte
des alten Orients*, p. 42, Abb. 20. Cf. Furlani, pp. 80–1, and Tav. I.
[2] Tab. I, ll. 107–161.
[3] Tab. II, ll. 1–91.

> Unalterable shall be what I may bring into being;
> Neither recalled nor changed shall be the command of my lips.[1]

The motive behind the account of this episode is obvious. Although they could not claim that their own local god had been originally the first of the gods and although they recognised some earlier subordination of Marduk to Ea, the Babylonian theologians sought thus to show that, when once in the fateful past the older gods had failed, Marduk had been accepted both as their champion and their lord.

The gods readily accept Marduk's condition, and the supreme position that they confer upon him is made uncompromisingly clear:

> They erected for him a princely throne.
> Facing his fathers, he sat down, presiding.
> "Thou art the most honoured of the great gods
> Thy decree is unrivalled, thy command is Anu".
> . . . . .
> O Marduk, thou art indeed our avenger.
> We have granted thee kingship over the universe entire.[2]

A demonstration is then proposed of Marduk's newly acquired power—here clearly conceived as the power of magical utterance:

> Having placed in their midst a piece of cloth,
> They addressed themselves to Marduk, their first-born:
> "Lord, truly thy decree is first among the gods.
> Say but to wreck or create; it shall be.
> Open thy mouth: the cloth will vanish!
> Speak again, and the cloth shall be whole!"
> At the word of his mouth the cloth vanished.
> He spoke again, and the cloth was restored.[3]

---

[1] Tab. III, ll. 116–22, in *A.N.E.T.*, p. 65b. Cf. Heidel, p. 29, n. 60: "When therefore the gods, at the New Year's festival, convened in the Court of Assembly, 'they reverently waited' on Marduk, the 'king of the gods of heaven and earth', and in that spirit they decided the destinies".

[2] Tab. IV, ll. 1–6, 13–14, in *A.N.E.T.*, p. 66a. "*Parak rubūtum* del nostro testo è quasi sinonimo di *parak šarrūtim* di altri testi babilonesi, e significa quindi seggio o trono regale, principesco, maestoso", Furlani, p. 86.

[3] Tab. IV, ll. 19–26, in *A.N.E.T.*, p. 66a. Furlani, p. 89, thinks that the test consisted of annihilating the cloth and then reconstituting it from nothing. Heidel, p. 37, n. 73, disagrees with such an interpretation, maintaining that "the dogma of a *creatio ex nihilo* was not shared by the Babylonians and Assyrians". "Par sa parole, il crée ou il anéantit. Cette puissance est rendue sensible par l'expérience du vêtement", Dhorme, *Choix de Textes*, p. 43, n. 22. This demonstration of Marduk's power is to some degree reminiscent of that of Yahweh's to Gideon in *Judges*, vi. 36–40.

At this sign of his power, the gods rejoice, and they commission him:

> Go and cut off the life of Tiamat.
> May the winds bear her blood to places undisclosed.

Marduk then arms himself for the encounter with Ti'âmat. His weapons are various: some belong to the armoury of the Mesopotamian warrior, but others take the form of winds and the rain-flood, which suggest that Marduk must have been closely associated with the phenomena of the storms so well known and feared on the Mesopotamian plains.[1]

The fateful encounter duly takes place, and it is vividly described. In the dialogue that precedes the actual struggle, Marduk significantly accuses Ti'âmat of having usurped the authority of Anu—an accusation of which the grounds are certainly not manifest in the narrative of the *Enuma elish*: the charge probably reflects the traditional view that Anu, as the original head of the pantheon, was the embodiment of the fundamental order of the universe.[2] From the references made to the reactions of Ti'âmat at this stage it is difficult to understand the manner in which she is conceived. The personification of the sea, Ti'âmat had previously been referred to as a female being who, presumably through intercourse with Apsû, had given birth to the first gods. Later she is depicted as producing fearsome serpents, dragons and other monsters to aid her in destroying the gods—a representation that would seem to imply that she was conceived as being herself of some monstrous serpentine or dragon form, an image that has some iconographic support.[3] However, at the time of her encounter with Marduk, Ti'âmat not only speaks, but reference is made to her having two legs, and, in order to subdue Marduk, she is depicted as uttering an incantation and as casting a

[1] Tab. IV, ll. 35–58; cf. Tab. VI, l. 125. Cf. Furlani, pp. 90–1.

[2] Tab. IV, ll. 76–84.

[3] Cf. *Bilderatlas zur Religionsgeschichte*, 6. Lief., Abb. 24, 127; Jeremias, Abb. 23–7; *Myth and Ritual* (ed. S. H. Hooke), fig. 6; Wiseman, *Cylinder Seals of Western Asia*, p. 75; Furlani, pp. 27–33, Tav. II; Frankfort, *Kingship and the Gods*, p. 327; *Cylinder Seals*, p. 199. According to a text given by Ebeling, p. 36, "Ein Kamel ist der Totendämon der *Tiâmat*". "Mais rien ne prouve péremptoirement qu'elle (Ti'âmat) ait été un dragon, un serpent gigantesque. Cette conception est née des représentations figurées qui reproduisent fréquemment le thème de la lutte contre le dragon", Garelli et Leibovici in *Sources orientales*, I, p. 120. See Plate IV.

magical spell—*traits* that are scarcely consistent with a dragon form and nature.[1]

The actual struggle is quickly over, though its manner is curious. Marduk drives an evil wind into the body of Ti'âmat, which distends her and enables him to shoot an arrow through her opened mouth that cleaves her heart. Her death demoralises her followers, who are rounded up and imprisoned. From the vanquished Kingu Marduk takes the tablet of fate or destinies, sealing it and fastening it on his own breast. He then turns back to the carcass of Ti'âmat:[2]

> The lord trod upon the legs of Tiamat,
> With his unsparing mace he crushed her skull.
> When the arteries of her blood he had severed,
> The North wind bore (it) to places undisclosed.
> On seeing this, his fathers were joyful and jubilant,
> They brought gifts of homage, they to him.
> Then the lord paused to view her dead body,
> That he might divide the monster and do artful works.
> He split her like a shellfish into two parts:
> Half of her he set up and ceiled it as the sky,
> Pulled down the bar and posted guards.
> He bade them to allow not her waters to escape.[3]

The change in the conception of Ti'âmat implied here is frankly baffling, and so is the cosmology which evidently inspires it. As we have already seen, the *Enuma elish* begins by personifying the sea under the name of Ti'âmat: although the form in which the sea was thus personified was obscure and allusions or references to it contradictory, it has so far appeared that the personification was consis-

---

[1] See Tab. IV, ll. 90–1. According to Dhorme, *Choix de Textes*, p. 51, n. 90, "L'adverbe *šuršiš* = 'à la racine', d'où 'jusqu'au fond'. Jensen revendique pour *išdā* le sens des 'deux jambes', tout en reconnaissant qu'il peut signifier aussi le fondement de l'individu". Heidel, Speiser, Furlani, and Garelli-Leibovici include the reference to the two legs.

[2] Tab. IV, ll. 93–127; cf. Tab. VII, ll. 132–4.

[3] Tab. IV. ll. 128–140, in *A.N.E.T.*, p. 67b. The word *ku-bu*, which Speiser translates as 'monster' in l. 136, Garelli and Leibovici, p. 120, are intent on pointing out as having the meaning of 'foetus'; Heidel, p. 42, n. 93, clearly has this in mind when he says: "the monstrous corpse of Ti'âmat is here compared to a thing as repulsive as an abortion". Cf. Dhorme, *Choix de Textes*, p. 56, n. 136. In the commentary on the New Year ritual, which Ebeling, p. 35, translates, reference is made to the division of Ti'âmat: "*Tiâmat*, der 'Herr' hat [sie] bezwungen, sie gepackt, sie (dazu) bestimmt und gehälftet wie . . . Fische in 2 [Hälften]". See Plate III.

tently envisaged in terms of a single monstrous living entity. But the deed of Marduk, now described, implies a very different view. For starting with the idea of Ti'âmat as some monstrous being, whose carcase could be sliced in two, we are next given the impression that one half of the body was of such a nature that it could be utilised to form the sky—nothing is said of what happened to the other half.[1] Moreover, since Anu, the sky or heaven god, had been the first of the gods of the traditional pantheon to be born, and since reference has been made earlier in the poem to 'the Abode of Heaven', it is puzzling to find that half of Ti'âmat is now used by Marduk to form the sky, thus implying that the sky had not existed hitherto. Nor is this all the ground for puzzlement here. Having used half of the body of Ti'âmat to form the sky, a use that would suggest that it had the necessary degree of solidity,[2] Marduk is then depicted as taking measures to prevent the escape of the waters of Ti'âmat, i.e. presumably to stop them from flooding into the universe which he had now created. In terms of the imagery employed here we are back with the simple conception of Ti'âmat as the sea. From what is known of the traditional cosmology of Mesopotamia it is possible to understand the implications of this last act of Marduk, namely, that since the whole universe was imagined as being surrounded by the ocean, the integrity of the fabric of the sky had to be preserved lest the outer waters should burst in.[3] But, while the imagery here is intelligible, it is impossible to follow the thought of the mythographer when he describes how half of the body of Ti'âmat, i.e. the sea, was used to form the sky that served to keep out the sea from the universe that Marduk had thus formed. Probably any attempt to reconcile this conflicting imagery would be mistaken, since it would seem likely that in this part of the *Enuma elish* there has also been some fusion of earlier myths. Reference has already been made to a Sumerian myth concerning the slaying of a monstrous dragon, named Kur, by

[1] According to Berossos (see p. 112), the other half of Ti'âmat was used to form the earth.

[2] Meissner, II, p. 179, renders l. 138 as: *"eine Hälfte setzte er hin/und machte sie zum Himmelsdach"*. Furlani, p. 94, comments: "Qui s'intende dire, senza dubbio, che il dio pose metà del corps di Tiāmat quale sostegno e trabeazione della superficie del cielo, della volta celeste; questa è rinforzata dal corps di Tiāmat".

[3] Cf. Meissner, II, pp. 108–9, 111–12.

Ninurta, a warrior-god who was the son of Enlil. This dragon was, significantly, connected with the primaeval waters, in that he held them in check. As a result of his destruction, these waters begin to rise to the surface, and they also have the effect of cutting off the flow of the sweet waters from the land. Ninurta has to remedy the situation, which he does by piling up heaps of stones on the body of the dead Kur, so that they might hold back the 'mighty waters'.[1] It would, accordingly, be reasonable to suppose that the author of the *Enuma elish*, intent on exalting Marduk, was led to ascribe to him something of the exploits of Ninurta as well as of Enlil.[2] Consequently, in seeking to show Marduk both as the slayer of a monster, connected with the primaeval waters, and the builder of the heavens, he fused together two very different myths, with a resulting confusion of *motifs* and imagery. Thus, he made the personification of the sea, the original Sumerian creatrix, into the monster that menaced the existence of the gods. The event of her destruction by Marduk he then utilises as the occasion for the creation of the sky by the same deity, an act which implies the separation of heaven and earth, thus emulating the deed of Enlil.[3] After this, he turns back again to the Ninurta myth, and he parallels Ninurta's exploit in using the body of Kur as the foundation of the barrier against the primaeval waters, by depicting Marduk as using part of the body of Ti'âmat as the protective canopy of the sky that holds back the surrounding ocean.

Having thus introduced Marduk as the demiurge, the poem continues with a detailed account of his creative activities. The Babylonian god, accordingly, is next depicted as surveying and ordering the proportions of the universe:

> He crossed the heavens and surveyed the regions.
> He squared Apsu's quarter, the abode of Nudimmud,
> As the lord measured the dimensions of Apsu.
> The Great Abode, its likeness, he fixed as Esharra,
> The Great Abode, Esharra, which he made as the firmament.
> Anu, Enlil, and Ea he made occupy their places.[4]

[1] Cf. Kramer, *Sumerian Mythology*, pp. 80–2; *Tablets of Sumer*, pp. 198–200.

[2] Cf. Furlani, pp. 11–12; Jacobsen in *I.A.A.M.*, pp. 179–80. See also L. W. King, *Legends of Babylon and Egypt*, pp. 116–19. On Ninurta see Dhorme, *Les religions*, pp. 102–5, 128–31.   [3] See p. 71.

[4] Tab. IV, ll. 141–6, in *A.N.E.T.*, p. 67b. What Esharra is meant to denote here is not certain. According to Heidel p. 43, n. 96, it is "a poetic

The tendentious character of the *Enuma elish* is very apparent in these lines. According to their logic, the three great cosmic deities of the traditional pantheon had to wait on Marduk for their establishment in those parts of the universe over which they presided. It is significant of the rather naïve literary ability of the author of the poem that he does not seem aware here, and also elsewhere, that the claims which he makes on behalf of the patron god of his city in fact contradicted the earlier traditions that he had chosen to incorporate into his work. The fact may also perhaps tacitly attest the strength of Mesopotamian religious tradition, in that such contradictions could have been removed, if Marduk had been represented as the original god. But great as was the Babylonian god and immense the power and prestige of his city, such a claim evidently could not be made. The author of the *Enuma elish* had to recognise Marduk as the son of Ea, and the most that he could do was to arrogate to his god such a superiority of status and such a plenitude of powers that he is betrayed into those contradictions that are so apparent to the modern scholar.

After determining the proportions of the universe, Marduk then turns to ordering the astral bodies, the movements of which the Mesopotamians believed were the 'writing of the heavens', ordaining the fates of nations and men:[1]

> He constructed stations for the great gods,
> Fixing their astral likenesses as constellations.
> He determined the year by designating the zones:
> He set up three constellations for each of the twelve months.
> . . . . .
> In her belly (Ti'âmat's) he established the zenith.
> The Moon he caused to shine, the night (to him) entrusting.[2]

designation of the earth, which is pictured as a great structure, in the shape of a canopy, placed over the *Apsû*". As he rightly remarks, the latter part of l. 145 cannot refer to the sky, since Marduk has already made this from the body of Ti'âmat. Differing interpretations are offered by other scholars; e.g. Meissner, II, pp. 179–80: "Nach dem Bilde des Apsû schafft er (Marduk) E-scharra, die himmlische Erde, wo die Hauptgötter ihre Standorte zugewiesen erhalten"; Furlani, p. 94: "Marduk construisse anzitutto Ešarra, vale a dire il cielo. Ešarra è parola sumera e vuol dire 'casa universale'. Di solito è un nome della terra, ma qui designa il cielo".

[1] Cf. Meissner, II, pp. 110, 400; Dhorme, *Les religions*, pp. 282–3, 284–7, 296–8.

[2] Tab. V, ll. 1–4, 11–12, in *A.N.E.T.*, p. 67b–68a. Cf. Furlani, pp. 95–7.

When he had completed his work of creating and ordering the universe, Marduk then turns to the creation of mankind. Once more we discern signs of the utilisation of an earlier tradition to enhance the renown of Babylon's god. The narrative here starts on the sixth tablet of the seven on which the poem was written; it would appear that there should have been some preamble to the episode that is now related—possibly it was contained on the destroyed final portion of the fifth tablet. The scene opens with Marduk's meditating on some statement of the other gods—possibly a request to make their existence easier for them:[1]

> When Marduk hears the words of the gods,
> His heart prompts (him) to fashion artful works.
> Opening his mouth, he addresses Ea.
> To impart the plan he had conceived in his heart:
> "Blood will I mass and cause bones to be.[2]
> I will establish a savage, 'man' shall be his name.[3]
> Verily, savage-man will I create.
> He shall be charged with the service of the gods,[4]
>   That they might be at ease!
> The ways of the gods I will artfully alter.
> Though alike revered, into two (groups) they shall be divided".[5]
> Ea answered him, speaking a word to him,

[1] Tab. VI, ll. 1–14, in *A.N.E.T.*, p. 68a.

[2] It is notable that there is no suggestion here of moulding man from clay: there is no apparent reason for this innovation in the tradition which we have noticed. Furlani, p. 98, translates the verb *kaṣarū* as 'legherò', commenting that it "ha poi il valore di fare". Garelli-Leibovici, p. 143, render l. 5 as: "Je veux faire un réseau de sang, former une ossature". Heidel, p. 46, has: "Blood will I form and cause bone to be". Dhorme, *Choix de textes*, p. 65, translates it as: "Mon sang je le pétrirai et des os je . . .". He explains (p. 64, n. 5) his rendering of *da-mi* as 'mon sang' by reference to the account of Berossos which we shall study below; King, *Seven Tablets of Creation*, pp. 86–7, does likewise. Cf. Brandon, *Man of his Destiny*, pp. 85–6.

[3] The word *lullū* used here as an eponym for 'man' means 'stupid', 'foolish', hence 'primitive' or 'savage'. Cf. Furlani, p. 98; Speiser, *ib.*, n. 86.

[4] " 'I riti' = *dullu*; questa parola ha il significato originario di 'servizio, lavoro', infatti i riti religiosi non sono altro che il servizio che l'uomo presta al dio", Furlani, p. 98.

[5] This possibly refers to the traditional division of the Mesopotamian pantheon into the Anunnaki and the Igigi. Cf. Dhorme, *Les religions*, p. 45.

Giving him another plan for the relief of the gods:
"Let but one of their brothers be handed over;
He alone shall perish that mankind may be fashioned".

The proposal of Ea introduces a new factor; but one possibly that had already been anticipated, as we have seen.[1] The import of his reply to Marduk is not immediately apparent, because it refers to the gods, now held captive, who had sided with Ti'âmat; in the extant form of the poem no immediate reference is made to them, so that it would seem that their unexplained appearance as the subject of Ea's proposal now is due to the unskilful introduction here of extraneous tradition.[2] However that may be, Ea is depicted as suggesting a significant amendment to Marduk's original intention, which was apparently to create man out of the basic materials that he, Marduk, would himself produce. Instead, Ea proposes a substitution sacrifice to provide the material for mankind, the victim being one of the rebel gods, which fact in turn introduces a *motif* of expiation for evil done.

To determine the victim an assembly of the gods is called, and Marduk addresses it, his leading question presuming a previous situation which is not described in the poem:

Who was it that contrived the uprising,
And made Tiamat rebel, and joined battle?
Let him be handed over who contrived the uprising.
His guilt I will make him bear. You shall dwell in peace!

To his question the assembled gods reply:

It was Kingu who contrived the uprising,
And made Tiamat rebel, and joined battle.[3]

[1] See p. 89.

[2] Cf. Tab. VI, ll. 152–3, Tab. VII, ll. 27, 90. Furlani, p. 98, suggests that, according to Mesopotamian custom, the conquered followers of Ti'âmat should have been made the slaves of the gods, but Marduk sought to spare them this fate. This interpretation encounters the difficulty constituted by the fact of the subsequent acceptance of Ea's proposal. There seems to be no justification for the view of Garelli and Leibovici, p. 144, n. 71, that the Anunnaki, the gods of the earth, were the partisans of Ti'âmat, and the Igigi, the gods of heaven, the supporters of Marduk; see p. 104, n. 5.

[3] Tab. VI, ll. 22–6, 29–30, in *A.N.E.T.*, p. 68b. "Il pantheon è insomma riunito di nuovo senza distinzione di categoria tra gli dèi stessi. Marduk fa opera di pacificazione", Furlani, p. 99.

According to the earlier narrative, Kingu had indeed been appointed by Ti'âmat as her consort and the commander of her forces, but it had not been made plain that he was the instigator of the so-called revolt. The fact that he is now selected as the sole victim perhaps indicates that the author here draws upon some other unknown source in which Kingu was more obviously cast for the rôle that he is now obliged to play:[1]

> They bound him, holding him before Ea.
> They imposed on him his guilt and severed his blood (vessels).
> Out of his blood they fashioned mankind.
> He (Ea) imposed the service and let free the gods.
> After Ea, the wise, had created mankind,
> Had imposed upon it the service of the gods—
> That work was beyond comprehension;
> As artfully planned by Marduk, did Nudimmud create it—[2].

These lines contain a number of problems that have severally caused much speculation among scholars and inspired some ingenious theories concerning the Babylonian conception of human nature and destiny. It will perhaps be well to deal with the least complex of them first. It is constituted by the part played by Ea *vis-à-vis* Marduk. Not only does Ea suggest a radical amendment of Marduk's original plan for the creation of mankind, but in the actual undertaking itself he seems progressively to assume the chief rôle until the point is reached at which it is categorically stated that Ea created mankind. The most obvious explanation is undoubtedly the likeliest here, namely, that the author is so consciously drawing on the well-established tradition that Ea was the creator of mankind, that, despite his clear intention to claim this rôle for Marduk, he insensibly slips into the older version.

Next, we have to consider the problem implicit in the fact that mankind is represented as being formed of the blood of one who was regarded as guilty of rebellion against the gods. Logically this derivation would make men partake of a sinful nature, and it might reasonably be interpreted as an attempt to explain the origin of the evil in mankind—indeed, it has been cited as a kind of Meso-

---

[1] Cf. Meissner, II, p. 98. For the ritual representation of the sacrifice of Kingu in the New Year festival see Ebeling, pp. 31, 36.

[2] Tab. VI. ll. 31–8, in *A.N.E.T.*, p. 68b.

potamian anticipation of the Hebrew account of the original sin of the human race.[1] Such an interpretation would do credit to Babylonian theological thinking. However, not only must it be noted that such a doctrine never became an established feature of Mesopotamian religious tradition, but there is even some evidence that Marduk made possible the creation of mankind by sacrificing himself. This version of the legend comes from fragments that have been preserved of a history of Babylonia which was written in Greek about 275 B.C. by Berossus, a priest of the temple of Bêl Marduk at Babylon.[2] In one of the passages concerned we are told that Marduk, or Bêl as he is here called, because the newly created land was desolate and bore no fruit, "ordered one of the gods, having cut off his own head, to mix the earth with the blood that flowed forth and to form men and beasts, capable of bearing the air".[3] Marduk did this, according to the other version of the episode, "so that (men) might be rational and partake of divine understanding".[4] There are admittedly many uncertainties and obscurities in the accounts that have survived to us of the record of Berossus; however, it would seem reasonable to conclude that, if a Babylonian priest in the third century B.C. could interpret Marduk's act in this manner, there could have been no established tradition that the moral imperfections of men were traceable to the material out of which their progenitors were originally made.[5]

---

[1] "L'homme n'est donc pas, à sa naissance, un être innocent et pur. Dans ses veines coulent sans doute, le sang d'un dieu, mais d'un dieu coupable et condamné. C'est un sang vicié qui charrie le péché et la mort. L'homme, en définitive, assume le châtiment d'un crime qu'il n'a pas commis. Ce sont les dieux qui ont lâché dans le monde le couple Péché-Mort", Garelli et Leibovici, p. 127.

[2] Cf. P. Schnabel, *Berossos und die babylonisch-hellenistische Literatur*, pp. 3–10; *R.G.G.*, I (3 Aufl.), 1069.

[3] κελεῦσαι ἑνὶ τῶν θεῶν τὴν κεφαλὴν ἀφελόντι ἑαυτοῦ τῷ ἀπορρυέντι αἵματι φυρᾶσαι τὴν γῆν καὶ διαπλάσαι ἀνθρώπους καὶ θηρία τὰ δυνάμενα τὸν ἀέρα φέρειν, in Schnabel, p. 256b. Heidel, p. 78, n. 88, maintains that the passage means that Marduk ordered a god to cut off his (not Marduk's) head, and he identifies this god with Kingu. However, to get this meaning, Heidel, has to supply in his translation the words "(that he also commanded the other gods)", otherwise he would be left with the ludicrous situation of a decapitated god creating mankind. Cf. Meissner, II, p. 106.

[4] τοῦτον τὸν θεὸν ἀφελεῖν τὴν ἑαυτοῦ κεφαλήν, καὶ τὸ ῥυὲν αἷμα τοὺς ἄλλους θεοὺς φυρᾶσαι τῇ γῇ, καὶ διαπλάσαι τοὺς ἀνθρώπους· διὸ νοεροὺς τε εἶναι καὶ φρονήσεως θείας μετέχειν, in Schnabel, p. 255b.

[5] Cf. Brandon, *Man and his Destiny*, pp. 85–7.

This conclusion bears also on another line of interpretation of this part of the myth, according to which, by man's formation from the blood of the guilty Kingu, he is doomed to bear the penalty of a crime which he did not commit—hence, in order to spare the rebel gods, by this sacrifice of Kingu, sin and death were brought into the world of men.[1] The profundity of theological thought implicit in such a notion would indeed greatly enhance the reputation of Babylonian religion, if it could be surely established that this is what the passage in the *Enuma elish* originally meant. Unfortunately this cannot be done, and the more likely explanation would seem to be that, in fusing the story of Marduk's conquest of Ti'âmat with the representation of him as the creator of mankind, the earlier tradition of Ea's creation of man from the blood of sacrificed gods has here been adapted to deal with the problem of the fate of the captured followers of the vanquished Ti'âmat.[2]

One other aspect of this *Enuma elish* version of the creation of man must be noticed. Man is made to "be charged with the service of the gods, that they may be at ease". This idea of the *raison d'être* of mankind was already ancient, and, as we shall see, it represented the established conviction of the Mesopotamians about the purpose of human life. It had a corollary, which we must later consider, but which does not overtly appear here. It is that the gods withheld the attribute of immortality from man when they created him, with the result that man, after serving his divine masters, has to die. It is conceivable that the author of the *Enuma elish* intended to suggest that man's mortal nature derives from the fact that he took his origin from one who had died; however, it must be recognised that this great Babylonian epic of creation does not clearly account for that aspect of human nature which, as we learn from other writings, so profoundly affected the Mesopotamian view of life.[3]

After the creation of mankind, Marduk assigns to the gods their various stations in the universe, and they, in gratitude for all that he has done for them, undertake the construction of his sanctuary at Babylon:[4]

> The Anunnaki applied the implement;
> For one whole year they moulded bricks.

[1] See n. 1, p. 107. [2] See p. 89, see also Tab. VII, l.90.
[3] See p. 115. [4] Tab. VI, ll. 39–58.

> When the second year arrived,
> They raised high the head of Esagila equalling Apsu.[1]

It may be considered strange that, after mankind had been created to serve them, we should now find the gods toiling as labourers to build a temple for Marduk. This apparent contradiction is undoubtedly to be explained as due to the desire of the author of the poem to ascribe Marduk's great sanctuary at Babylon to the work of the gods—intent on claiming this divine foundation, he ignored the contradiction which it constituted for the logic of his narrative.[2]

The rest of the *Enuma elish* is concerned with the honouring of Marduk, which chiefly takes the form of the gods' proclaiming of his fifty names connoting the plenitude of his power and glory. However, it is important to note, with reference to the probable ritual use of the *Enuma elish*, that, after the building of Marduk's sanctuary, the gods assemble for the determining of the destinies:

> The great gods took their seats,
> They set up festive drink, sat down to a banquet.
> After they had made merry within it,
> In Esagila, the *splendid*, had performed their rites,
> The norms had been fixed (and) *all* [their] portents,
> All the gods apportioned the stations of heaven and earth.
> The fifty great gods took their seats.
> The seven gods of destiny set up the three hundred [in heaven].[3]

That the Babylonian version of the creation exercised a considerable influence upon Mesopotamian mythology is evident both from the variety of the provenance of the texts and of the languages[4] in which it has been found, and also from the fact that Berossos witnesses to its currency in the third century B.C. But this influence did not mean that other accounts were superseded, and interesting proof of this is provided by yet another version of the creation of man that was known in the city of Ashur about 800 B.C. It is also

[1] Tab. VI, ll. 59–62, in *A.N.E.T.*, pp. 68b–69a.

[2] Furlani, p. 100, thinks that the building is located in the heavens: "Il poeta la chiama Babele, poiché si tratta del prototipo celeste della Babele terrena. Tutto in terra ha il suo prototipo in cielo: sopra la Babele di Mesopotamia ha il suo prototipo in cielo".

[3] Tab. VI, ll. 74–81, in *A.N.E.T.*, p. 69a. The 'seven gods of destiny' (*ilāni sīmāti*) are the seven planets. See p. 114.

[4] Cf. Heidel, pp. 1–2; Furlani, pp. 9–10.

notable for the fact that it too utilises the idea that mankind took its origin from the sacrifice of certain gods, though in this instance there is no suggestion of a guilt factor in the transaction. The myth opens with a description of the gods discussing future undertakings, after the establishment of the main features of the Mesopotamian world:[1]

(And) the Anunnaki, the great gods,
Seated themselves in the exalted sanctuary
And recounted among themselves what had been created.
"Now that the destinies of heaven and earth have been fixed,
Trench and canal have been given their right courses,
The banks of the Tigris and the Euphrates
Have been established,
What (else) shall we do?
What (else) shall we create?
O Anunnaki, ye great gods,

. . . . .

The Anunnaki, who fix the destinies,
Both (groups) of them, made answer to Enlil:
"In Uzumua, the bond of heaven and earth,
Let us slay (two) Lamga gods.[2]
With their blood let us create mankind.
The service of the gods be their portion,
For all times
To maintain the boundary ditch,
To place the hoe and the basket
Into their hands
For the dwelling of the great gods,
Which is fit to be an exalted sanctuary,

. . . . .

To increase the abundance in the land,
To celebrate the festivals of the gods,
To pour out cold water
In the great house of the gods, which is fit to be an exalted sanctuary.
Ulligarra (and) Zalgarra
Thou shalt call their names".[3]

. . . . .

[1] Trans. Heidel, pp. 69–70, cf. p. 68. Cf. Ungnad, pp. 56–7; Garelli et Leibovici, pp. 148–50.
[2] "The Lamga deities were craftsmen gods", Heidel, p. 69, n. 52.
[3] The names probably mean respectively "the establisher of abundance" and "the establisher of plenty", Heidel, p. 70, n. 56. Cf. Garelli et Leibovici, p. 149, n. 98; Ungnad, p. 57, n. 3.

To complete our survey of the creation legends of Mesopotamia, we must now notice at greater length the account of the Babylonian priest, Berossos, to which reference has already been made. Our knowledge of what Berossos wrote has unfortunately reached us in a very indirect manner, namely, in the fragments that have been preserved of the *Chronica* of the fourth century bishop Eusebius, who in turn quotes from what an earlier writer, Alexander Polyhistor (1st cent. B.C.), had reported of the lost writings of Berossos.[1] However, despite this lack of direct access to the original record, what we do learn is remarkable alike for the fact of its general consistency with the ancient tradition recovered from the tablets and for its witness to the continuity of that tradition into the third century B.C.

According to the record as it apparently existed in the *Chronica* of Eusebius, it would seem that, after describing Chaldaea as being originally populated by a mass of strange men, living a life of brutish ignorance and disorder, Berossos went on to describe the way in which civilisation first came to mankind here: "Now, in the first year (after the creation?) there appeared out of the Red Sea, where it borders Babylonia, a fearsome being named Oannes, as Apollodorus also relates; his whole body was that of a fish, and under the head of the fish grew out another head, and feet as those of a man, growing out from the tail of the fish. He had also a human voice. His image has been preserved until the present day".[2] There can be little doubt that in this strange being, as the sequel also shows, Berossos was describing the water-god Enki or Ea, who was also the god of wisdom; there is indeed evidence that the deity was served by priests who wore a fish-like costume.[3] The account continues: "And this being (τὸ ζῷον), he (Berossos) relates, daily consorted with the people, partaking of no food, and imparting to them the knowledge of letters and all kinds of learning (μαθημάτων) and skills, and teaching them

[1] Cf. Schnabel, pp. 134–6.

[2] In Schnabel, p. 253. For Polyhistor's or Eusebius's reference to the record of Apollodorus see Schnabel, pp. 261, 262. Schnabel, p. 173, interprets 'the first year' as that of Aloros, 'des ersten Urkönigs'; but, since Oannes imparts to mankind their first knowledge of laws and all that constitutes *politeia*, it would be reasonable to think that the reference is to the first year after the creation. Cf. Jeremias, *Das Alte Testament im Lichte des alten Orients*, p. 5.

[3] Cf. Dhorme, *Les religions*, p. 33; C. J. Gadd, *History and Monuments of Ur*, pp. 7–8, and Plate I.

to found cities and establish temples, to formulate laws and to survey the land. He showed them the use of seeds and the cultivation of fruits—indeed he taught men all that is necessary to the daily support of life. Since his day no further discoveries had been made. And at the setting of the sun this being, Oannes, sunk back again into the sea and tarried by night in the ocean. For he was amphibious. Later, other beings also appeared similar to this one, concerning which, he said, there is an account in the record of the kings. And he relates that Oannes wrote about the creation and political affairs, and that he gave this record (λόγον) to men".[1]

After this strange legend, which undoubtedly preserves a reminiscence of the Sumerian tradition of Enki as the founder of the arts of civilised living, Berossos apparently related the myth of the creation as he knew it in his day—it would seem too that he believed that it had been part of Oannes' primordial revelation: "He (Berossos) says that once there was a time when all was darkness and water, and in this there came into existence beings of wondrous and peculiar forms (ἰδέας). For there were born men with two wings, some also with four wings and double faces, and bodies having one or two heads, male and female; moreover, their genitals were both male and female". The account continues with a description of many more of these strange beings, with a note that their images were to be found in the temple of Bêl (Marduk). Over all these beings, it is said, there ruled a woman named Omorka. "Now this in Chaldaean is *thalatth*, meaning in Greek the sea (*thalassa*), and equalling numerically the moon. And all things being thus situated, (Berossos says) Bêl came and clove the woman in two; and of one half of her he made the earth and of the other the heaven, and he destroyed the beings within her."[2] Berossos apparently recognised this as an allegorical account of the beginning of things, and he continues with a more rationalised version of the process of creation:[3] "For the universe was moisture, and living things were generated in it". Then, after the second of the passages already cited above about Bel's creation of mankind,[4] there follows a further statement about the creation of the universe: "that

[1] In Schnabel, pp. 253–4; τὸν δὲ Ὠάννην φησι (Berossos) περὶ γενεᾶς . . . γράψαι . . . .

[2] In Schnabel, pp. 254–5. Cf. Heidel, pp. 77–8; Meissner, II, pp. 103–4.

[3] Ἀλληγορικῶς δέ φησι ταῦτα πεφυσιολογῆσθαι.

[4] See p. 107, n. 4.

Bêl, i.e. Zeus according to the customary interpretation, cleaving the darkness in twain, separated earth and heaven from each other, and set in order the world (τὸν κόσμον). But the living beings, not able to bear the light, perished". To deal with this latter contingency, as we have already noticed, Bêl created men and beasts, who were able to sustain the air. The work of creation was completed by Bêl's making of the stars, and the sun and moon, and the five planets.[1]

It is worth noting also that some knowledge of the Babylonian creation myth had reached the last of the Neoplatonist philosophers, Damascius (c. A.D.480), but whether from Berossos's account is not known. Damascius, who naturally attempts some rationalisation of the myth, mentions a series of beings between the primordial pair, whom he names Tauthe and Apasōn, and Bêl, whom he calls the demiurge (δημιουργός)—a series that can be reasonably identified with the divine generations given in the *Enuma elish*.[2]

There can be no doubt both from the narrative of the *Enuma elish* and from other material that one of the main themes of the *akîtu* festival at Babylon was the decreeing of the destinies of the state by Marduk for the coming year.[3] There was apparently in the Esagila, Marduk's temple, a *du-azag*, i.e. a 'chamber of destiny', where Marduk and the other gods were believed to assemble on the eighth and eleventh days of the festival for the purpose of deciding what was to come to pass;[4] it would seem also that at *akîtu* festivals elsewhere in Mesopotamia a similar occasion was annually commemorated.[5] The idea of destiny, and that of the power to determine it, were clearly basic notions in Mesopotamian thought, and they were closely associated with the idea of creation. As we have already seen in our study of the Sumerian cosmogonies, creation meant not only bringing a thing into existence, but also the ability to conceive its purpose and the power to decree that it should fulfil that purpose. Quite clearly the idea of the magical potency of knowing and pronouncing a name was operative here, although it also possibly involved some primitive

---

[1] In Schnabel, pp. 255–6. See p. 107.
[2] Cf. Meissner, II, p. 103; Heidel, pp. 75–6.
[3] Cf. Pallis, pp. 186, 189–97, 296–7; Frankfort, *Kingship and the Gods*, pp. 325–6, 331–3; Thureau-Dangin, p. 134.
[4] Cf. Pallis, pp. 99, 184; Frankfort, *ibid*.
[5] Cf. Jean, pp. 170–1; Pallis, pp. 92–4.

analysis of the intellectual processes of conception and planning, together with the authority to achieve what was conceived. In Mesopotamian literature the notion finds a variety of expression, some forms of which appear to be mutually contradictory.[1] Some examples may be briefly mentioned: whereas Enki is often depicted decreeing the fates of various individual things,[2] the strange 'myth of Zu' envisages the Tablets of Destiny as in the possession of Enlil, until they are stolen by the Zu-bird and Enlil is thus rendered impotent[3]—here the Tablets appear to be regarded as a kind of talisman which conferred supreme power on its possessor. A rather similar conception seems to underlie the references to the Tablets of Destiny in the *Enuma elish*. Ti'âmat, the primaeval creatrix, gives the Tablets to her consort Kingu, and one of Marduk's first acts after his victory is to seize them for himself [4]—on the other hand, it is to be noted that Marduk demands, before undertaking to fight Ti'âmat, that "my word, instead of you, determines the fates",[5] but the test set to discover that he has become endowed with this power takes the form of his destroying and restoring again a piece of cloth.[6] Some contradiction about the nature of destiny is also to be found in the fact that, while according to current astrological notions the pattern of all things had been fixed "from far days", the *akîtu* festival presupposed an annual determination of fates.[7] However, we should perhaps regard these contradictions of concept as more apparent than real; for behind them there seems to lie a profound conviction on the part of the inhabitants of Mesopotamia that there was a law or principle according to which all things must conform. They naturally sought to associate the gods, who were for them the embodiment of the order of the universe, with the creation or determination of this law; but it is evident that at times they almost reached to a personification

[1] Cf. M. David, *Les Dieux et le Destin en Babylonie*, pp. 21–37, 89–94; Pallis, pp. 191–3; Furlani, p. 87.

[2] See pp. 72, 75, 77–8.

[3] Cf. *A.N.E.T.*, pp. 111–13. See also T. Fish, "The Zu Bird", in *B.J.R.L.*, 31 (1948).

[4] "disposer des tablettes revient à disposer de l'ordre universel ou, plus précisément, à détenir une sorte de pouvoir général de création, d'ordonnancement et d'action, *la légitimité* de ce pouvoir étant d'une importance suprême", David, p. 89.

[5] Tab. III, l. 120.   [6] See p. 98.

[7] Cf. Meissner, II, p. 125; Dhorme, *Les religions*, pp. 282–3, 284–7.

The Creation of the Sun and Moon, by Michelangelo (Sistine Chapel). This representation of the Creator is instinct with the awful dynamism implied by the brief statement of *Genesis* i. 16. It has been suggested that the figure to the left also represents God turning to create the earth and its vegetation. (Photo: Anderson.)

PLATE

V

The Creation of Woman, by Michelangelo (Sistine Chapel). God is represented as though He calls forth Eve, from the side of the unconscious Adam, by the power of conceptual thought. Possibly Michelangelo had also in mind here the ancient myth of Pallas Athene springing forth from the head of Zeus. (Photo: Anderson.)

PLATE VI

of destiny itself, perhaps rather after the fashion of the Egyptian *maat* or the Indo-Iranian *rta-aša*.[1]

With the concept of destiny the *raison d'être* of mankind as a whole and as individuals was essentially related. As we have learned from a number of texts, men had been expressly created to serve the gods by building their temples and maintaining the regular services of praise and sacrifice in them. The acceptance of, and indeed the emphasis upon, this rôle which we find in Mesopotamian literature is very remarkable, and it contrasts notably with the apparent lack of concern in Egypt about defining the purpose of human existence. And the *trait* is even more remarkable, when it is recalled that this divine service carried no *post-mortem* reward, and, moreover, that the gods had ordained that it should be thus—"When the gods created mankind, Death for mankind they set aside, Life in their own hands retaining", to quote the bitter refrain of the *Epic of Gilgamesh*.[2] But this estimate of man's life was closely integrated with the evaluation of destiny. Indeed, in terms of the Mesopotamian *Weltanschauung* to have a destiny, a *šimtu*, 'that which is attributed, or decreed', meant to have a *raison d'être*, to have a part in the scheme of the universe.[3] In other words, while the gods had a purpose for a man, he lived; and, if he served them well, they blessed him and gave him prosperity; but, when they no longer decreed his destiny, he died and departed to the miserable half-life in *kur-nu-gi-a*, the awful 'land of no return'. Why such an arrangement should be, the Mesopotamians never asked. They appear essentially to have been realists, and their eschatology expresses the realism of their estimate of death.[4] It is probably for this reason that in their cosmogonies they felt no need

---

[1] Cf. J. Bottéro, *La religion babylonienne*, p. 80: "Il est possible que les hautes sphères de penseurs soient arrivées assez près de l'idée d'une Loi universelle, laquelle gisait au fond du mythe de la marche du monde réglé par la Décision des Dieux". Cf. David, p. 55. See also Brandon, *Man and his Destiny*, pp. 263–4, 320–1.

[2] *Epic of Gilgamesh*, Tab. X, col. iii, 3–4. Cf. Brandon, pp. 92–5.

[3] Cf. David, pp. 23, 26, 39–40, 43; Bottéro, p. 79; Furlani, p. 87.

[4] Cf. Brandon, pp. 70–105. It is significant that F. R. Kraus in his valuable article entitled "Altmesopotamisches Lebensgefühl" (*J.N.E.S.*, XIX, pp. 117–32), in which he seeks to prove that the Mesopotamian philosophy of life was not profoundly pessimistic, does not discuss this aspect of the concept of destiny.

to account for the origin of the dismal underworld of the dead or for that of death itself. Although they conceived of a death-god, Uggae, death itself was a negative thing, and it was sufficiently explained by the action of the gods in making men to serve them only here in this world.[1] In their orderly manner they assigned the realm of the dead a divine ruler, Nergal, since it constituted one of the clearly defined parts of the universe; but in their mythology they never apparently felt it necessary to account for its origin or awful nature.[2]

In conclusion it may be asked whether in Mesopotamian thought creation implies an ultimate destruction, whether an *Urzeit* connotes an *Endzeit*? The cuneiform evidence is not clear, particularly because it is almost non-existent. As we have seen, the tradition of a great flood that destroyed almost all living things had fixed itself firmly in the Mesopotamian mind, thereby making familiar the idea of a universal destruction. Moreover, the concern with omens, especially in connection with astral phenomena, suggests both a profound awareness of the incalculable factor in life and a belief that its operations may in some ways be foreseen. On the other hand, a notable passage in the *Epic of Gilgamesh* seems to reveal a weary pessimism about the inconsequence of life:

> Do we build a house for ever?
> Do we seal (contracts) for ever?
> . . . . .
> Since the days of yore there has been no [permanence];
> The *resting* and the dead, how alike [they are]!
> Do they not compose a picture of death,
> The commoner and the noble,
> Once they are near to [their fate]?[3]

But it is to Berossos, or rather to fragments of his work quoted by later writers, that we owe the clearest statement on this issue.

---

[1] Cf. Brandon in *B.J.R.L.*, 43 (1961), pp. 322–4.

[2] Cf. Dhorme, *Les religions*, pp. 38–44, 51–2; Jean, pp. 19, 91; Kramer, *Tablets of Sumer*, pp. 81–8, 182–3.

[3] *Epic of Gilgamesh*, Tab. X, col. vi, 26–39, trans. E. A. Speiser in A.N.E.T., pp. 92b–93a. Cf. W. G. Lambert, *Babylonian Wisdom Literature*, pp. 11–12, 17–18; Kraus in *J.N.E.S.*, XIX, pp. 121–5; Brandon, *Man and his Destiny*, pp. 94–6. See also the cynical dialogue translated by S. H. Langdon, *Babylonian Wisdom*, pp. 67 ff.

Although what is reported of his views has not yet found confirmation in the native sources, it would seem not impossible that Mesopotamian astrology contemplated a situation that would reverse or undo that which produced the creation: "Berossos, who is the interpreter of Bêl, says that everything takes place according to the course of the stars; further he affirms this so confidently that he assigns times for the conflagration (*conflagrationi*) of the world and the flood (*diluvio*). For he asserts that the world (*terrena*) will burn, when all the stars, which now pursue diverse courses, come together in (the constellation of) the Crab, thus positioned under the same sign so that a straight line may pass through all their orbs. As to the future inundation, (it will happen) when the same body of stars meet in (the constellation of) Capricorn. The former constellation denotes the summer solstice, the latter the winter solstice: they are the signs of great power, since in them the turning-points of the year lie".[1]

That some form of the 'myth of the eternal return' should have existed in ancient Mesopotamia would not be surprising;[2] but it is probable that it exercised no more effective influence on the *Weltanschauung* of the individual person than it did in the sister civilisation of Egypt, if indeed the myth were current in some fashion there.[3] In each instance personal destiny was conceived in terms of the accepted evaluation of man, and, accordingly, they differed fundamentally—while the Egyptian could look forward with some measure of confidence to a *post-mortem* existence of eternal beatitude, the Mesopotamian contemplated beyond death only the hopeless doom of the 'land of no-return'.[4]

[1] Quoted by Seneca, *Nat. Quest.* III, 29, 1; in Schnabel, pp. 266–7, see also pp. 251–2. Cf. Meissner, II, pp. 117–18.
[2] Cf. M. Eliade, *Traité d'Histoire des Religions*, pp. 341 ff.; *Le Mythe de l'Éternel Retour*, pp. 89–94.
[3] See p. 62.   [4] Cf. Brandon, pp. 103–5.

CHAPTER FOUR

ISRAEL: COSMOGONY AS A FACTOR IN AN ETHNIC RELIGION

OF all the many accounts of the Creation known to the historian of religions none arrests the attention more than that contained in the first two chapters of the book called *Genesis*. Its narrative form and dramatic quality evoke a lively impression both of the primordial acts of the Creator and the fateful tragedy that so soon befalls the progenitors of mankind. It is surely significant that the story inspired Michelangelo to some of the greatest achievements of his mighty genius: indeed the walls of the Sistine Chapel are an abiding witness to the fact that the ancient Hebrew legend could provide both the *rationale* of the Christian doctrine of salvation and a worthy theme for that Renaissance artist in whom the spirit of classical Greece seems most manifest.

The *Genesis* story of the Creation, in its extant form, has long been recognised by scholars as incorporating two distinct versions: that which runs from i.1–ii.4a being assigned to what is known as the Priestly tradition, and dating from the post-Exilic period (5th cent. B.C.); the other, and the older, commencing at ii.4b and described as the Yahwist tradition, the date of its original composition being possibly about 900–750 B.C.[1] Before we enter, however, into a study

---

[1] Cf. R. H. Pfeiffer, *Intro. to Old Test.*, pp. 147–8, 159 f., 188, 190–1; O. Eissfeldt, *Geschichtsschreibung im Alten Testament*, pp. 8–45; C. R. North in *The Old Testament and Modern Study* (ed. H. H. Rowley), p. 81; A. Lods, *Histoire de la Littérature hebraïque et juive*, pp. 180–2; H. H. Rowley, *The Growth of the Old Test.*, pp. 28, 31–6. I. Engnell (in *Wisdom in Israel and in the Ancient Near East*, pp. 108–111) has contended that "the Creation story and the Paradise myth form part of the first great tradition work of a narrative character, Genesis to Numbers". He, accordingly, refuses to recognise a distinctive Yahwist tradition; however, he does admit that the Priestly creation story in *Gen.* i: "really consists of the 'P circle's' own tradition material" (*note:* the Yahwist tradition is so-called from the use of 'Yahweh' (i.e. Lord), which was the distinctive name of the god of Israel. See the references concerning the origin of Yahwism in n. 1, p. 121).

118

of these versions and their many complicated problems, we must briefly consider the question whether those people who inhabited Canaan or Palestine before the Hebrews effectively settled themselves there possessed any cosmogonic traditions, since it is now known that there was much intermingling of the two peoples and the Hebrews absorbed much of the culture of their predecessors.

Until the now famous excavations of the site of the ancient city of Ugarit, near the modern Ras Shamra, and the decipherment of the inscribed tablets found there, nothing was known of Canaanite, or Phoenician cosmogony, beyond the obviously distorted accounts of the teaching of Sanchuniathon, preserved by the Christian bishop Eusebius of Caesarea.[1] Now, through the Ugaritic tablets, a rich treasury of Canaanite mythology has been made known, although its full evaluation still awaits the solution of many problems of decipherment and interpretation. However, it must be admitted that, despite the comparative abundance of material, very little has been learned about the contemporary cosmogonic tradition. We find that El, the chief god of the Ugaritic pantheon, has the title *âb âdm*, i.e. the 'father of mankind', a title that is significant in the light of other fragmentary evidence, and which may perhaps be connected with the mysterious god 'El-'Elyōn, 'creator of heaven and earth' of Genesis xiv. 19, who was served by Melchizedek, the priest-king of Salem.[2] It seems possible that El was a kind of Canaanite counterpart of the Mesopotamian god Ea, for, as Ea was the lord of wisdom and dwelt in the *apsû*, so was the wisdom of El specially commemorated and he resided "at the source of the rivers, amid the channels of the two

[1] For the relevant passages of Sanchuniathon see A. Jeremias, *Das Alte Test. im Lichte des alten Orients*, pp. 62–4; cf. A. Caquot in *Sources orientales*, I, pp. 182–3; G. Contenau, *La civilisation phénicienne*, pp. 85–88, 88–9 (for the cosmogony of Mochus). On Ugarit see generally C. F. Schaeffer, *The Cuneiform Texts of Ras Shamra-Ugarit*; R. de Langhe, *Les textes de Ras Shamra-Ugarit et leurs rapports avec le milieu biblique de l'Ancien Testament*, 2 tomes, also in *Myth, Ritual and Kingship* (ed. S. H. Hooke), pp. 122–132; W. F. Albright in *The Old Test. and Modern Study*, pp. 29–34; G. R. Driver, *Canaanite Myths and Legends*, pp. 1–2; C. H. Gordon in *M.A.W.*, pp. 183–215.

[2] *Keret* I, i. 35–7, 43, in Driver, p. 29; cf. Caquot, pp. 179–180; R. Dussaud, *Les religions des Hittites et des Hourrites, des Phéniciens et des Syriens*, pp. 359–61. A Hittite text mentions a god Elkunirsa and his wife Ashertu who are probably the Canaanite *El qônê eres*, i.e. 'El, the Creator of the Earth' and Asherah; cf. H. Güterbock in *M.A.W.*, p. 155.

oceans . . ."[1] Another Ugaritic deity, Baal, is recorded to have struggled with and overcome Yam, the 'god of the seas and rivers, including subterranean waters as the reputed source of lakes and rivers';[2] the act at once reminds us of Marduk's victory over Ti'âmat, but the Ugaritic text concerned contains no reference to Baal as a creator. Baal also appears in another interesting rôle which again reminds us of the Babylonian god's conquest of the monster of chaos, at least in some of its later depictions. Thus Baal is reminded: "When thou smotest Leviathan the slippery serpent, (and) madest an end of the wriggling serpent, the tyrant with seven heads . . ."[3] However, whether this monster was a personification of the primaeval chaos as was Ti'âmat, its overthrow is not connected with any subsequent creative activity on the part of Baal. Accordingly, so far as our sources allow us to know at present, we can only conclude that the Canaanites regarded their god El as the creator of the world, including mankind, and that this conception may have been influenced by the Mesopotamian conception of Ea. The idea of a conflict between another god, Baal, and what appears to have been some monstrous being connected with the sea seems to have been part of an established tradition,[4] but it was unconnected with any divine act of creation. Until further evidence should come to light, it would seem, therefore, that cosmogony did not greatly command the interest of the Canaanites, which is the more remarkable in view of the fact that Mesopotamian influence was clearly considerable at Ugarit.

Our studies of Egyptian and Mesopotamian cosmogonies have shown us that such accounts of the origin of the world were not generally motivated by a desire to speculate about the beginning of

[1] *Baal* III* C, I. 4, in Driver, p. 77; cf. Caquot, p. 179 .

[2] *Baal* III* A, 8–34, in Driver, pp. 80–3, cf. p. 20b. Cf. Caquot, pp. 181–2; C. Virolleaud, *Légendes de Babylon et de Canaan*, pp. 75–82; Gordon, pp. 191–4.

[3] *Baal* II I*, ii. 1–3, 28–30, in Driver, pp. 102. 103, 104, 105. Cf. G. Widengren in *Myth, Ritual and Kingship*, pp. 172–3. In *Baal* V, iii. 55–6, the goddess Anat claims to have slain the seven-headed serpent (Driver, pp. 86, 87). See Plate IV.

[4] "Il (El) n'est, en tout cas, nullement combatif, et ce n'est pas lui qui frappera, pour les anéantir, Tannin et Léviathan, ou tels autres monstres incarnant les forces mauvaises de la nature", Virolleaud, p. 62.

things: instead they were designed to promote the interests of some sanctuary or city. In view of the great antiquity of most of the systems which we examined, it was not surprising to find that the pursuit of such purpose was crudely managed, taking the form of a brief exposition of the priority of some deity in certain basic acts of creation. It was notable also that in these cosmogonies little or no attention was given to describing the origin of man or to accounting for his nature and place in the scheme of things. When we turn to Hebrew cosmogonic thought, or rather to that of the Yahwist tradition, we find a very different situation. The account of the origin of things, particularly that of man and his destiny, is an integral part of a veritable philosophy of history designed to trace out the purpose of Israel's god, Yahweh, from the very creation to the settlement of his chosen people in the land of Canaan. This mighty theme, which is presented in a superb narrative of great dramatic quality, has three distinct parts, namely, a kind of Primaeval History that runs from the Creation (*Gen.* ii. 4) to the story of the Tower of Babel and the Dispersion of Mankind (*Gen.* xi 1–9), the Patriarchal Sagas which trace out the fortunes of the Israel's ancestors until the nation settles in Egypt, and the account of Yahweh's deliverance of his people from their bondage in Egypt and their establishment in the Promised Land. In this great conspectus of the past the primary purpose of the Yahwist writer (or writers) was to give the various Semite tribes that came to form the nation of Israel a sense of unity through the providence of Yahweh, who seems to have been the deity under whose leadership the conquest of Canaan was effected.[1] This purpose is essentially achieved in the Patriarchal Sagas and the story of the Exodus and Settlement. The Primaeval History, however, although not concerned with the nationalist theme, has nevertheless an important function in the Yahwist scheme.[2] This is, briefly, apart from the impressive prelude which it provides to the story of Yahweh's providence for Israel, to set forth an account of human nature that would accord with Yahwist theology. For, in order to maintain and

[1] Cf. S. G. F. Brandon, *Time and Mankind*, pp. 63–76, 82–4. On the origins of Yahweh and his worship by Israel see A. Lods, *Israël: des origines au milieu du viiie. siècle*, pp. 150–1, 370–7; Rowley, *From Joseph to Joshua*, pp. 149–160, *The Faith of Israel*, pp. 53–6; G. W. Anderson, in *The Old Test. and Modern Study*, pp. 286 f.
[2] Cf. Brandon, *Time and Mankind*, pp. 76–82.

further the supremacy of their god, the devotees of Yahweh felt it necessary to suppress the ancient mortuary cults that presupposed a *post-mortem* existence of the dead and which those cults were designed to assist. The subject cannot be pursued here, and it has been discussed at length elsewhere:[1] suffice it to say that the Yahwists accordingly denied that the dead had any effective *post-mortem* life, and that what remained of a person after the dissolution of death departed to a miserable and hopeless existence in Sheol, which was very much the counterpart of the grim *kur-nu-gi-a*, the 'land of no-return' of Mesopotamian eschatology. Consequently, the needs of Yahwist theology would be well served, if an account of the origins of human nature could be given that would preclude any possibility of an effective survival of death. As we shall see, this is done with considerable skill in the Yahwist account of the creation and fall of man.

By the general consensus of critical opinion the Yahwist cosmogony commences with the second part of verse 4 of *Genesis* ii: "in the day that the Lord God made earth and heaven". That in effect is all that the Yahwist writer says about the actual creation of the world; as such it scarcely merits the designation 'cosmogony'. The grammatical construction of this part of the verse, and its relation to the next verse, raises certain difficulties which suggest that some adjustment has been made to the beginning of the Yahwist account, in order to accommodate it to the Priestly cosmogony that precedes it.[2] However that may be, it is certain that the Yahwist story that follows envisages a different process of creation so far as the earth is concerned, and, as quickly becomes evident, it is concerned rather with the origins of the human situation than with those of the cosmos.

In the following two verses (5–6) a significant indication is given of the geographical environment familiar to the author of the narrative: "And no plant of the field was yet in the earth, and no herb of the field had yet sprung up: for the Lord God had not caused it to rain upon the earth, and there was not a man to till the ground; but there went up a mist from the earth, and watered the whole face of the ground". The general impression which this description gives is

---

[1] Brandon, *Man and his Destiny in the Great Religions*, pp. 108–129.
[2] Cf. E. König, *Die Genesis*, pp. 193–4; J. Skinner, *Genesis*, p. 54.

that of a desert land that depends for its fertility upon a rain-fall. Such an habitat would well accord with the conditions of Palestine, especially in the south; it would, moreover, suggest a contrast with Egypt and Mesopotamia where agriculture depends upon the utilisation of the waters of great rivers. What is puzzling, however, is the statement that the primaeval state of aridity was ended by the rising of a mist which presumably condensed and fell as rain. The word '*ēd* translated as 'mist' occurs only in one other place in ancient Hebrew literature, namely, *Job* xxxvi. 27; it appears to be related to an Assyrian word *êdû* meaning the flooding of a river, undoubtedly with reference to the Euphrates. This latter connotation would, of course, imply a different situation from that of Palestine; since, however, v. 8 would seem to rule out a Mesopotamian location in the present passage, it would probably be wiser to see in the reference to rain the outlook of an inhabitant of Palestine. It should also be noticed that that outlook is essentially one of an agriculturist—the earth only has significance when it is cultivated.[1]

The next verse (7) is one of crucial importance: "And the Lord God formed man of the dust of the ground, and breathed into his nostrils the breath of life; and man became a living soul". The idea of the fashioning of man out of clay, after the manner in which the potter moulds his vessels, is one with which we are already familiar. The Egyptian god Khnum shaped the new infant on his potter's wheel out of clay and straw, while in Mesopotamia the goddess Mami was pictured making men severally from handfuls of clay:[2] we may also usefully recall that in our preliminary reflections we noted the stimulus which must have been given to the imagination of the Palaeolithic peoples when they learned to make clay images of animals.[3] The Hebrew conception of the initial fashioning of man has, however, a greater depth of meaning. The word for man ('*ādām*) suggests a pregnant relationship with that for the clay or dust of the

---

[1] Cf. J. Bottéro in *Sources orientales*, I, p. 219; Skinner, p. 55; König, pp. 194–6. The apparent discrepancy involved in the references to rain and the 'ēd, if it means the flooding of a river, has caused some commentators to think that two different traditions underlie this passage: "Vielleicht gehört der 'Strom' nicht der Schöpfungs—, sondern der Paradieses-Geschichte an", H. Gunkel, *Die Urgeschichte und die Patriarchen*, p. 55; cf. K. Budde, *Die biblische Paradiesesgeschichte*, pp. 6–7.   [2] See pp. 60–1, 77, 84, 88–9.

[3] See p. 4 (the bison are moulded of clay).

ground (*'ădāmāh*), a relationship that, as we shall see, is made a crucial factor in the presentation of the nature and destiny of man with which the Yahwist is so earnestly concerned.[1] The formation of man is conceived as a twofold process: after the making of the body comes the animating of it. The parallel here to the Egyptian concept is very close. As we have seen in the depiction of the birth of Amenhotep III, the goddess Hathor animated the manikins made by Khnum by holding, evidently to their mouth and nostrils, the *ankh*, the symbol of life. Similarly, then, is Yahweh depicted as breathing 'the breath of life' (נִשְׁמַת חַיִּים) into the nostrils of the body which he had fashioned, with the result that the inanimate Adam becomes a 'living soul' (נֶפֶשׁ חַיָּה). This divine inflation of the 'breath of life' might reasonably be taken as indicating that man received the non-material or spiritual side of his being from his Maker, and that to be a 'living soul' was the distinctive characteristic of man.[2] This, however, is not so, because a little further on in the narrative (ii. 19), when the creation of the animals is described, the animals are referred to singly as נֶפֶשׁ חַיָּה ('living soul'). Consequently, since Yahweh also forms the animals out of the earth (*'ădāmāh*), they too presumably, although the fact is not mentioned, were animated by him in a manner similar to that which he had used to make Adam a 'living soul'.[3] It is important to note this similarity, for it surely indicates that in the Yahwist's mind the nature of man differed in no essential way from that of the animals. This unconscious assumption is particularly significant, because, as we shall see, it does in fact conflict with the assertion that is soon to be made that man was originally immortal by nature—hence the tragic consequence of his fall.

[1] Engnell, pp. 110–114, maintains that Adam does not represent the 'primaeval Man', but the 'sacral king'. It is surely significant that in his supporting argument that the idea of the 'primaeval Man' has no real place in the thinking of both the Eastern and Western Semites, he makes no reference to the figure of Enkidu in the *Epic of Gilgamesh* (see p. 82, n. 1, also pp. 126–8, 131–2).

[2] Cf. Gunkel, *Urgesch.*, pp. 55–6; Fr. Ceuppens, *Genèse I–III*, pp. 115–16.

[3] Cf. Budde, pp. 11–12; König, pp. 196–7; O. Procksch, *Die Genesis*, p. 23; Brandon, *Man and his Destiny*, pp. 123–4. A. R. Johnson (*The Vitality of the Individual in the Thought of Ancient Israel*, p. 23, n. 2), points out that there exists no example of נֶפֶשׁ by *itself* as a term of reference for the animal world.

It is notable that the Yahwist writer in the next verse (8) lays the scene of the fateful drama of the ensuing fall of man not in Palestine, but in some area to the east: "And the Lord God planted a garden eastward, in Eden; and there he put the man whom he had formed. (9) And out of the ground made the Lord God to grow every tree that is pleasant to the sight, and good for food; the tree of life also in the midst of the garden, and the tree of the knowledge of good and evil". The location of this divine garden has long been a subject of speculation, and it has inspired many flights of the poetic imagination as well as the theories of the learned. The word 'Eden' may give some clue, since it can reasonably be connected with a Sumerian word *édinu* meaning 'plain' or 'steppe' or 'desert', which would suggest that the idea was of Mesopotamian origin, a suggestion that would appear to find some confirmation in the Sumerian myth of Dilmun and of a primaeval Golden Age.[1] Possibly the Yahwist conceived of the garden rather in terms of an oasis, and it is likely that he also imagined it as surrounded by a wall as was the general custom for a place of special cultivation.[2] However, it would clearly be unwise to interrogate the description too closely, for it is evident that it was rather vaguely conceived—for example, as a garden it would be definitely limited in area, yet it would seem that all the animals lived there with Adam and nothing is said of their dispersal after his expulsion from the place. The mention of the two trees, each of a supernatural character, at the end of verse 9, introduces us to a problem of basic concern for the understanding of the original meaning of this account of the creation and fall of man. However, since the mention of these trees occurs here in isolation, and because the problem which these trees constitute will require an extended discussion later, it is better that we pass on now to complete our commentary on the remaining part of the narrative that deals with the setting of the great drama of man's temptation and fall. The five verses that follow (10–14) have the appearance of an interpolation designed to locate the position of the garden more precisely. Of the four rivers, which are described as having their source in Eden, only two can be certainly identified, namely, the Euphrates and the Tigris ('Hiddekel'). This

[1] Cf. Skinner, p. 57; S. R. Driver, *The Book of Genesis*, p. 38; Jeremias, p. 92; S. H. Hooke, *In the Beginning*, p. 28. See also pp. 73–5.
[2] Cf. H. J. Stoebe in *Z.A.T.W.*, 65 (1953), p. 190.

identification naturally suggests a Mesopotamian derivation for the tradition, which in turn suggests that the rivers Pishon and Gihon are equated with the *Apsû* that encompasses the earth, as we have seen in our study of Mesopotamian cosmology.[1]

After this apparent interpolation, the narrative returns to its theme in verse 15, where it is related that Yahweh put Adam in the garden to maintain it and guard it.[2] Again the meaning of the statement must not be pressed by asking whether this work of cultivation was easy compared to that spoken of in iii. 17–19, or against what menace had the garden to be guarded.[3] The next verses (16–17) are of crucial importance to the theme in their record of the divine prohibition that, while Adam may eat freely of all the other trees in the garden, the fruit of the tree of the knowledge of good and evil he must not touch. However, consideration of this statement we must now leave to a more appropriate occasion. The verses that follow (18–24) are clearly aetiological in character and intended to prepare the way for the great drama that is to be unfolded in chapter iii. Thus the *raison d'être* of the animals is represented in this passage as being that of providing companionship for the man, which they fail to do, so incidentally frustrating the divine plan, although the Yahwist does not notice the fact. In turn it is explained that the animals received their names from Adam—we may perhaps legitimately ask whether, on the analogy of Mesopotamian thought in this connection, as we have noticed, this naming of the animals meant rather the decreeing of their particular functions.[4] This idyllic picture of the primordial man living in a state of harmony with the animals also recalls a Mesopotamian parallel, namely, of Enkidu and his communion with the animals before he is civilised.[5]

[1] Cf. Bottéro, pp. 219–20; Procksch, pp. 23–7.

[2] An attempt has been made to relate the Yahwist story of Adam's sojourn in Paradise with an 'Eden-cherub myth' that seems to lie behind *Ezekiel* xxviii. 1–14 and *Isaiah* xiv. 12–15, according to which a supernatural being was expelled from Eden for the sin of *hubris*: cf. T. H. Robinson in *Myth and Ritual*, pp. 180–3; Widengren in *Myth, Ritual and Kingship*, pp. 165–9. It would seem that there must have been some prototype to the Lucifer myth; but, whatever it was, it has not yet been identified in Mesopotamian mythology (the Adapa myth is certainly not relevant), nor in any other mythology of the ancient Near East. Moreover, if the existence of such a prototype be assumed, no light is thrown thereby on the sources of the Yahwist story. Cf. G. Fohrer, *Das Buch Jesaja*, I, 179–80.   [3] Cf. Budde, p. 21.

[4] See pp. 113–14. [5] *Epic of Gilgamesh*, Tab. I, col. i 35–41. See p. 82, n. 1.

The failure of the animals to provide an adequate companionship for Adam is given as the reason for the creation of woman (20–3).[1] The writer here is obviously concerned to show the derivative, and, therefore, the subordinate character of the female sex, while at the same time attesting the essential unity of man and woman and their complementary natures. The curious means by which Yahweh procures the substance from which to make the woman has long puzzled commentators, who have naturally sought to find some relevant parallel to the extraordinary idea. The most likely one found so far comes from the interesting fact that the Sumerian words for 'side' (*ti*) and life (*til*) are depicted by the same ideogram; however, no instance of Sumerian interest in this homonymity has yet come to light.[2] The Yahwist clearly found his own explanation of the union of the sexes and the institution of marriage in the fact that the Hebrew word for woman (*'isshāh*) is constructed from that for man (*'ish*).[3] The concluding verse (25) of this section is obviously intended to prepare for the sequel, but it raises a problem that may be conveniently discussed at this point. The Yahwist records: "And they were both naked, the man (*'ādām*) and his wife (*'isshāh*), and they were not ashamed". The verb (בּוֹשׁ), translated here as meaning 'to feel ashamed', signifies in this context specifically 'to change colour, to blush', and its employment surely indicates the author's attitude towards nudity. To the Hebrew the exposure of the sexual organs, whether of man or woman, was a shameful thing;[4] but possibly the real point of the Yahwist's remark in this verse is to be seen by way of comparison with what is said of Enkidu in the *Epic of Gilgamesh*. As we have seen, in his original state Enkidu represents mankind before civilisation. Accordingly, he is shown as living with and as the

[1] "Of the revolting idea that man lived for a time in sexual intercourse with the beasts, there is no trace", Skinner, p. 67. This commentator's suggestion (p. 91) that this is implied in the story of Enkidu appears to be quite unwarranted.

[2] Cf. Bottéro, p. 221. "Der Name bezeichnet zutreffend das Wesen eines jeden Geschöpfes: es dürfte nicht überflüssig sein zu betonen, welches hohe Mass von Einsicht und von schneller Gedankenarbeit dem Menschen damit zugemutet und zugeschrieben wird", Budde, p. 35.

[3] "Wahrend er bei den Tieren keinen Namen fand, der eine Ähnlichkeit mit ihm wiedergab, muss sie אִשָּׁה nach ihm selbst heissen, da sie aus ihm stammt", Procksch, p. 29. Cf. Skinner, pp. 69–70.

[4] Cf. J. Pedersen, *Israel: its Life and Culture*, I, pp. 241–2.

animals and wearing no clothes—instead his body is covered with hair.[1] In this picture of the primordial state the Mesopotamian author is clearly only concerned with nudity as the natural result of primitive ignorance—man is just brutish, and to emphasise this aspect he is depicted as having a hairy pelt. It is interesting, therefore, to note that the Yahwist writer, in envisaging the primordial state, thinks especially of the first human pair as naked, and that it is necessary to explain that they were not ashamed of the fact. As becomes evident in the sequel, the significance of the comment on their nudity is that they are male and female.[2]

How long this idyllic existence of the first human pair continued in the divine garden the Yahwist does not tell us.[3] Indeed the question is irrelevant, because time, in the sense of the past conditioning the future, only really commences with the fateful transaction that the writer now proceeds to relate. The account opens in chapter iii by introducing the mysterious agent of the tragedy that now befalls Adam and his wife: "Now the serpent was more subtil than any beast of the field which the Lord God had made". The rôle played by this famous *dramatis persona* in the story of the Temptation and Fall of Man has, understandably, become involved in much subsequent theological speculation, both Jewish and Christian, so that it is difficult to evaluate it in its proper context in the Yahwist narrative. Traditionally the serpent has been identified with Satan, and his part in the Fall of Man is consequently interpreted in terms of the veiled dualism that has its place in both Jewish and Christian theological thought.[4] But we must be careful to note that in the text itself the serpent is consistently represented as an animal. Thus in iii. 1, as we have just seen, the serpent is specifically associated with 'the beasts of the field', and in the divine condemnation that falls on the serpent in iii. 14 for its part in the Fall of Man, its essential animal

---

[1] *Epic of Gilgamesh*, Tab. I, col. ii. 36, cf. Tab. II, col. iii. 22–6.

[2] Cf. Procksch, p. 30 on verse 25.

[3] According to later rabbinic speculation the period of primaeval innocence varied from six hours to seven years; cf. Skinner, p. 71.

[4] The identification of the serpent of *Genesis* with the devil first appears in *Wisdom* ii. 24 (1st cent. B.C.); possibly an earlier reference is to be found in *Enoch* lxix. 6 (*Apoc. u. Pseudep.*, ed. E. Kautzsch, II, p. 275). Cf. Skinner, pp. 72–3; J. A. MacCulloch in *E.R.E.*, XI, p. 403b; N. P. Williams, *Ideas of the Fall and of Original Sin*, pp. 191–2.

nature is made even plainer: "And the Lord God said unto the serpent, Because thou hast done this, cursed art thou above all cattle, and above every beast of the field; upon thy belly shalt thou go, and dust shalt thou eat all the days of thy life"—the latter clause being obviously intended as an explanation of the curious locomotion of the snake and its lowly habitat.

That the author envisaged the serpent essentially as an animal there can, therefore, be no doubt. However, it is also endowed with one attribute, namely, the power of (human?) speech, which makes it something more than a beast. Whether that was the author's conscious intention may be doubted, since to play its part the serpent had to speak—perhaps also, on the analogy of Enkidu's originally complete accord with the animals, it may have been thought that in Paradise before the Fall, man and beast could communicate with each other.[1] That the serpent was 'more subtil' than all other animals suggests in the light of the sequel a malevolent mind or disposition, although the epithet עָרוּם ('subtil') is used in Hebrew literature in both a good and a bad sense.[2] However, it must be recognised that the Yahwist clearly depicts the intention of the serpent as malevolent, which in turn suggests some unexplained enmity on its part either towards God or Adam. This apparent trait raises the question why the serpent was chosen by the Yahwist as the agent through whom man was tempted to disobey his creator. On general grounds it could be answered that there is a widespread fear and detestation of the serpent because of its silent sinuous movements and the deadly power of its bite.[3] The fact of this attitude is undoubted, and it must be reckoned with; however, among the Semites the serpent had other significant aspects of a more specific kind. There is evidence of a belief in the serpent as an emblem of healing and of the use of a bronze serpent as a cult object.[4] The serpent also was associated with the worship of the goddess Astarte and thus had some fertility symbolism—the serpent's tempting of the woman, and the consequences of the Fall, as we shall see, appear accordingly to have a possible sig-

---

[1] Cf. MacCulloch in *E.R.E.*, XI, p. 409a(g).
[2] Cf. Skinner, p. 71; Procksch, p. 32.
[3] Cf. Gunkel, *Urgeschichte*, p. 60.
[4] Cf. Lods, *Israël*, pp. 101–2, 274–5, 498–9; W. O. E. Oesterley and T. H. Robinson, *Hebrew Religion*, p. 34; Pederson, III–IV, pp. 452, 711–12.

nificance in this connection.[1] There is yet another aspect of the symbolism of the serpent that could conceivably be also relevant here. It is significant that, it is a serpent in the *Epic of Gilgamesh* that robs the hero of his opportunity to acquire immortal youth; also, we may note, this incident in the career of Gilgamesh appears to be our earliest known instance of a *motif* that occurs in the folklore of many peoples.[2] It is inspired by the phenomenon of the snake's ability to slough off its old skin. To the primitive mind it appeared that the snake had learned the secret of renewing its youth—a secret that man so earnestly sought to learn for himself, and of which it was easy to believe that he had been cheated by the serpent. As we shall see in the Yahwist narrative, the serpent, although it does not win immortality for itself, becomes the effective agent through whom man loses the inestimable attribute with which he had been originally endowed. It would, accordingly, appear that the Yahwist writer, while conceiving of the serpent primarily as an animal, was probably influenced in his choice of it for the rôle of the Tempter of Man by the ambivalent symbolism which it had in current Semitic folklore, namely, in the cult of the fertility goddess and in the legend of the robbing of Gilgamesh of the secret of perpetual youth.

In the dialogue that follows (iii. 1b–7) between the serpent and the woman, and the act to which it leads, we reach the heart of the problem that faces us in seeking to understand this Yahwist interpretation of human nature and destiny: "And he (the serpent) said unto the woman, Yea, hath God said, Ye shall not eat of any tree of the garden? And the woman said unto the serpent, Of the fruit of the trees of the garden we may eat: but the fruit of the tree which is in the midst of the garden, God hath said, Ye shall not eat of it, neither shall ye touch it, lest ye die. And the serpent said unto the woman, Ye shall not surely die: for God doth know that in the day ye eat thereof, then your eyes shall be opened, and ye shall be as God, knowing good and evil. And when the woman saw that the tree was good for food, and that it was a delight to the eyes, and that the tree

[1] Cf. Lods, *Israël*, pp. 154–5; MacCulloch in *E.R.E.*, XI, pp. 403b, 409b–411a. Philo regards the serpent as a symbol of pleasure (ἡδονῆς), including sexual lust (*On the Creation*, lvi, 157–160).

[2] *Epic of Gilgamesh*, XI, 266–95. Cf. Brandon, *Man and his Destiny*, pp. 93, 126; J. G. Frazer, *The Folklore of the Old Testament*, pp. 18–19, 26–33; MacCulloch in *E.R.E.*, XI, p. 408b(f).

The Temptation of Adam and Eve, by Michelangelo (Sistine Chapel). Michelangelo follows a tradition, probably inspired by psychological motives, that represented the Serpent as feminine (the arm of the serpent is seen offering the fruit to Eve).

PLATE VII

The Creation of Eve (top left), from an early Christian sarcophagus. In this representation the three Persons of the Trinity are shown as involved in the act of creation. The actual agent seems to be Christ, in accordance with the Christian belief that first finds expression in *John* i, 2. Museo Lateranese, Rome. (Photo: Alinari.)

PLATE V

was to be desired to make one wise, she took of the fruit thereof, and did eat; and she gave also unto her husband with her, and he did eat".

The dialogue is written with great skill, and it attests the psychological insight of the author. The serpent's opening remark shows great subtlety by inviting the woman's correction, namely, that God had not forbidden all the trees of the garden to them, and so leading her on to be the first to mention the one tree that was forbidden. It is natural to ask why the woman is chosen by the Yahwist to be, as it were, the mediator of the serpent's temptation, and why the serpent is not depicted as approaching the man directly with his fatal suggestions.[1] Hebrew society was essentially a patriarchal society, and in the organisation of family life, in public affairs, and in religious thought and practice women had a very subordinate, in fact almost a passive, part.[2] It is remarkable, therefore, that in the account of this fateful transaction the man is represented as following the woman's lead. Indeed it would seem that the Yahwist writer was intent on stressing Adam's subordination to his wife on this occasion. Thus, when Adam encounters Yahweh after his act of disobedience, he seeks to excuse himself by blaming the woman: "The woman whom thou gavest to be with me, she gave me of the tree, and I did eat" (iii. 12). Then, the subservience is again mentioned in Yahweh's reply: "And to Adam he said, Because thou hast hearkened unto the voice of thy wife, . . ." (iii. 17). From this emphasis it would seem that the Yahwist, while not seeking to abate the guilt of Adam, regards Eve as a temptress and as the means by which Adam's integrity was successfully assaulted. With Eve cast in this rôle, at once a classic parallel springs to mind, namely, Hesiod's myth of Pandora, the original and veritable *femme fatale*, whose eager reception by Epimetheus, heedless of his brother's warning, brings sorrow to the race of man.[3] But interesting though the parallel be which this Greek myth affords, it could not have been known to the Yahwist in view of its date and location. A more likely source of influence for the Yahwist's conception of Eve in this respect is provided once more by the *Epic of Gilgamesh*, and most notably too in the story of Enkidu, to which we have already made reference. This wild man, representative as we have seen of humanity

[1] Cf. Procksch, p. 32. [2] Cf. Pedersen, I–II, pp. 60 f.
[3] Hesiod, *Works and Days*, 48–82; cf. Brandon, *Man and his Destiny*, pp. 166–7. See also pp. 177–8.

before civilisation, is lured away from his simple harmonious life with the animals, by a sacred courtesan who is sent out for the purpose from the city of Erech. By her wiles she makes him sexually conscious, she teaches him to eat bread and wear clothes, and finally brings him into the city and so ultimately to his doom. In describing this process of weaning the primaeval man from his natural innocence, the *Epic* contains one passage of especial significance for our interpretation of the Yahwist story, as we shall see. Having seduced him and with him sitting tamely at her feet, the courtesan exclaims: "Thou art wise, Enkidu, art become like a god!"[1] Later, however, when he lays dying, Enkidu curses the woman who had tempted him away from his original simple life.[2] We have, then, in the *Epic of Gilgamesh* the figure of a woman, undoubtedly one of the temple prostitutes of Ishtar, the great fertility goddess, who seduces the type-figure of a primitive man from his original innocence and well-being by giving him sexual experience, which makes him god-like, but which sets him on the course that leads inevitably to his death. In view of the wide dispersion of texts of the *Epic*, if we seek for some precedent for Eve's rôle in the fall of Adam, it would seem, therefore, that it is in the story of Enkidu that we shall find it.

We must deal now with the problem which we have already encountered but have deferred for later discussion, namely, that of the meaning of the 'tree of the knowledge of good and evil'. The eating of the fruit of this tree clearly constitutes the crisis of the drama of Adam's fall, so that upon a proper understanding of the nature of the tree the interpretation of the myth essentially depends. That the problem involved here is fundamentally obscure is obvious from the conflict of opinion that is found when the relevant commentaries and monographs are consulted.[3] The interpretation that will be put forward here is built partly upon earlier suggestions, as will be seen from the notes; the new elements which it contains seem to have the virtue of providing a consistently intelligible explanation of the

---

[1] *Epic of Gilgamesh*, Tab. I, col. iv 34; cf. Tab. II, col. ii. 10–11.

[2] *Op. cit.*, Tab. VII, col. iii. 5–37. Philo (*On the Creation*, liii. 151) emphasises the bliss of Adam's solitary life—"woman becomes for him the beginning of blameworthy life".

[3] A useful list of references to studies of the subject is given by Bo Reicke at the beginning of his article "The Knowledge Hidden in the Tree of Paradise", in *J.S.S.*, I (1956), p. 193, n. 1.

Yahwist's intention which otherwise is exceedingly obscure. Before entering upon this interpretation it is, however, necessary to remove what most scholars recognise as a basic contradiction in the Yahwist narrative as we now have it. This contradiction is constituted by the mention in two places of the existence of a 'tree of life' as well as the 'tree of the knowledge of good and evil' in the garden.[1] The first mention is very brief; it occurs in ii. 9, where it is recorded that "out of the ground made the Lord God to grow every tree that is pleasant to the sight, and good for food; the tree of life also in the midst of the garden, and the tree of the knowledge of good and evil". Now, after this brief mention, this 'tree of life' plays no part in the subsequent narrative of Adam's cultivation of the garden or the drama of his temptation and fall. Reference is only made to it again in iii. 22-4, where it then features in a kind of appendix to the *dénouement* of the story of the temptation and fall. If these two mentions of the 'tree of life' are to be considered part of the original form of the tragedy of man, then a number of self-evident contradictions have to be faced. The first is constituted by the fact that in ii. 16-17 it is recorded that, "the Lord God commanded the man, saying, Of every tree of the garden thou mayest freely eat: but of the tree of the knowledge of good and evil, thou shalt not eat of it: for in the day that thou eatest thereof thou shalt surely die". Why, it must be asked, did God prohibit Adam only from eating of the 'tree of knowledge of good and evil' and not from eating of the 'tree of life', if both grew in the garden?[2] Presumably, in the light of what is said in iii. 22, if Adam

---

[1] It must be recognised that a number of scholars maintain that the two trees figured in the original form of the Yahwist narrative. e.g. G. Pidoux in *Z.A.T.W.*, 66 (1954), who thinks that, before the Fall, man maintained his life from the 'tree of life', although he did not know it (p. 43); H. J. Stoebe in *Z.A.T.W.*, 65 (1953), explains the two trees as due to the fusion of 'doublets' and that the obvious difficulty that the presence of both raises is due to a theological thinker who was more intent on his theme than on the logic of his narrative (pp. 189, 194); F. J. Leenhardt in *Das Menschenbild im Lichte des Evangeliums*, p. 7, maintains that the 'tree of life' was part of the original story on the ground that, if man had continued to be obedient, God would, Himself, have given him of its fruit. S. H. Hooke (*In the Beginning*, pp. 31-2) suggests that the 'tree of life' had originally been hidden, and its location was revealed to Adam on eating the fruit of the 'tree of the knowledge of good and evil'. Cf. G. von Rad, *Genesis*, pp. 76-7.

[2] According to Pidoux, *op. cit.*, p. 39, "En un sens la vie ou l'immortalité était accordée au premier homme pour autant qu'il demeurait dans le

had eaten of the 'tree of life', he would "live for ever"—yet God only bars him from the 'tree of the knowledge of good and evil', warning him that death would be the penalty of eating its fruit.[1] The contradiction here is reinforced by Eve's answer to the serpent in iii. 2–3: "Of the fruit of the trees of the garden we may eat: but of the fruit of the tree that is in the midst of the garden, God hath said, Ye shall not eat of it, neither shall ye touch it, lest ye die". Now, the tree concerned here is obviously the 'tree of the knowledge of good and evil' and it is located "in the midst of the garden" (בְּתוֹךְ־הַגָּן); but, according to ii. 9, this was the location of the 'tree of life'—once more it is exceedingly strange that there should be no mention of this tree, which, if the reference to it in ii. 9 is original, must have been standing at the very place of, or alongside, the 'tree of the knowledge of good and evil'.[2] Moreover, if the 'tree of life' appeared in the original form of the story, we then have the rather improbable situation that, in the midst of the garden, there stood two trees of unique virtue, one giving immortality and the other giving death; but Adam is only barred from eating of the latter, so that it follows that he would normally have eaten of the 'tree of life'—action is only taken to prevent him from doing this as a kind of afterthought, after he had eaten of the 'tree of the knowledge of good and evil'. These contradictions and inconsistencies are at once removed and a logically

voisinage de l'arbre de la vie"; hence his exclusion from after his fall (pp. 41, 43). This seems to be rather an instance of special pleading, since there is no indication that the virtue acquired by eating the fruit of the tree of life was only of temporary duration: indeed the whole logic of iii. 22 completely contradicts such a view.

[1] W. Vollborn in *T.L-Z.*, 77 (1952), 712, suggests that the knowledge which 'the tree of the knowledge of good and evil' gave to man was consciousness of his mortality, of which he had hitherto been ignorant—"Er war zwar sterblich, aber weil er davon nichts wusste, lebte er im Urstand ganz unreflektiert wie das Kind, vom dem Hölderlin sagt, dass er unsterblich ist, weil es nichts vom Tode weiss". The profundity of idea here would seem to be beyond the range of the Yahwist writer. Stoebe, *op. cit.*, p. 201, argues that 'knowledge of good and evil' means knowing what is or is not profitable for life . . . "*das crimen laesae majestatis* ist, dass der Mensch für sich selbst entscheiden will". Because the aim of such a decision will always be life, therefore, according to Stoebe, the 'tree of life' stands next to the 'tree of knowledge'. Stoebe avoids the obvious difficulty, that there is no mention that man was originally prohibited from eating of the 'tree of life', by assuming the theological preoccupation of the author, as noticed above in n. 1, p. 133.

[2] Cf. H. Holzinger, Genesis, p. 27; Budde, pp. 17–20.

coherent narrative is obtained, if the brief reference to the 'tree of life' in ii. 9 is omitted as an interpolation designed to prepare for the passage about this tree (iii. 22–4) that has been added on to the story of the temptation and fall which properly ends at iii. 21. The reason for this addition is not far to seek. As we have seen,[1] a plant, conferring perpetual youth on its possessor, features in the *Epic of Gilgamesh*, the influence of which, or of some of the *motifs* which it incorporates, we have already noticed in the Yahwist narrative. It would, accordingly, be legitimate to conclude that either the original writer himself or some later editor, impressed by the idea of such a marvellous plant or tree, sought to incorporate it in the story, howbeit at the expense of logical consistency—as we shall see, the story of the Flood was in a rather similar manner inserted into the original narrative of the Yahwist Primaeval History.

If we may thus reasonably account for the references to the 'tree of life', we are left with the drama of Adam's temptation and fall in which only one supernatural tree is involved, namely, the 'tree of the knowledge of good and evil'. Now we have the task of investigating the nature of this mysterious tree. Its description is not self-explanatory, since 'knowledge of good and evil' in itself is ambiguous and can be interpreted to mean various things, as indeed has been done.[2] Some clue is, however, given of the author's meaning in the warning with which Yahweh reinforces his prohibition of this tree to Adam: "thou shalt not eat of it: for in the day that thou eatest thereof thou shalt surely die" (ii. 17, cf. iii. 3). The author evidently intended, then, that it should be understood that this knowledge, whatever it be, would be fatal to man. The obvious inference from this is, of course, that Adam was already immortal by nature, or rather perhaps that his Maker had not decreed death as his end—it is useful to recall here that in the *Pyramid Texts* a primordial state was envisaged when there was no death.[3] But, not only would this knowledge be fatal, it is explained by the serpent that by its acquisition "your eyes shall be opened, and ye shall be as God (or, gods), knowing good and evil" (iii. 5). This statement of the serpent is apparently reflected in Eve's

---

[1] See p. 130. Cf. Brandon, *Man and his Destiny*, pp. 93, 124–5.
[2] Cf. Skinner, pp. 94–7; König, pp. 200–1.
[3] See p. 16. It is obvious from the context and sequel, that the warning did not just mean that the fruit was lethal, in that it was poisonous.

estimate of the forbidden fruit as "to be desired to make one wise" (iii. 6), and it is surely confirmed by Yahweh when he is represented as saying: "Behold, man is become as one of us, to know good and evil; . . ." (iii. 22). We see, then, that the Yahwist regarded this knowledge as something that it was only proper for God to have, and that its acquisition by man would bring death upon him.

It is, accordingly, surprising to find that the first consequence of the eating of the forbidden fruit is not immediate death, as was threatened, but that the man and the woman become aware of their nudity: "And the eyes of them both were opened, and they knew that they were naked; and they sewed fig leaves together, and made themselves aprons" (iii. 7).[1] Next, significantly, when Adam hides himself from his Maker, saying that he did so because he was naked, Yahweh in his reply immediately connects man's consciousness of his nudity with the forbidden fruit: "And he said, Who told thee that thou wast naked? Hast thou eaten of the tree whereof I commanded thee that thou shouldest not eat?" (iii. 11).

It would appear, then, that the knowledge which the first man and woman acquired by eating of the 'tree of the knowledge of good and evil' was the realisation that they were naked, which, in the light of our previous discussion, must surely mean consciousness of sex.[2] Sexual consciousness, let us also recall, was represented as the first stage in the process of changing Enkidu from his primordial state. But why, we may ask, was such knowledge considered as something that man should not have? It would seem that we may perhaps have a clue to the answer to this question in the fact, which we have already noted, that such knowledge would make man like God (iii. 5, 22). Now, for sexual consciousness to have such effect, it must surely follow that the author was thinking rather of the potentiality of such consciousness and not just the fact in itself. In other words, the knowledge that was acquired by eating of the forbidden fruit was that of the means of producing or reproducing life. It was this knowledge

[1] It has been suggested that fig-leaves were used because that was the tree from which the fruit had been taken, see Reicke in *J.S.S.*, I, p. 196. The 'tree of life' has also been identified with the fig tree, cf. Widengren, *The King and the Tree of Life in Ancient Near Eastern Religion*, p. 38.

[2] Cf. Reicke, *op. cit.*, pp. 196–7, 201; see also Engnell, p. 115; Gunkel, *Urgeschichte*, p. 61; Brandon, *Man and his Destiny*, p. 125, in *History Today*, XI (1961), pp. 386–7.

that now made Adam like his Maker—indeed, when we consider the presentation of Yahweh in these chapters of *Genesis*, we see that it is essentially as the Creator of living things that he appears. By his awareness of the potentiality of sex, Adam can now emulate Yahweh in creating new beings like himself. But why should the acquisition of this creative power bring death upon him? The answer would seem to lie in a widespread folk-belief concerning the origin of death which has been aptly entitled the myth of the 'Overcrowded Earth'. It is based on what might be termed a shrewd appraisal by the primitive mind of a kind of 'Malthusian exigency'. Old people become an economic burden to the tribe; if they did not die and children continued to be born, a dire situation would obviously be created in which all would be involved—hence death is the solution, and its origin as such is explained in a variety of myths or legends.[1] That such an interpretation of the necessity of death was known in Israel, although the evidence itself comes from a much later period than that of the Yahwist story, is attested by a passage from the apocalyptic work known as the *Fourth Book of Ezra* (v. 43–4). There Ezra is represented as asking God: "Couldst thou not have created at one time all the generations of the past, the present, and the future, so that thy judgement might have been manifested the sooner?' He answered me and said: 'The creation cannot anticipate the creator; moreover, the world could not support all the generations at one moment'."[2]

[1] H. Schwarzbaum, "The Overcrowded Earth", in *Numen*, IV (1957), pp. 59–71.

[2] In *Apoc. u. Pseudepig.* (ed. E. Kautzsch), II, p. 363. This part of the document is dated for the 1st century A.D., cf. *op. cit.*, p. 252. Schwarzbaum, *op. cit.*, p. 62, thinks that the idea is reflected in *Eccles.* i. 4: "One generation goeth, and another generation cometh; and the earth abideth for ever". See also the passage, purporting to come from the *Gospel according to the Egyptians*, preserved by Clement of Alexandria (*Strom.* iii. 6.45): "The Lord said to Salome when she inquired: How long shall death prevail 'As long as ye women bear *children*', not because life is an ill, and the creation evil: but as showing the sequence of nature: for in all cases birth is followed by decay" (in M. R. James, *The Apocryphal New Testament*, p. 11). It would seem that Philo (*On the Creation*, liii, 1152) was also inclined to interpret the myth along these lines: "Love supervenes, brings together and fits into one the divided halves, as it were, of a single living creature, and sets up in each of them a desire for fellowship with the other with a view to the production of their like. And this desire begat likewise bodily pleasure, that pleasure, which is the beginning of wrongs and violation of law, the pleasure for the

Seen, then, in such a context, the decree of death that follows on man's acquisition of the knowledge of procreation becomes intelligible as the inevitable consequence of his ability to increase his species. It is, accordingly, significant that the Yahwist writer also explains the pain of child-birth as the penalty that now falls upon the woman for her part in acquiring this knowledge: "Unto the woman he said, I will greatly multiply thy sorrow and thy pregnancy (הֵרֹנֵךְ); in pain (בְּעֶצֶב) thou shalt bring forth children; and thy desire shall be to thy husband, and he shall rule over thee" (iii. 16).[1] And, immediately after their expulsion from the garden of Eden, the Yahwist records: "And the man knew Eve his wife; and she conceived, and bare Cain, and said, I have gotten a man with *the help* of the Lord (iv. 1).[2] Adam, therefore, had won a knowledge that was fatal to him as an individual, for he had acquired and soon used the power to create children who would supplant him. Accordingly, having decreed his own fate by his disobedience to his creator, the man (*'ādām*) must, as an individual, return to the earth (*'ădāmāh*) out of which he had been formed (iii. 19).[3]

sake of which men bring on themselves the life of mortality (τὸν θνητὸν) and wretchedness in lieu of immortality (ἀντ' ἀθανάτου) and bliss" (Loeb ed., vol. i, pp. 120, 121, tr. G. H. Whitaker).

[1] "I will cause thee to have much suffering and pregnancy", Skinner, p. 82. "Woher dies Elend? Das ist Gottes Fluch. Das Weib hat ihr Geschlecht durch eine Sünde entdeckt; so ist ihr Geschlechtsleben verflucht worden", Gunkel, *Urgeschichte*, p. 64. "Diese Strafübel bekommen eine intensivere Steigerung, indem das Weib selbst zu ihrer Wiederholung beiträgt", König, p. 246.

[2] According to *Gen.* iii. 20, "the man called his wife's name Eve: because she was the mother of all living". Since the verse appears to break the theme of the narrative at this point and to anticipate the statement of iv. 1, it has been regarded as an interpolation. Moreover, it is curious that a proper name is given to the woman, whereas the man is only called "*ādām*' (הָאָדָם), signifying '(the) man'. It is possible that behind the name there may be some earlier myth concerning the 'Great Mother' of all life. On whether the suggested derivation of חַוָּה (Ḥawwah) from חַיָּה=חַיִּים ('life)', (LXX ζωή), see the pertinent remark of Budde, p. 75: "Dass der Name aber nicht *ad hoc* geschaffen ist, sondern in der Überlieferung sich vorfand, dafür bürgt allein das statt des hebräischen". Cf. Skinner, p. 86.

[3] It is interesting to note that Engnell, pp. 115–18, has also seen that the decisive point of the story is that Adam and Eve, by their act of disobedience, gain the ability to procreate. However, he fails to connect this with the ensuing divine decree of death. It would seem that, intent on pursuing his

In thus presenting the essential nature and the destiny of man, the Yahwist writer also skilfully provided a *rationale* to support that doctrinal position which accepted the Sheol eschatology and rejected the faith that inspired the old mortuary cults. In a superb drama, calculated to arrest the imagination, it was shown that the constitution of human nature contained nothing significant that might survive the dissolution of death; "for dust thou art, and unto dust shalt thou return" (iii. 19). It was perhaps as an afterthought, as we have noted, that either the original author or an early redactor thought it well also, mindful of the quest of Gilgamesh, to forestall any hope that man might by some means acquire immortality. Accordingly, the *motif* of the 'tree of life' was introduced only to show the decisive measures which Yahweh had taken to keep man from it (iii. 22–4).[1]

As a good story-teller, the Yahwist was able also to use his narrative to express his views on a number of subsidiary issues. Thus, possibly in accord with the prophetic view that Israel's golden age was when the people lived as nomads and were uncorrupted by the agrarian civilisation of Canaan, agriculture is represented as part of the divine penalty imposed on man for his disobedience to his creator: instead of the easy life in the fruitful garden, man has now to labour hardly on ground which is barren and productive only of weeds (iii. 17–19).[2] The strange curse that is laid upon the serpent is undoubtedly intended, as we have already noted, to explain its repulsive form and movement; [3] but the enmity which is placed between the woman and the serpent and between their respective progeny (iii. 14–15) seems to suggest some deeper meaning than that of mankind's instinctive dislike of snakes because of the menace of their insidious habits.

theory that Adam represents the sacral king, Engnell is concerned to work in here the royal *hieros gamos* motive as a feature of an annual ritual to renew and sustain fertility.

[1] Cf. Brandon, *Man and his Destiny*, pp. 122–7; in *History Today*, X (1961).

[2] Cf. Budde, pp. 67–73. Vollborn in *T.L-Z.* 77 (1952), 713, sees a peculiar theological meaning in the cursing in iii. 17: "diese verfluchte אדמה muss der Mensch im Tode zurückkehren". Such a *motif* is certainly found in later literature, e.g. in the Coptic document entitled the "Discourse on Abbatôn by Timothy, Archbishop of Alexandria" (in *Coptic Martyrdoms*, ed. E. A. Wallis Budge, British Museum, 1914, pp. 232 f., 481 f.). A somewhat similar view of the toil of agriculture as a mark of divine jealousy towards mankind finds expression in Hesiod, *Works and Days*, 42–4; see p. 177.

[3] Cf. König, pp. 241–3.

Possibly the Yahwist is mindful here of the connection of the serpent with the fertility cults of Canaan. We have already noticed the ambivalence of his attitude towards Eve in that, like the sacred courtesan who brought doom to Enkidu in seducing him from his simple life, Eve is the means whereby the serpent's temptation is presented to Adam—perhaps Eve and the serpent, with whom she conspired to bring Adam into possession of that fatal knowledge, reminded him of Astarte and the serpents of her licentious rites.[1] The third piece of aetiology in this story is the brief explanation of the wearing of clothes, which incidentally suggests some awareness that the art of weaving was a later invention: "And the Lord God made for Adam and his wife coats of skins, and clothed them" (iii. 21).[2]

As we have already noted, the Yahwist story of the creation and fall of man was part of a narrative sequence designed to provide a prelude to the Patriarchal Sagas in which the beginnings of Yahweh's providential shaping of Israel's destiny are traced out. Consequently, the drama of the Temptation and Fall, in which the Yahwist doctrine of Man is impressively presented, is linked on to an account of the origin of various human activities and institutions that gradually develops the story of mankind to the point at which its primaeval unity is broken and migration takes place from its original home (xi. 1–9). Now, it is obvious that the Yahwist writer drew upon much traditional material in compiling this account. What was the original nature of this material and its derivation, and to what extent it had already been organised in some sequential form, are questions which

[1] For other interpretations see Budde, pp. 61–4; Gunkel, *Urgeschichte*, pp. 63–4; Skinner, pp. 79–82. On the connection between snakes and the fertility goddess see E. Dhorme, *Les religions de Babylonie et d'Assyrie*, p. 121; S. R. Driver, *Modern Research as illustrating the Bible*. pp. 56–9; W. F. Albright, *The Archaeology of Palestine*, pp. 104–7; Lods, *Israël*, pp. 151–6, Pl. IX, 1; E. O. James, *The Cult of the Mother Goddess*, pp. 69–84, see also pp. 129–131; MacCulloch in *E.R.E.*, XI, pp. 403–4, 406a, 409b–411a; E. Neumann, *The Great Mother*, Plates 11a, 55b–61.

[2] According to the Phoenician legend of Usōos (given in Eusebius, *Praep. ev.* I, 10.7f), the wearing of skins resulted from the first hunting of animals; cf. Skinner, p. 87; König, pp. 250–1. The divine precautions taken to keep man from re-entering the garden of Eden and approaching the 'tree of life' in iii. 24 certainly seem to indicate imagery of Mesopotamian derivation. Cf. Jeremias, pp. 115–16 .

have greatly occupied scholars. There does appear to be some grounds for thinking that the Yahwist may have utilised an already existing cycle of legend of what is known as the *Heilbringer* type, which told how man's hard lot as an agriculturalist was alleviated by a hero who discovered the art of making wine, thus making glad the heart of man.[1] How the origin of agriculture, and the hard toil which it involved, was related in the original form of this legend is difficult to discern, because in the Yahwist narrative two different accounts are given of why agriculture is so toilsome. The one we have already discussed, namely, that it was part of the penalty inflicted on Adam for his disobedience. The other occurs in the celebrated story of the first murder (iv. 2–15). In this story we have a clear statement, which is very significant of the Yahwist's attitude, that Yahweh preferred the offerings of the pastoralist Abel and rejected those of Cain, the agriculturalist. The curse that Cain brings upon himself by his consequent killing of Abel takes the form of an infliction of sterility upon the earth similar to that incurred by Adam's sin: "And now cursed art thou from the ground, which hath opened her mouth to receive thy brother's blood from thy hand; when thou tillest the ground, it shall not henceforth yield unto thee her strength; . . ." (iv. 11–12). That the same curse should be twice imposed to explain the unremitting toil of agriculture is certainly suspicious; it would suggest that some not very expert fusion of traditions has taken place here[2]— a possible solution might be that the curse existed originally in the Cain and Abel story, and that the Yahwist was so impressed by its aptness as a penalty for Adam's sin that he transferred it to the earlier place in his narrative, thus creating this awkward repetition of what can intrinsically be only of single occurence.[3] However that may be, it would appear that in the original form of the legend Noah was designated the hero who mitigated the hard toil of the agriculturalist's life by the invention of viniculture. An indication that this was to be the rôle of Noah is skilfully introduced in the form of a

[1] Cf. Brandon, *Time and Mankind*, pp. 78 f.; Skinner, pp. 133–4; Gunkel, *Urgeschichte*, p. 76.

[2] It would appear that several different themes have been fused together in the story of Cain and Abel; cf. Skinner, pp. 111–15.

[3] Holzinger, p. 49, recognises the difficulty here and discusses whether, the two cursings are to be assigned to different writers or sources; he thinks, however, that iv. 1–15 can be regarded as a continuation of iii.

prophecy placed in the mouth of Lamech, Noah's father, on the birth of his son: "and he called his name Noah, saying, This same shall comfort us for our work, and for the toil of our hands, because of the ground which the Lord hath cursed" (v. 29).[1]

Consistency of theme naturally requires that the narrative should soon show how Noah came to fulfil his father's prophecy. However, this is not done in the extant form of the Yahwist narrative; instead there follows, first, what has aptly been termed a piece of 'unassimilated mythology' in vi. 1–4, which tells of a race of giants, the offspring of 'sons of God' and 'daughters of men'. There has been much discussion among scholars both as to the source of this strange legend and the purpose of its incorporation in *Genesis*. Folk-belief in an ancient race of giants is fairly widespread, and we have a notable instance of its occurence among the Israelites in *Numbers* xiii. 33.[2] We may also note, in view of the many indications that we have seen of the possible influence of the *Epic of Gilgamesh*, that the hero himself, Gilgamesh, was reputed to be 'two thirds god and one third man', as well as being of gigantic stature.[3] Whatever may have been the source of the belief, the problem of its introduction at this point in the narrative is even more baffling. It has been suggested that this liaison between divinities and mortals was regarded as an instance of the signal wickedness of mankind and is designed to illustrate why in the following verses (vi. 5–7)[4] Yahweh decided to destroy the race because of its wickedness. This explanation is possible; but there is no clear evidence in vi. 1–4 that any moral issue is involved, and in vi. 5–7 there is no reference back to the liaison between gods and humans. On the other hand, vi. 5–7 constitutes an explicit and independent statement of the reason why Yahweh now determined to destroy mankind, and it brings us more closely to understanding why the legend concerning Noah's rôle as the *Heilbringer* to the human race by his invention of viniculture is interrupted by the insertion of

[1] König's discussion (pp. 309–11) of the points involved here is important; but he does not seem to have reckoned with two factors, namely, the displacement of theme caused by the interpolation of the Flood legend and the Yahwist's desire to utilise the story of Noah's sons to further the development of his *Heilsgeschichte*.

[2] Cf. Skinner, 139–140, 145–7; M. Burrows, *What Mean These Stones?*, 180; von Rad, pp. 109–12.

[3] *Epic of Gilgamesh*, Tab. I, col. ii. 1, cf. Tab. I, col. i. 7–9.

[4] Cf. Driver, *Genesis*, p. 83.

the story of the Flood; it may also help us to understand why the section vi. 1–4 is introduced by the statement that, at this time, "men began to multiply on the face of the earth".

We have already noticed evidence of the influence of Mesopotamian tradition on the Yahwist narrative. Mindful of this, we may also recall that we noted, in our study of Mesopotamian cosmogony, that the memory of a flood of such catastrophic proportions that it seemed to destroy all living things upon earth was firmly established in Mesopotamian tradition.[1] Indeed so firmly established was it, and so much had it impressed itself upon the imagination, that the author of the *Epic of Gilgamesh* worked it, howbeit very skilfully, into his narrative which had quite a different theme. Without doubt the Yahwist knew of this great Flood and felt it incumbent upon himself also to introduce it into his account of the early history of mankind. Now, according to Mesopotamian tradition, the Flood had been caused by the fact that mankind, having multiplied exceedingly, disturbed the great god Enlil and led him to decree its destruction.[2] In seeking to introduce the legend into his narrative, the Yahwist in turn had also to find an occasion for it. It would, accordingly, seem that, still perhaps influenced by the *motif* of the 'overcrowded earth', he thought that he had found that occasion when he came to record the multiplication of the human race (vi. 1); and, in accordance too with Mesopotamian precedent, he depicted the cause of the Flood as the annoyance of Yahweh at what amounted to the *hubris* of man (vi. 5–7).[3]

The story of the Flood (vii. 1 ff.), which follows this explanation of its cause, constitutes a long interpolation and the theme of Noah as the *Heilbringer* is only resumed at ix. 20, where we are told that, "Noah began to be an husbandman, and planted a vineyard: and he drank of the wine, and was drunken; . . ." But, by this time, the Yahwist had evidently forgotten that consistency of theme demanded

---

[1] See pp. 87–8.

[2] In *A.N.E.T.*, p. 104, A(i), 1 f. The *Epic of Gilgamesh* does not explicitly state what was the cause of the Flood, but it is implied that human sin was in some way a factor, cf. Tab. XI, 180 f.

[3] It is remarkable that Schwarzbaum in his valuable study of the myth of 'the overcrowded earth', to which reference has already been made, while seeking to use it (cf. *Numen*, IV, pp. 72–3) to explain *Gen.* vi. 1–3, does not notice its much greater relevance to the Yahwist legend of the fall of Adam.

that he should show how Lamech's prophecy in v. 29 had really been fulfilled by Noah. Consequently, instead of doing this now that he had at last reached the point of recording Noah's invention of wine, we find that another issue is attracting his interest. Noah's discovery of the use of wine does not lead on to a demonstration of how he comforted mankind "for our work, and for the toil of our hands, because of the ground which the Lord hath cursed"; it is used instead as an occasion to pass on to the curious story of how Noah came to bless or to curse each of his sons (ix. 21b–28). Because of the shocking act that results from Noah's drunkenness, it has been easy to mistake the intention of the Yahwist writer here. Thus it has been said in explanation that "the story of Noah's drunkenness expresses the healthy recoil of primitive Semitic morality from the licentious habits engendered by a civilization of which the salient feature was the enjoyment and abuse of wine".[1] It is indeed correct that there was a puritanic tradition in ancient Israel concerning the use of wine; but to find its operation here leads to a complete mistaking of the original nature of the passage. As we have seen, Noah was destined to be a benefactor of mankind, and the sense of elation, indeed the experience of intoxication itself, has been regarded by primitive peoples as quasi-sacred and certainly not something to be condemned.[2] What the Yahwist appears to have done here is to fuse this ancient culture legend about Noah's invention of viniculture with another of a very different kind concerning the destiny of Noah's sons. What was the original form of this latter legend cannot now be discerned; but what is clear is the use to which the Yahwist has put it. The three sons of Noah, first given as Shem, Ham, and Japheth, are the eponymous ancestors of the chief racial groups with which the Hebrews were involved.[3] The Yahwist's intention here is to justify Israel's dispossessing the Canaanites of their land which is to be the

[1] Skinner, p. 185. However, Skinner recognises (p. 186) that "the cultural motive is crossed by an ethnographic problem, which is still more difficult to unravel".

[2] Reference may be made to the part played in various religions by such intoxicating beverages as soma, haoma, nectar and wine; cf. N. Soederblom, *The Living God*, pp. 2 f.; J. G. Frazer, *Taboo and Perils of the Soul* (*The Golden Bough*), pp. 248–50; E. B. Tylor, *Primitive Culture*, II, pp. 417–18. For the Hebrew attitude to wine see Pedersen, III–IV, pp. 264–6, 418–19; Lods, *Israël*, pp. 70–1, 353–5, 451, 476–7.

[3] Cf. Skinner, pp. 186–223; König, pp. 386–423.

climax of his history. Hence, he shows how Ham, the father of the ancestor of the Canaanites, had by a deed of shame incurred the curse of the great patriarch who had survived the Flood and from whom mankind was descended (ix. 22 ff.). However, so intent is he on making clear the accursed nature of the Canaanites that, in recording Noah's curse, the one upon whom the curse falls is not Ham, who had actually done the deed, but his son Canaan: "Cursed be Canaan; A servant of servants shall he be unto his brethren" (ix. 24–7).[1]

By thus utilising these traditions concerning Noah, the Yahwist prepares for his passage from the Primaeval History to the Patriarchal Sagas, in which he will begin to develop his true theme, namely, of Israel's original unity and of Yahweh's promise to settle the nation in the land of Canaan. The transition from the story of mankind as a whole to that of the Israelite nation is effected by the account of the building of the so-called Tower of Babel and its consequences. By this aetiological story the origin of the multiplicity of languages is explained, and the shattering of the primaeval unity of mankind is accounted for, together with the geographical dispersion of its members, so that the narrative can now conveniently pass on to record the movements of Terah, the father of Abram (xi. 1–9, 28 ff.), and thus to the great patriarch himself.[2]

The achievement of the Yahwist in these chapters of *Genesis* is truly superb. In a well-articulated narrative of great dramatic quality he accounts for the nature and destiny of man, showing why man as an individual is wholly mortal, according to the tenets of Yahwist

[1] Cf. Brandon, *Time and Mankind*, pp. 79–81.

[2] "The thesis of the *Heilsgeschichte* gives the answer to the obvious question of the Primaeval History, namely, of the relations of God with mankind. The definition of the theme of the *Heilsgeschichte* in *Gen.* xii. 1–3 constitutes not only the conclusion to the Primaeval History, as Budde (*Die biblische Urgeschichte*, s. 404) has rightly noted, but the proper key to it . . . In this fusion of the Primaeval History and the *Heilsgeschichte* there is provided the Yahwist justification of the meaning and purpose of the Salvation-relationship (Heilsverhältnis), which Yahweh has granted to Israel. It affords the aetiology of all aetiologies of Israel and is such for the true prophets", G. von Rad, *Das formgeschichtliche Problem des Hexateuchs*, p. 60. Cf. Brandon, *Time and Mankind*, pp. 81–2; Procksch, pp. 85–6; Gunkel, *Urgeschichte*, pp. 98–9.

theology. Incidentally he is able to provide an explanation of a number of other things from the pain of child-birth to that of the variety of languages. Drawing upon various older traditions, he fabricates a consequential survey of the evolution of mankind from the creation to a point at which he is able, without any obvious dislocation of theme, to pursue his real purpose of demonstrating the providence of Yahweh for his chosen people, Israel, from the calling of their ancestor Abram to their settlement in the Promised Land. The subsequent influence of this veritable philosophy of history has been immense; for it has truly provided the *rationale* of Judaism, and through that faith it has powerfully affected the development of Christian theology.

The Yahwist story of the creation and fall of man is preceded, as we have noted, by an account of the creation of the universe which comes from what is termed the Priestly tradition. This tradition, which can be traced throughout the Pentateuch, constitutes a kind of editorial commentary on the older traditions that have been bonded together to make a continuous narrative—indeed the Priestly tradition has been aptly described as "a fifth century midrash, or historical commentary, on the embryonic Pentateuch (JED)".[1] It must, therefore, be considered significant that the Priestly editor, while not excising or rewriting the Yahwist account of the creation and fall of man, obviously felt it necessary to add to this account the story of the creation of the universe that runs from *Genesis* i. 1 to ii. 4. Whether, in doing this, he cut out a Yahwist cosmogony with which he did not approve, or whether he thought that the Yahwist account of the creation of man alone (if that was its original form) was insufficient, we cannot know. That the later editor made no attempt to remove the inconsistency constituted by the fact that the Yahwist story presents the creation of the animals as subsequent to that of man (ii. 7, 18–19), whereas the Priestly version places the creation of man last in the order of creation (i. 24–7), suggests that the latter, as an already existing account, was added to the established Yahwist record. It has been suggested that, since the divine action in the Priestly cosmogony is carefully related to a period of seven days, the document may originally have been composed for liturgical

[1] Pfeiffer, p. 188.

146

use at a Hebrew New Year Festival, after the manner in which the *Enuma elish* was ritually recited at the *akîtu* festival in Babylon, as we have seen.[1] Such an origin would explain its appearance of being a well established and revered composition, so that it was joined as a whole to the existing Yahwist story, despite the discrepancy between its account of the origin of man and that of the older tradition.

It has long been recognised by Biblical scholars that this Priestly cosmogony reveals obvious traces of Mesopotamian influence, although, as we shall see, against the similarities must be set one notable exception. Mesopotamian influence is most apparent in the cosmological presuppositions, and in this sense the Priestly account differs significantly in its outlook from that of the Yahwist. Thus, whereas the Yahwist record envisages the primordial state as one of a desert needing water to fructify it, the Priestly presupposes the existence of a watery chaos invested in primaeval darkness: "And the earth was waste and void; and darkness was upon the face of the deep: and the spirit of God moved upon the face of the deep" (i. 2). This truly majestic imagery requires some commentary to make its full significance plain. The Hebrew words *tōhū wā-bōhū*, translated as 'waste and void', mean essentially in this context 'non-existent', as, of course, is evident from the statement in i. 9–10.[2] In other words, in the beginning the earth did not exist; there was only 'the deep'. In the concept of this 'deep' we certainly seem to discern Mesopotamian influence; for it is generally recognised that the Hebrew word *tᵉhōm* ('deep') is akin to the Babylonian Ti'āmat, the primordial watery chaos, which we have already discussed at some length.[3] But with the following statement, that "the spirit of God moved upon the face of the deep", we appear to be in another sphere of imagery. The word (רוּחַ), used for the 'spirit' of God, essentially connotes the idea of air, breath or wind, while that translated 'moved' (מְרַחֶפֶת) seems rather to mean 'brood' or 'hover', thus sug-

---

[1] Cf. Hooke, *In the Beginning*, p. 36; Widengren in *Myth, Ritual and Kingship*, p. 175; Anderson in *The Old Testament and Modern Study*, pp. 291–3; E. O. James, *Myth and Ritual in the Ancient Near East*, pp. 169–70. I. Engnell (in *Wisdom in Israel and in the Ancient Near East*, p. 105) thinks that in its extant form the Priestly cosmogony has been 'de-culticized'.

[2] Cf. Skinner, p. 16; König, pp. 138–9.

[3] Cf. Skinner, p. 17; Gunkel, *Urgeschichte*, p. 102; T. H. Robinson in *Myth and Ritual*, p. 176; A. Heidel, *The Babylonian Genesis*, pp. 98–101.

gesting the action of a bird.[1] No parallel to the imagery implicit here is found in Mesopotamian cosmogonic thought. The most obvious analogy is provided by the Hermopolitan-Theban cosmogony, in which, as we have seen, Amun is envisaged as the primaeval wind (or breath) that moves across the surface of the stagnant Nun, imparting to it the motion necessary for creation.[2] This Egyptian parallel could be further extended by comparing the emphasis that is laid upon the primaeval darkness in the Hebrew account (i. 2–3) with the personification, Kuk-Kauket, of the darkness that covers the primordial Nun.[3] The analogy could, with the necessary adjustments, be still further pursued in the divine action recorded in i. 3: "And God said, Let there be light: and there was light". For, as we have seen, in the Egyptian cosmogonies the very appearance of the sun-god as the creator dispelled the primaeval darkness. However, although an interesting parallelism of imagery is afforded by this reference to Egyptian cosmogonic thought, it seems improbable that Egypt actually provided the prototype here to the Hebrew conception.[4] On the other hand, it must be recognised that, while Mesopotamian influence appears to be very evident in the Priestly cosmology, it is possible that a wider syncretism contributed to this post-Exilic picture of the creation. Thus, it is very remarkable that in verse 4, prior to the creation of the sun, God is represented as separating the light from the darkness. What is the source of this light is not explained,

[1] Procksch, p. 426, maintains that 'spirit of God' does not mean 'der Geist Gottes', but 'Gottesgeist', so that it is rather the divine potentiality, not the personality, that is emphasised. Accordingly, the 'Prinzip des Geistes' is contrasted here with the 'Prinzip des Chaos. König, pp. 139–140, argues strongly against this view, maintaining that the 'spirit of God' means essentially the 'breath of God'—"Der Geist Gottes ist der Hauch oder Atem der Gotterheit, den der Dichter in einer tiefblickenden Stelle (Ps. 104, 29 f.) gleichsam aus dem pulsierenden Weltherzen hervorströmen und so den Urquell alles Weltlebens bilden lässt". Cf. Skinner, pp. 17–18; Johnson, pp. 26–39.

[2] See pp. 46–7.   [3] See p. 46.

[4] Whether or in what manner the Hermopolitan-Theban cosmogony could have been known to a learned Jew of the fifth century B.C., it is impossible to tell. By that time the cult of Amun had lost much of the prestige which it had enjoyed in the New Kingdom period; however, it was still influential under the Ethiopian pharaohs, and Amun and his oracle at Siwah were well known to the Greeks (cf. E. Bevan, *A Hist. of Egypt under the Ptolemaic Dynasty*, pp. 8–14), by whom he was identified with Zeus (Diodorus Siculus, I, 13.2, 15.3). Cf. Bonnet, *Reallexikon*, pp. 36b–37a.

although we are informed that "God called the light Day, and the darkness he called Night"[1] (i. 5); we are also told that God found the light to be good, but nothing is said of his evaluation of the darkness. That the first act of creation should concern light and darkness, and this without reference to the sun, has no precedent in Mesopotamian cosmogonic thought; but it has in Iranian religion, where light and darkness, personified in Ahura Mazdah and Ahriman, were regarded as the two primaeval forces which unceasingly struggle for cosmic mastery.[2] Possibly the Hebrew thinker, in depicting his god as manifesting himself in his first creative act as the master of light and darkness, was mindful of the cosmic dualism of Iran and sought thus to emphasise the superiority of his own deity.[3] If such was the purpose of the Priestly author, it is possible also that he knew something of Egyptian cosmogony and tacitly claimed for his god a form of creative activity that had been attributed to Amun.

In verses 6 and 8 we are firmly back in the tradition of Mesopotamian cosmology: "And God said, Let there be a firmament in the midst of the waters, and let it divide the waters from the waters. And God made the firmament, and divided the waters which were under the firmament from the waters which were above the firmament; and it was so. And God called the firmament Heaven". The imagery here reproduces with an amazing fidelity that implicit in Marduk's creative act in the *Enuma elish*, but with one notable difference. As we have seen, the Babylonian god used half of the body of Ti'âmat to form the vault of heaven, the solid canopy of the sky, to hold back the encompassing waters; after that he dealt with the Apsû, the deep of the sweet waters, and placed the earth ('Esharra')

---

[1] The statement in i. 5b: "And there was evening and there was morning, one day", presents a difficulty which cannot be explained by the fact that the Jews reckon a day as the period from one sunset to another. Possibly König, pp. 143–4, is right in suggesting that due weight must be given to the mention of 'Day' and 'Night' in the first part of the verse concerned. Cf. Skinner, pp. 20–1; Procksch, p. 427.

[2] Cf. R. C. Zaehner, *The Dawn and Twilight of Zoroastrianism*, pp. 42–3, 64. See also Brandon, *Man and his Destiny*, pp. 264 f., and pp. 194–9.

[3] On the question of a dualistic factor in Judaism see A. E. Suffrin in *E.R.E.*, V, pp. 112a–114a. The idea of two opposing spirits in the Dead Sea Scrolls probably derives from Iranian sources; cf. Zaehner, pp. 51–2; H. W. Huppenbauer, *Der Mensch zwischen zwei Welten*, pp. 26–30, 71–3; J. Duchesne-Guillemin, *The Western Response to Zoroaster*, pp. 91–6.

as a kind of canopy over the Apsû.[1] The creation of the earth that follows in the Priestly account also conforms to this further feature of the Babylonian cosmological scheme: "And God said, Let the waters under the heaven be gathered together unto one place, and let the dry land appear: and it was so. And God called the dry land Earth; and the gathering together of the waters called he Seas: and God saw that it was good" (i. 9–10). The notable point of difference in the Hebrew story, which was alluded to above, is that, whereas Marduk is represented in a thoroughly mythological manner fashioning the solid canopy of the sky out of the carcase of a primaeval monster, nothing is said of the material employed by the Hebrew deity for the same purpose.[2] In this connection, too, it will be convenient to comment here upon the fact that in this Priestly cosmogony the various acts of creation are accomplished by the pronouncement of the divine *fiat*. However, although this manner contrasts favourably with the action of Marduk in slicing up the body of Ti'âmat, it does not really imply any advance in conceptual thought, because, as we have already seen, the idea of creation by divine decree was known long before in both Egypt and Sumer.[3]

The consequent acts of creating vegetation, the heavenly bodies, the birds and fishes, and the terrestrial animals do not call for special comment,[4] although we may note with interest that, whereas the Yahwist was particularly concerned about the necessity of water for vegetation, the subject is ignored by the Priestly writer—possibly he reflects the

---

[1] See pp. 102–3. The word (רָקִיעַ) translated 'firmament' (LXX στερέωμα, Vul. *fundamentum*) connotes the idea of solidity; it can be rendered as 'pavement' or 'floor'. Cf. Skinner, pp. 21–2; A. Heidel, *The Babylonian Genesis*, p. 116. Reference is made to the Apsû in *Deut.* xxxiii. 17.

[2] It cannot be inferred from this fact that the Priestly writer conceived of a creation *ex nihilo*, thus anticipating the later Christian formulation of this dogma; as we have seen, in the Priestly account the t°hōm preexists the first divine act of creation.

[3] See pp. 33–4, 37–8, 72, 86–7, 98. It must also be noted that, after the pronouncement of the *fiat* in i. 6, in i. 7 God was described as making (וַיַּעַשׂ) the firmament, and as dividing (וַיַּבְדֵּל) the waters.

[4] i. 11–25. The record in i. 21 that God created the 'great sea-monsters' calls perhaps for comment. These הַתַּנִּינִם recall the monsters created by Ti'âmat (*Enuma elish*, Tab. I. 132–142), although these were not marine creatures. Cf. Bottéro, pp. 227–8.

mentality of a civilisation based on irrigation from great perennial rivers. According to the Priestly view, the process of creation reached its climax in the creation of man. But, not only does the Priestly version here differ from the Yahwist in the matter of chronological order, the Priestly concept of human nature and of man's relation to the other animals also diverges notably from the Yahwist estimate: "And God said, Let us make man in our image, after our likeness: and let them have dominion over the fish of the sea, and over the fowl of the air, and over the cattle, and over all the earth, and over every creeping thing that creepeth upon the earth. And God created man in his own image, in the image of God created he him; male and female created he them" (i. 26–7). The problems of interpretation in this passage have, down the centuries, led to much debate and speculation.[1] Attention has inevitably been focused upon the meaning of the use of the plural in "Let us make man in our image, after our likeness" and on that of the words translated 'image' and 'likeness'. With regard to the first difficulty, explanations based upon the fact that the Hebrew word for God (*Elōhīm*) is plural in form or upon the use of the 'royal we' are not really apposite. A more likely interpretation would seem to be that, in his account of the creation of man, the Priestly writer had in mind Mesopotamian tradition, which, as we have seen, represented the making of the human species as the concerted plan and action of a number of deities, the basic idea being that mankind was created to serve the gods—an idea which finds reflection, if perhaps not so overtly, in Hebrew thought.[2] The expressions 'in our image, after our likeness' (בְּצַלְמֵנוּ כִּדְמוּתֵנוּ) surely connote the idea of following a model or pattern,[3] and, despite the well-known Hebrew iconomachy, it is obvious that the Priestly writer was here holding some definite picture of God in mind as the pattern of man.[4] In other words, in view of the context of this passage,

---

[1] Cf. Skinner, pp. 31–2; Holzinger, pp. 10–11.
[2] See pp. 76–7, 89, 104–6. Cf. Skinner, pp. 30–1, 46, König, pp. 153–5; Gunkel, *Urgeschichte*, p. 106.   [3] Cf. König, pp. 156–8.
[4] An interesting parallel is afforded by the *Epic of Gilgamesh*, Tab. I, col. ii. 3–5, where the goddess Aruru's creation of Enkidu is described: "When Aruru heard this, she conceived in her heart an image of Anu (i.e. the god of heaven); (A)raru washed her hands, pinched off clay, (and) threw (it) on the steppe: (. . .) valiant Enkidu she created, . . ." (trans. A. Heidel), *The Gilgamesh Epic*, pp. 18–19.

a contrast is evidently being made between the form and nature of the animals and of men, the latter differing fundamentally from the former in that they were modelled on the pattern of the divine Creator. It is possible that the Priestly writer felt a need to emphasise this difference, being mindful of the deification of animals in the neighbouring state of Egypt.

In the concluding section of the Priestly account (i. 28–ii. 4), attention is concentrated on two subjects, namely, the providence of God for man and the *raison d'être* of the Sabbath rest[1]. In describing the bounty of God, the Priestly writer reveals a very different spirit from that of the Yahwist. He surveys the situation of mankind optimistically; in his fair picture nothing mars or menaces the idyllic relationship of God and man—there is no whisper of human defection, of the hard toil of agriculture, and of death. Moreover, in the divine command to man to "be fruitful, and multiply, and replenish the earth, and subdue it" (i. 28), we are far from any suggestion of the 'overcrowded earth', that man's acquisition of the ability to procreate inevitably brought the sentence of death upon him as an individual. However, in his generation the Priestly writer clearly had not the same theological task as that of his predecessor, the Yahwist.

In one notable way the Priestly account of creation appears to differ, tacitly, from the Mesopotamian tradition as exemplified in the *Enuma elish*. This is in the absence of any suggestion that God accomplished the creation of the world after subduing a monster which personified the primaeval chaos of water. As we have noted, the Priestly writer does conceive of a primaeval chaos of water which he designates *t^ehōm*, thus seemingly equating it with Ti'âmat, the primaeval monster conquered by Marduk, the Babylonian creator-deity; but in the Hebrew story this chaos is not personified, nothing is said of its needing to be subdued before the work of creation can begin, and the world is not fashioned out of its substance as in the *Enuma elish*. If the Priestly writer did know the Babylonian creation tradition, and there is certainly much other reason for thinking that he did, he clearly refrained from following it in this matter. What was his reason for so doing we can only surmise; but even to surmise is difficult, because, as we must now notice, the idea of a primaeval con-

[1] Cf. Skinner, pp. 35–9.

flict between Yahweh and some monster was a well established belief of Hebrew folk-lore.

The Ugarit texts have revealed to us that already, during the second millennium B.C., the *motif* of a struggle between a god and a 'slippery', 'wriggling', seven-headed serpent, named Leviathan, was known to the Canaanites, as well as the idea of a conflict between a god and a personification of the waters or sea.[1] That the Hebrews, before the Babylonian Exile (586 B.C.), imagined that a great serpent lived in the sea or personified it, is attested by an interesting passage from the prophetic writings attributed to Amos. The prophet depicts Yahweh as saying of his enemies, "though they be hid from my sight in the bottom of the sea, thence will I command the serpent, and he shall bite them" (*Amos* ix. 3).[2] The 'sea-serpent' here would appear to be under the command of Yahweh; there is, however, much evidence, probably post-Exilic, which shows that the idea of a primaeval conflict between Yahweh and the sea, or a monster personifying it, was familiar to the Hebrew mind. Thus, to start with *Psalm* civ,[3] which may even ante-date the Exile and so anticipate the Priestly cosmogony, we have evidence of a belief that Yahweh, in his work of creation, had to contend with the sea or primaeval waters. Yahweh is being addressed:

> Who laid the foundations of the earth,
> That it should not be moved for ever.
> Thou coveredst it with the deep as with a vesture;
> The waters stood above the mountains.
> At thy rebuke they fled;
> At the voice of thy thunder they hasted away;
> They went up by the mountains, they went down by the valleys,

---

[1] See p. 120. Cf. T. H. Gaster, *Thespis*, pp. 125–6, 135–8.

[2] "Wir würden aus dieser Anspielung allein mit Sicherheit erkennen, dass diese 'Schlange' ein mythologisches Ungeheuer, das personificierte Meer ist", H. Gunkel, *Schöpfung und Chaos*, p. 81.

[3] Cf. Pfeiffer, p. 631. J. H. Breasted (*The Dawn of Conscience*, pp. 282–4) suggested that certain ideas in the *Psalm* civ had been anticipated by the famous Egyptian *Hymn to the Aten*. The parallels cited do not concern the verses quoted here; moreover, the Egyptian poem does not regard the primaeval waters as a violent menace that the creator-god overcomes—indeed the Aten cosmogony is in line with Egyptian tradition on this point, as we have seen. Bottéro, p. 196, sees *Psalm* civ as "une sorte de commentaire poétique et d'envolée lyrique" on the Priestly cosmogony.

Unto the place which thou hadst founded for them.
Thou hast set a bound that they may not pass over;
That they turn not again to cover the earth" (5–9)[1]

In the majestic imagery of this Psalm the primaeval chaos of waters is not personified; the personification is, however, well attested in other documents. For example, *Psalm* lxxiv. 12–17:

Yet God (*Elōhim*) is my King of old,
Working salvation in the midst of the earth.
Thou didst divide the sea by thy strength:
Thou breakest the heads of the dragons (תַּנִּינִים) in the waters.

Thou breakest the heads of Leviathan in pieces,
Thou gavest him to be meat to the people
    inhabiting the wilderness.
Thou didst cleave fountain and flood:
Thou driest up mighty rivers.
The day is thine, the night also is thine:
Thou hast prepared the light and the sun.
Thou hast set the borders of the earth:
Thou hast made summer and winter.[2]

In this passage we surely have preserved a statement of the creative activity of Israel's god which is much more akin to the Babylonian tradition of Marduk's conquest of Ti'âmat and his subsequent work of cosmic creation. The name 'Leviathan' given to the monster and the allusion to its several heads naturally recalls the Ugaritic mythology, reminding us that both the name and the concept had a long ancestry in Canaan, although the concept itself may well have found its way there from Mesopotamia.[3]

---

[1] Cf. Gunkel, *Schöpfung*, pp. 91–2; R. Kittel, *Die Psalmen*, pp. 338–9. In the mention of the leviathan in verse 26 there seems to be a reference back to *Genesis* i. 21; cf. W. Stärk, *Lyrik*, p. 81.

[2] Cf. Gunkel, *Schöpfung*, pp. 41–5, who rightly points out a new feature which has no Babylonian parallel, namely, the giving of the body of Leviathan to feed the denizens of the desert—צִיִּים surely means the wild beasts

which live in the desert. Kittel, p.252, thinks that an ancient popular myth may here have been renewed by the Mesopotamian contacts of the Exile—"Was im Volksglauben immer gelebt hat, findet jetzt wieder neue Nahrung. Die Seele des Volkes sucht 'die alten Heimlichkeiten' wieder auf".

[3] Cf. Pedersen, I–II, pp. 472–4; Widengren in *Myth, Ritual, and Kingship*, pp. 170–3; Bottéro, pp. 226–8; J. P. Peters in *E.R.E.*, IV, pp. 153b–154a Gaster, pp. 142–9.

The primaeval monster was also named Rahab, a word signifying 'violence', 'defiance', and obviously appropriate for a personification of the sea.[1] Thus in *Psalm* lxxxix, 10–12 (Hebrew), the achievement of Yahweh is commemorated:

It is thou who hast conquered the pride of the sea!
Thou who hast quietened its bounding waves!
Thou who hast broken Rahab, as one that is slain,
And scattered thy enemies with the arm of thy strength.
The heavens are thine, the earth also is thine:
The world and the fulness thereof, thou hast founded them.[2]

In the so-called *Deutero-Isaiah* (li. 9–10) this ancient exploit of Yahweh is also recalled: "Awake, awake, put on strength, O arm of the Lord; awake, as in the days of old, the generations of ancient times. Art thou not it that cut Rahab in pieces, that pierced the dragon? Art thou not it which dried up the sea, the waters of the great deep; . . ."[3] It is commemorated, too, in *Job* xxvi. 10–13:

He hath described a boundary upon the face of the waters,
Unto the confines of light and darkness.
The pillars of heaven tremble
And are astonished at his rebuke,
He causeth the sea to tremble by his power,
And by his understanding he smiteth through Rahab.
By his spirit the heavens are garnished;
His hand hath pierced the slippery (בָּרִ֫חַ) serpent.[4]

The evidence of these passages attest the existence in Israel of a well established tradition that represented Yahweh as having in the beginning overcome a monster that either personified, or was closely associated with, a primaeval chaos of waters. The subduing or controlling of this primordial deep had been the first necessary stage in the process of creating the world. Since this was clearly a popular tradition and it occurs in psalms, it would seem likely that this tradition had some liturgical expression, and it is possible that it formed part of the myth and ritual pattern of a Hebrew New Year festival after the manner in which the *Enuma elish* was used in

[1] Cf. Gunkel, *Schöpfung*, pp. 31–2; Pedersen, I–II, pp. 472–3, 476 f.; Pfeiffer, p. 36.
[2] Cf. Bottéro, p. 226; Gunkel, *Schöpfung*, pp. 36–7.
[3] Cf. Gunkel, *Schöpfung*, pp. 30–3.
[4] Cf. Gunkel, *Schöpfung*, pp. 36–7. See p. 120.

Babylon, as we have seen.[1] If this were so, it is significant that this tradition, with its primitive mythological imagery, was not incorporated by the Priestly writer into his account of the creation of the world which was to preface the Yahwist story of the creation and destiny of man. The idea of some primaeval monster, co-existent with Yahweh from the beginning, was doubtlessly felt to be incompatible with the monotheistic outlook that had already found noble expression in *Isaiah* xliii. 10: "Ye are my witnesses, saith the Lord, and my servant whom I have chosen: that ye may know and believe me, and understand that I am he; before me there was no God formed, neither shall there be after me". And so, although not sufficiently a metaphysician to notice that he was tacitly allowing the pre-existence of some form of matter when he described the primordial deep, the Priestly writer was careful not to personify this deep; moreover, he ascribed the creation of its very monsters to the action of the god in whose service he wrote.[2]

Such, then, was the achievement of that unknown writer who finally fused together into an apparently continuous narrative the Priestly and the Yahwist traditions concerning the creation of the world and the origin of man and his fatal act of disobedience. When seen in the context of the Egyptian and Mesopotamian cosmogonies, this Hebrew account at once impresses by its greater lucidity, its comparative freedom from the more primitive mythological imagery, and the high quality of its drama. For a proper evaluation it must, however, be recognised that the *Genesis* story of the creation is the product of that peculiar Hebrew interest in the past that first finds expression in the Yahwist attempt to demonstrate the providence of Yahweh for Israel by means of a philosophy of history. The success

[1] Cf. Pedersen, III–IV, pp. 443–4; W. O. E. Oesterly in *Myth and Ritual*, pp. 128–9; Widengren in *Myth, Ritual, and Kingship*, pp. 170–3; James, pp. 199–201; S. H. Hooke, *The Siege Perilous*, pp. 140–3.

[2] In *Proverbs* viii. 22–30. Wisdom is virtually hypostatised and is represented as pre-existent and associated with Yahweh in his work of cosmic creation. The account given of the process of creation appears to be free of mythological imagery. The passage is surely late, perhaps not before 300 B.C. (Pfeiffer, p. 659); the source of the conception remains much disputed, cf. W. Baumgartner in *The Old Testament and Modern Study*, pp. 215–16; P. A. H. De Boer in *Wisdom in Israel and in the Ancient Near East*, pp. 42–71. See also Bottéro, pp. 216–17.

of that original attempt was immense, and it set the pattern for all subsequent Hebrew thinking. Its requirements determined that current cosmogonic tradition should be shaped to form a consequential narrative of Yahweh's creative activity in accordance with the monotheistic outlook that was gradually being established as the faith of Israel. The measure of that achievement is to be seen when reference is made to the cosmogonic mythology that also existed concerning Yahweh's struggle with the monster of primaeval chaos. For that mythology truly represented the earlier popular tradition of Israel, and, for that reason doubtlessly, it was more in keeping with the neighbouring traditions of Egypt and Mesopotamia.

CHAPTER FIVE

GREECE: THE INTUITIONS OF MYTHOLOGY
AND OF A DAWNING RATIONALISM

WE have now examined the three main traditions of cosmogonic speculation in the ancient Near East. As we have seen, each of those traditions was closely, or perhaps rather essentially, bound up with the religious faith and practice of the peoples concerned. Thus in Egypt certain great sanctuaries based their claims to precedence on the assertion that they each severally marked the site, and their own patron god had performed, the first essential acts of creation. The Mesopotamian cosmogonies all ascribed the beginnings of the world, of mankind and the institutions of civilised life to divine action, and in the case of the celebrated *Enuma elish* cosmogony was used to vindicate the supremacy of Babylon and its god, Marduk. Among the Hebrews cosmogony became a potent instrument for advancing the claim that Yahweh was the only God by virtue of his creation of the universe, while at the same time it helped to provide a superb introduction to that great philosophy of history in which Yahweh's providence for Israel was set forth. When we turn, as we now do, to consider Greek tradition about the beginning of things, we find a striking difference in ethos and purpose: the religious factor is diminished and a spirit of secular rationalisation begins to show itself.

It is, of course, to the peculiar genius of the Greeks for rational enquiry that the origins of Western science and philosophy are to be traced. Now, this genius manifested itself early, and with increasing strength, in speculation concerning the origin of the world and the institutions of human life. Consequently Greek cosmogonic thought quickly became part of the tradition of Greek philosophy, and as such it falls outside the proper scope of our subject, i.e. creation-legends. However, the earliest Greek thinkers did not come to consider the problem of the beginning of things with minds untouched or unformed by more ancient traditions. It will, accordingly, be our task to evaluate Greek cosmogonic thought during that formative period before mythopoeic speculation had been generally superseded by philosophical reflection on natural phenomena as the accepted means of understanding the way in which the universe had come into being.

Before proceeding to examine the relevant material, we must, however, notice certain factors of geographical environment and of the historical situation that may possibly be of significance for evaluating the peculiar nature of early Greek cosmogony.

We have seen that certain features of their physical environment very probably suggested to both the Egyptians and the peoples of Mesopotamia imagery in terms of which to conceive the process of creation: in particular, we noted the effect of the Nile's annual inundation and the peculiar conditions faced by those who sought to settle in the delta area of the Tigris and Euphrates. Water, in its varying aspects of an encompassing featureless deep or the destructive violence of rivers in spate, dominated the cosmogonies of these two peoples. In Israel physical environment provided one factor of the Yahwist story of the creation, namely, the need of rain for the production of vegetation;[1] but the Priestly cosmology, as we saw, was derived from Mesopotamian tradition, with perhaps some reference to that of Egypt. When we turn to consider the geography of the area of Hellenic culture, comprising as it did the Greek mainland, Ionia and the Aegean islands, we are at once struck by its difference from that of Egypt or Mesopotamia. The Greeks had no experience of life in an environment dominated by mighty rivers; instead, almost on every side the sea formed part of their horizon. In this respect their situation was to a certain degree similar to that of the Hebrews, whose land had a comparatively long coastline; however, whereas the Hebrews seem persistently to have turned their backs on the sea, the Greeks embraced it willingly as their natural environment and studied to live with it and use it.[2] We might, accordingly, be led to expect that the sea should have constituted a

[1] See pp. 122–3.
[2] Cf. A. Lesky, *Thalatta*, pp. 1–37, who traces out the gradual transformation of the original 'Seefremdheit' of the Greeks; M. Cary, *The Geographic Background of Greek and Roman History*, pp. 35–6, 47.

basic factor in both their cosmology and cosmogony; but we should also bear in mind the fact, apparent from *a priori* consideration, that the sea itself would not immediately have provided features of possible cosmogonic significance as did the Nile and the great rivers of Mesopotamia.[1]

The complex of Greek culture and civilisation, as it is known to us through literature and art, represents a fusion of two distinctive traditions. The earlier inhabitants of the area, whose way of life may be conveniently termed Aegean and of which the centre and source of inspiration lay in Crete, had differed profoundly in their *Weltanschauung* from the Indo-European people who gradually dispossessed them during the latter half of the second millennium B.C. Unfortunately, owing to our continuing inability to decipher their written records, we can still only know the Aegean peoples through their archaeological remains and from such inferences as may reasonably be drawn from the later literature of the Greeks. So far as this evidence concerns our own subject, we may note that the religion of these peoples seems to have centred on the cult of a mother goddess who embodied the principle of fertility and as such was closely associated, if not identified, with the earth.[2] The fact is significant, because it would suggest that Aegean cosmogony, if indeed such existed, was likely to have been especially concerned with the earth as the source of life. On the other hand, it must also be noted that the surviving monuments are singularly free from fertility symbolism.[3] Of what this fact might be significant it is impossible to say, and we may well reflect in this connection on a kindred fact, namely, that the remains of contemporary Greek art similarly provide no evidence of the currency of such a conception of the beginning of things as appears in the *Theogony* of Hesiod, to which we must shortly turn

[1] The phenomena of bradyseism could conceivably have provided apparent evidence of the creative property of the sea, if it had operated in ancient times in the Mediterranean area to raise the coastline. However, the legend of Atlantis presents the sea in a contrary guise. On the later effects of bradyseism in the bay of Naples see A. Maiuri, *The Phlegraean Fields*, pp. 21–30. Cf. J. O. Thomson, *History of Ancient Geography*, pp. 54, 90–3.

[2] Cf. M. P. Nilsson, *Minoan-Mycenaean Religion*, pp. 328–9, 389–412; C. Picard, *Les religions préhelléniques*, pp. 74–80; J. Charbonneaux, in *H.G.R.*, II, pp. 10–11. See also L. A. Stella in *Numen* V (1958), pp. 38–9.

[3] Cf. Nilsson, *Minoan-Mycenaean Religion*, p. 573; but see also Picard, pp. 110–11.

our attention. However that may be, it is certain that Greek religious faith and practice, as they find expression in literature, incorporate elements that derive from both the Aegean and Indo-European traditions[1]—as we shall see when we study the Hesiodic cosmogony, the portrait of Zeus combines the concept of the sky-god of the northern invaders with some myth of a divine child that had its location in Crete.

Another factor with which we must reckon in these *a proiri* considerations is the absence in Greece of any powerfully organised cult, located at some particular centre, that might have been concerned with advancing its claims by means of a kind of cosmogonic propaganda after the manner of that which was done in Egypt and in Babylon, as we have seen. Greece did not, of course, lack important sanctuaries; but it is interesting to note how the foundation-legends of two of the most famous of these sanctuaries, which might well have developed cosmogonic claims, failed to do so. In an awe-inspiring setting, the temple of Delphi, through the fame of its oracle, acquired immense prestige. In the *adyton* of Apollo's shrine there a navel-shaped stone, called the *omphalos*, was shown as marking the centre of the earth. It might accordingly be expected that so significant a possession, curiously reminiscent of the 'primaeval hills' of the Egyptian sanctuaries, would have been explained by some legend which made clear the temple's unique status as the *locus* of the first acts of creation. But this was not so: instead the position of the *omphalos* was explained by a jejune tale, while the origin of Apollo's cult there was accounted for in terms of the god's victory over the mysterious Python, the chthonic being that first possessed the site.[2] A similar apparent lack of cosmogonic interest shows itself in the foundation-legend of the sanctuary of Eleusis in the form in which

[1] Cf. Nilsson, *Geschichte der griechischen Religion*, I, pp. 281–359; *Minoan-Mycenaean Religion*, pp. 2–6; Picard, pp. 185–6; G. Glotz, *La civilisation égéenne*, pp. 445–52; Stella in *Numen*, V, pp. 18–57 (on what may be learned from the so-called 'Linear B' texts).

[2] Cf. Nilsson, *Gesch. d. griech. Rel.*, I, pp. 189, cf. p. 599; *O.C.D.*, *sub* 'Omphalos', p. 622a; H. J. Rose, *Handbook of Greek Mythology*, pp. 136–8. The myth concerned is that Zeus discovered that the centre of the earth was located at Delphi by marking the meeting point of two eagles, of equal speed, started respectively from the eastern and western limits of the world. On the possibility that the *omphalos* was the tomb of Python cf. J. Fontenrose, *Python*, pp. 374–94.

it has been preserved in the so-called *Homeric Hymn to Demeter*. The beautiful story of Demeter, the corn-goddess, in her quest for her lost daughter, might conceivably have been exploited to prove that agriculture had originated in Eleusis; instead the legend is concerned to explain how the celebrated mystery-cult came to be located there.[1] It would, accordingly, seem that the Greek priesthoods, while mindful of the need of accounting for the origin of their own particular temples, did not instinctively think in terms of primordial creation; instead they were content to appeal to the authority of some event alleged to have happened in a remote 'age of the gods', which, however, was subsequent to the beginning of the world.

As with so much else in Greek culture and civilisation, it is with Homer that we have to begin our study of the literary evidence for Greek cosmogonic thought. That the *Iliad* and *Odyssey*, which in their extant form probably date from some time before 700 B.C., embody much earlier tradition is a generally accepted principle of classical scholarship, although the determination of the original nature of that tradition remains in most instances a problem around which controversy still rages.[2] We meet this kind of problem in all the, very meagre, references that have to do with the Homeric view of the constitution of the world. Thus, in the graphic description that is given of the mighty shield that the artificer-god, Hephaestus, made for the hero Achilles, we are told that on the outer surface "Therein he wrought the earth (γαῖαν), therein the heavens, therein the sea, and the unwearied sun, and the moon at full, and therein all the constellations wherewith heaven is crowned—" Then, after having represented the main features of the universe on the surface of the shield, Hephaestus is recorded to have "set also the great might of the river Oceanus, around the uttermost rim of the strongly-wrought shield".[3] In other words, the poet clearly conceives of the universe, i.e. the earth, the sea, and the heavens with its stars, as surrounded

---

[1] *Hymn to Demeter*, 268–74, 480–2. It is significant that in ll. 470–3 no attempt is made to locate Demeter's bountiful act at Eleusis. Cf. W. K. C. Guthrie, *In the Beginning*, pp. 97–8.

[2] Cf. *O.C.D.*, p. 435 ('Homer'); A. Rostagni, *Storia della Letteratura greca*, pp. 34–7; H. L. Lorimer, *Homer and the Monuments*, pp. 452–93.

[3] *Iliad* xviii. 483–5 (trans. A. T. Murray, Loeb ed., II, pp. 322–5). Cf. Lesky, p. 15.

by a great river named Oceanus. Another passage supplies further details of this all-encompassing Oceanus. The mighty power of Zeus, the supreme god of the Homeric pantheon, is here being celebrated by a series of comparisons: "With him (Zeus) doth not even king Achelous vie, nor the great might of the deep-flowing Ocean ('Ωκεανοῖο), from which all rivers flow and every sea, and all the springs and deep wells".[1] We see, then, that this Oceanus, which encircles the universe, was also regarded as the source of every form of water, both of the bitter and the sweet. It is natural to ask whether such a concept was one that was likely to have been suggested to a Greek by the features of his physical environment or whether it contains imagery that might have been derived from some foreign tradition. We have noted the predominance of the sea as a factor of the Greek environment; however, the Mediterranean, although doubtlessly appearing vast in expanse to a primitive people, was known to have its limits, since the Greeks were a seafaring people. The Atlantic Ocean, which stretched away westward to apparent infinity beyond the Pillars of Hercules, might well have suggested an all-encompassing waste of waters; but it is unlikely that Greek mariners had ventured so far west to have known the Atlantic by the time of the composition of the *Iliad*.[2] Oceanus is actually described as a river (ποταμός), not as the sea. If the usual meaning of the word is to be pressed here, it is doubtful whether the Greeks at this period were acquainted with any great river that might have suggested the concept of Oceanus to them. The word Oceanus ('Ωκεανός) is not self-explanatory; it has been thought to be a non-personal descriptive term possibly related to Hittite or Sanskrit terms meaning 'circle' or 'that which surrounds'.[3] The idea of the universe as being surrounded by water is, of course, reminiscent of Babylonian cosmology; the origin of the Homeric concept of Oceanus may, therefore, be conveniently attributed ultimately to Mesopotamian influence,

---

[1] *Iliad* xxi. 194–7 (trans. A. T. Murray, *op.cit.*, pp. 422–3).

[2] Cf. Thomson, pp. 19–27.

[3] Cf. G. S. Kirk and J. E. Raven, *The Presocratic Philosophers* (abbr. Kirk-Raven), p. 14 (3). Lesky, pp. 65–6, suggests another derivation: "wir es bei 'Okeanos' mit einem Worte zu tun haben, das zusammen mit der Vorstellung den Griechen aus dem vorindogermanischen Bereiche zuwuchs. Das phoinikische uk und Okeanos mögen trotzdem zusammengehören, sind aber dann von demselben 'aegaeischen' Worte abzuleiten".

although it must be recognised that the line of derivation cannot be traced.[1]

Two other references that Homer makes to Oceanus are especially puzzling. In the one the goddess Hera is represented as saying that she was going to visit "the limits of the all-nurturing earth, and Oceanus, from whom the gods are sprung, and mother Tethys, even them that lovingly nursed me and cherished me in their halls, when they had taken me from Rhea, what time Zeus, whose voice is borne afar, thrust Cronos down to dwell beneath earth and the unresting sea".[2] Before commenting upon the very interesting implications of this passage, it will be well to notice the other passage to which reference has been made. Hypnos, the personification of Sleep, is therein depicted as telling Hera: "another of the gods, that are for ever, might I lightly lull to sleep, aye, were it even the streams of the river Oceanus, from whom all are sprung".[3] These two references, taken together, represent Oceanus as the begetter of all (living?) things, including the gods. As such the lines concerned contain the only explicit cosmogonic statement in Homer. The brevity of reference, however, constitutes a problem that might be interpreted in two ways. It could be argued that so brief are the references that it would be unwise to regard them as containing a definitive statement of Homer's cosmogonic belief. On the other hand, the very brevity of the references might be interpreted as indicating that so familiar was the conception to his audience that the poet felt no need to expand or explain them. Whatever may be the correct interpretation, it is significant that the first passage, with which we are concerned, implies the existence of yet another myth about the origin of the gods. For, while Hera is represented as ascribing to Oceanus the genesis of the gods, this great goddess and spouse of Zeus alludes to her birth from Rhea—indeed, as we shall shortly see, the Olympian gods, of whom Homer tells, were held to be the offspring of more ancient gods. It would, accordingly, seem that Homer knew of various traditions concerning the origin of the gods; and, it would further appear that none had an exclusive validity for him. Quite clearly chronological pre-

[1] Cf. Lesky, pp. 58–87; Kirk-Raven, pp. 18–19, see also pp. 10–15. See also Thomson, pp. 27, 95–9.

[2] Iliad, xiv. 200–204 (trans. Murray, op. cit., pp. 80–1).

[3] Iliad, xiv. 244–6: Ὠκεανοῦ, ὅς περ γένεσις πάντεσσι τέτυκται· (trans. Murray, op. cit., pp. 84–5). Cf. Kirk-Raven, pp. 15–16.

cedence had no importance in his theology, as it obviously had in the other religions which we have studied, and he could easily regard Zeus as the supreme ruler of the universe and designate him 'father of gods and men', and yet hold him to have been begotten of earlier gods and in no wise to be the creator of either the world or mankind.[1]

The *Iliad* contains one further passage which seems to reveal the poet's acquaintance with another figure of possible cosmogonic significance. Hypnos relates how he barely escaped the vengeance of Zeus for having lulled him to sleep at the behest of Hera: "But Zeus, when he awakened, was wroth, and flung the gods hither and thither about his palace, and me above all he sought, and would have hurled me from heaven into the deep to be no more seen, had Night not saved me—Night that bends to her sway (δμήτειρα) both gods and men. To her I came in my flight, and besought her, and Zeus refrained him, albeit he was wroth, for he had awe lest he do aught displeasing to swift Night".[2] This description of Night is brief but very significant in its implications. Night is personified as a goddess, and one so mighty that the epithet δμήτειρα θεῶν ('subduer of the gods') is given to her; moreover, even Zeus, the supreme god of the Olympic pantheon, is said to stand in awe of her. Nothing is explicitly said or implied in this passage as to Night's having any cosmogonic rôle; however, the awesome power with which she is invested indicates that in some tradition known to Homer she must have played a more significant part than that of the personification of night. This intimation is confirmed by other evidence which, although being later than Homer, must surely preserve a very ancient tradition. Thus Aristotle briefly refers to "theologians (θεολόγοι) who generate (γεννῶντες) from Night",[3] and some information of such systems would appear to be preserved in the later records of the so-called Orphic cosmogonies. We may cite, for example, the record

[1] E.g. *Iliad* xvi. 458; πατὴρ ἀνδρῶν τε θεῶν τε· The epithet signified the supreme status of Zeus in a patriarchal-ordered society, and did not connote 'procreator'. Cf. Nilsson, *Gesch. d. griech. Religion*, I, p. 390: "der Name Vater bezeichnet Zeus nicht als den Erzeuger, sondern als den Hausherrn", see also p. 314. In the light of the Hittite myth of Kumarbis (see p. 171), H. Schwabl (in *P.W.*, 'Weltschöpfung', 5–6) thinks that Homer knew of a cosmic generation series comprising Okeanos-Uranos-Kronos-Zeus.

[2] *Iliad* xiv. 256–61(trans. Murray, *op. cit.*, pp. 84–7).

[3] *Metaphysics* Λ 6, 1071 27, in Kirk-Raven, p. 20.

165

of Damascius: "The theology ascribed to Orpheus in Eudemus the Peripatetic kept silence about the whole intelligible realm . . . but he made the origin from Night (ἀπὸ δὲ τῆς Νυκτὸς ἐποιήσατο τὴν ἀρχήν), from whom Homer too (even though he does not describe the succession of generations as continuous) establishes the beginning of things; for we must not accept it when Eudemus says that Homer begins from Okeanos and Tethys . . ."[1] If we must accept then, that there most probably existed an ancient cosmogonic tradition which made Night the original creatrix, it is natural to wonder how this idea arose.[2] Night must surely be associated with darkness, and as such might reasonably be supposed to have invested whatever may have been the primordial state before the creation of an ordered world—instances of such belief we have already met in the Egyptian cosmogonies and in that of the Priestly writer of *Genesis*.[3] However, conceived in this manner, Night or Darkness remained essentially a condition, even when personified, of the primordial situation: it could not as such be imagined as the original creatrix. Possibly the difficulty that confronts us here resides in the fact that in the evidence we have been considering Night is represented as the *original* creatrix; but we shall presently notice other evidence which indicates that Night was also regarded as one of the first, but not actually the first, of a series of generating entities that severally produced the various constituents of the universe—as such the concept appears to reflect an incipient rationalism rather than an ancient mythology.

We come next to the first consciously conceived cosmogony in Greek literature, and the one that set the pattern of subsequent Greek speculation about the beginning of things. It was composed by Hesiod, probably sometime in the eighth century B.C.[4] In the work

---

[1] *De principiis* 124, cited and trans. in Kirk-Raven, p. 21.

[2] "Nyx was primarily a mythographer's goddess, with little cult, but one may mention her connexion with oracles . . . and a dedication to her in the temple of Demeter in Graeco-Roman Perganum . . .", *O.C.D.*, *sub* "Nyx", p. 615b. Cf. Kirk-Raven, pp. 19–24; *P.W.*, XVII.2, 1663–70, Schwabl, 6/20–40.　　　[3] See pp. 46–7, 148.

[4] On Hesiod and the significance of his work see the introduction to the Loeb edition (*Hesiod, the Homeric Hymns and Homerica*) by H. G. Evelyn-White, pp. x–xxvi; Rostagni, pp. 60–4; A. W. Mair in *E.R.E.*, VI, pp. 668b–671b; W. Jaeger, *The Theology of the Early Greek Philosophers*, pp. 11–19; F. Schwenn, *Die Theogonie des Hesiods*, pp. 1–15; N. O. Brown, *Hesiod's Theogony*, pp. 7–48.

concerned, the *Theogony*, the poet claims that he was inspired by the Muses, who dwelt on Mount Helicon, to sing the hymn of praise to Zeus that is sung by the nine Muses on Olympus.[1] And so he enters upon his task with an invitation to these gracious beings:

Hail, children of Zeus! Grant lovely song and celebrate the holy race of the deathless gods who are for ever, those that were born of Earth (Γῆς) and starry heaven (Οὐρανοῦ) and gloomy Night (Νυκτός) and them that briny Sea (Πόντος) did rear. Tell how at the first gods and earth came to be (γένοντο), and rivers, and the boundless sea with its raging swell, and the gleaming stars, and the wide heaven above, and the gods who were born of them, givers of good things, and how they divided their wealth, and how they shared their honours amongst them, and also how at the first they took many-folded Olympus.[2]

This exordium is significant of the presuppositions of the poet. Although he proposes to sing in praise of Zeus, whom he also describes as 'the father of gods and men', he conceives of a primordial situation that logically makes Zeus as it were a derivative being—in other words, however great he thought Zeus to be in majesty and power, he did not claim for him the character of the Creator; he accepted without question that the creation of the world was affected by other beings who preceded Zeus and to whom he owed his genesis. However, while in this presentation of Zeus it would seem that Hesiod was following an established tradition, of which we have found some reflection in Homer, it soon becomes evident in his cosmogonic scheme that an element of rationalisation runs through its mythic imagery. Thus he begins to tell of things 'that were aforetime' (πρό τ'ἐόντα):

Verily at first Chaos came to be, but next wide-bosomed Earth, the ever-sure foundation of all the deathless ones who hold the peaks of snowy Olympus, and dim Tartarus in the depth of the wide-pathed Earth, and Eros (Love), fairest among the deathless gods, who unnerves the limbs and overcomes the mind and wise counsels of all gods and all men within them. From Chaos came forth Erebus and black Night; but of Night were born Aether and Day, whom she conceived and bare from union in love with Erebus. And Earth first bare starry Heaven, equal to herself, to cover her on every side, and to be an ever-sure abiding-place for the blessed gods. And she brought forth long Hills, graceful haunts of the goddess-Nymphs

[1] *Theogony*, 1–103.
[2] *Theogony*, 104–13 (trans. Evelyn-White, Loeb ed. pp. 85, 87). Cf. Schwenn, p. 5.

who dwell amongst the glens of the hills. She bare also the fruitless deep (i.e. the sea) with his raging swell, Pontus, without sweet union of love. But afterwards she lay with Heaven and bare deep-swirling Oceanus, Coeus and Crius and Hyperion and Iapetus, Theia and Rhea, Themis and Mnemosyne and gold-crowned Phoebe and lovely Tethys. After them was born Cronos the wily, youngest and most terrible of her children, and he hated his lusty sire.[1]

This strange medley of personified cosmic phenomena and virtues, together with mythical beings, appears at first sight quite nonsensical, and it is tempting to dismiss it as a piece of confused speculation about the beginning of things in which various and often non-related entities are invoked as the primordial agents. However, on closer analysis there is reason for thinking that the whole scheme is not just the product of Hesiod's imagination, but that it incorporates certain basic ideas that recur in the cosmogonies of other peoples, although the poet has sought to present them in, to him, a rationalised form.

A clue to the meaning of at least one aspect of what Hesiod seems here to conceive to have been the beginning of the cosmic process is perhaps provided in what he says about Chaos (Χάος). The concept itself is very puzzling, particularly so when it is remembered that to Hesiod it surely did not mean what the word 'chaos' now generally means to us, namely, a state of disorder. The root-meaning of the Greek word Χάος is that of 'gape, gap, yawn', thus signifying a movement of division or separation.[2] Consequently, the idea of 'Chaos' implies a change that takes place in some already existing entity or situation. That this is the essence of the idea with Hesiod seems to be confirmed by the verb which he uses in his statement about Chaos. He says that "at the first Chaos came to be (γένετ')"; presumably, if he had contemplated it as an existent situation, he would have written "at the first Chaos was (ἦν)". It would follow, therefore, that Hesiod must have envisaged some primaeval substance or state of being which became split, so that its parts were separated by a gap ('Chaos').[3] We also learn from a subsequent reference that he

---

[1] *Theog.* 116–38 (trans. Evelyn-White, Loeb ed., pp. 87, 89).

[2] Cf. Schwenn, p. 107; Cornford, *Principium Sapientiae*, pp. 194–5; Kirk-Raven, pp. 25–7; Jaeger, pp. 13–14.

[3] Cf. Cornford, *ibid*; Kirk-Raven, pp. 28–9. It is interesting to note that in the Hittite myth of Ullikummis reference is made by Ubelluris, the Hittite prototype of the Atlas of Greek mythology, to the cleaving asunder of heaven and earth: "When they came and severed the heaven from the earth with a

thought of this Chaos as gloomy (ζοφεροῖο). From this gap in the primaeval substance we are told that Earth (Γαῖ') next came into being, and Tartarus, and Eros.[1] Whether these three entities are to be considered as appearing at one and the same time or in succession is not clear; but it may be noted that Tartarus is described as a part of, or as located in, the Earth.[2] However, of these three Earth clearly has the greatest cosmological significance, and its appearance after Chaos is interesting. Now, if the appearance of the Earth had coincided with that of the Heaven (Οὐρανός), we should be reminded of Egyptian cosmogony in this respect, for therein we saw that the earth-god, Geb, was imagined at first as being in close embrace with Nut, the sky-goddess, until the two were separated by Shu, the god of the air.[3] Such a conception could possibly underlie Hesiod's view but have been obscured by that incipient rationalism of which his thought shows evidence. Thus it might be that, while working on the basis of some myth which told how the separation of a primaeval substance had produced the Earth, he felt a need to account for the origin of a number of other entities before describing the creation of the Heaven. Accordingly he relates the emergence of personifications of natural phenomena that might be considered proper to the situation consequent on that split of the primaeval matter which preceded the appearance of the Earth—Darkness (Erebus)[4] and Night, which in turn produce (ἐξεγένοντο) a pair of opposites: Aether and Day. We may note here that in Hesiod's scheme Night has not that primacy or power that Homer seems to recognise, although with Hesiod she has an important cosmogonic rôle. It is significant that, when he comes to describe the creation of Heaven, the poet seems insensibly to revert to a more primitive imagery according to which the Earth is pictured as

cleaver, . . .", in *A.N.E.T.*, p. 125a. Cf. M. Vieyra in *Sources orientales*, I, p. 172; O. R. Gurney, *The Hittites*, pp. 192–3, H. G. Güterbock in *M.A.W.*, p. 171. On the task of Atlas cf. Hesiod, *Theog.* 746–8.

[1] "He (Hesiod) does not say that Earth was born of Chaos, but that Earth came into being 'thereafter' (ἔπειτα)", Cornford, p. 195.

[2] μυχῷ χθονὸς l. 119: it must be noted that χθών is used here, not Γαῖα. On the location and nature of Tartarus see Kirk-Raven, pp. 30–1.

[3] See pp. 27–8. See also pp. 71, 100–3, and for other indications of a 'Trennungsmythos' see Schwabl, 35.

[4] " 'Erebos' ist das Dunkel ganz allgemein, bei Hesiodos synonym mit (v. 669 mit v. 653, 658), später Euphemismus für Totenreich, . . .", Schwenn, p. 108.

a woman who gives birth (ἐγείνατο) to Heaven, although the purpose for so doing is essentially cosmological, namely, "to cover herself on every side", and to provide "an ever-sure abiding-place for the blessed gods".[1] We may usefully notice here a certain parallelism with Marduk's use of the body of Ti'âmat in the Babylonian Creation Epic, although there can be no suggestion of the influence of Mesopotamian cosmogony here. According to the Babylonian view, the world needed a strong canopy over it, such a cover being seen in the over-arching vault of heaven which arose in a circle about the limits of the earth.[2]

The representation of Eros or Love as one of the original cosmogonic agents is curious, and it would seem best accounted for as another instance of Hesiod's tentative rationalism. For, in imaging the process of creation in sexual terms as the product of the intercourse of various cosmic entities, it would appear that he saw the need of some factor that would unite and make fruitful the union of the various pairs. The concept is indeed remarkable, and it may fairly be taken as the prototype or an anticipation of that idea so pregnant of consequence for philosophy, namely, the 'First Cause'. With Hesiod the connotation of Eros is essentially sexual, and it may possibly derive from a primitive folk-tradition that regarded rain as semen that fertilises the earth—a belief which finds eloquent expression in some lines of Aeschylus: "Love moves the pure Heaven to wed the Earth; and Love (ἔρως) takes hold on Earth to join in marriage. And the rain, dropping from the husband Heaven (ἀπ᾽ εὐνατῆρος οὐρανοῦ) impregnates Earth, and she brings forth for men pasture for flocks and corn, the life of man".[3]

The subsequent gestations of Earth have results which show that,

[1] On Gaia (Earth) as a goddess and her cult, which was not prominent, cf. O.C.D. sub 'Gaea', p. 375a; Nilsson, Gesch. d. griech. Religion, I, pp. 427–33; I. Opelt in R.A.C., V, 1125–30.

[2] See pp. 100–3. G. Vlastos in Gnomon, 27 (1955), p. 74, thinks that ll. 736 ff. of Hesiod's Theogony contains a "remarkable venture into cosmography", since "the 'sources and boundaries' of Earth, airy Tartarus, Sea, and Sky are located 'all in a row' in Chaos". It would seem that the passage might have this significance, if Χάσμα μέγ᾽ of l. 740 can be identified with Chaos. Cf. Kirk-Raven, p. 31, n. 1.

[3] Aeschylus, Danaids, frag. 44. Cf. Cornford, p. 196; Kirk-Raven, pp. 28–9; Schwenn, pp. 109–11. On the nature and cult of Eros see J. Harrison, Prolegomena to the Study of Greek Religion, pp. 630–45; O.C.D., sub 'Erōs', pp. 338b–339a. See also Schwabl, 36–7.

whatever traditions he may have known, Hesiod did not accept that, known apparently to Homer and probably of more ancient derivation, that made water or the sea the source of all things. This is clear from the fact that he makes Earth the genetrix of both Pontus (Sea) and Oceanus; the former she is curiously reported to have borne 'without sweet union of love', while Oceanus is described as her child by Ouranos (Heaven).[1]

This first section of the *Theogony*, with which we have been dealing, constitutes the cosmogony proper of Hesiod. The poem continues to describe the successive generations of monsters, deities, and personifications of various phenomena which Hesiod obviously felt had to be accounted for as significant entities or aspects of the universe. These have little relevance for our subject, but there are two episodes of the narration which we must notice. These episodes have a certain similarity of theme which causes suspicion as to their original relationship, particularly whether the one may not have inspired the other or been an elaboration of it.[2] According to the first version, Ouranos proved himself to be a tyrannous sire and imprisoned his offspring within the body of Earth, so that she groaned with the burden. Release came ultimately when one of the sons, Cronos, with the connivance of his mother, castrated his father. The severed genitals produced their own progeny, including the great goddess Aphrodite.[3]

This strange and primitive story appears to have a parallel in a Hittite myth which tells how the sky-god Alalus was emasculated by the divine hero Kumarbis, who swallowed the genitals and was impregnated thereby and produced the Storm-god.[4] In view of the early contacts of the Achaeans with the Hittites, and the fact of the greater antiquity of the Hittite story, it is possible that Hesiod drew

Cf. Lesky, p. 84, Schwabl, 13(9).
[2] The question of how far the extant text of the *Theogony* represents its original form and what sources underlie that form is one of the greatest complexity, some indication of which is given by Schwenn, pp. 144–5, in his 'Übersicht zur Echtheitsfrage'.
[3] *Theog.* 154–210. "Denn es kann ... kein Zweifel mehr daran aufkommen, dass dem Mythos von der Uranosentmannung eine Erzählung über die Trennung von Himmel und Erde zugrundeliegt", Schwabl, 10/60.
[4] Cf. *A.N.E.T.*, p. 120b (trans. A. Goetze); Vieyra in *Sources orientales*, I, pp. 161–2; O. R. Gurney, *The Hittites*, pp. 190–2; Güterbock in *M.A.W.*, pp. 156–7.

upon some tradition that derived ultimately from Asia Minor.[1] The second episode in the *Theogony* is concerned with Cronos and his son Zeus, and it involves a similar situation. Cronos, learning that he would be supplanted by his own son, devours the children whom Rhea bears to him. However, when she is about to bear Zeus, Rhea takes refuge in Crete and her child is successfully hid from Cronos, who is deceived into swallowing a stone instead of the infant. Reared in secrecy, Zeus grows quickly to strength and vanquishes his father and frees his brethren.[2] This quaint tale has, as we noted, a remarkable resemblance in many ways to the former story, but it differs notably from that in the fact that it concerns two gods of historical significance.[3] Although of the two deities Cronos is the lesser known, Zeus, the chief of the Hellenic pantheon, is habitually styled the son of Cronos, thus perhaps signifying a relationship rather of succession than of derivation. In other words, as the myth retailed by Hesiod clearly shows, Zeus displaced the older god Cronos. But in the myth as we have it, Zeus is depicted in a manner that seems scarcely consistent with the mature sky-god, the head of the pantheon of those northern invaders who overthrew the civilisation centred on Crete. Indeed the Zeus who is the infant son of the Earth-mother and who has to be saved from the virile god who impregnates her, appears to belong rather to Aegean religion than to the Hellenic, and this indication is strengthened by the location of the myth in Crete.[4] However, since the Zeus with which Hesoid was really concerned was the supreme Olympian deity, it would appear that the poet was here utilising an Aegean myth for a specific purpose. What that purpose was may reasonably be explained in terms of that historical situation which we noted earlier. Zeus, the chief god of the Indo-European invaders, had displaced the former chief male deity of the Aegean

[1] Cf. R. Cohen, *La Grèce et l'Hellénisation du Monde antique*, pp. 31–2, 38–9; Gurney, pp. 53–8; Güterbock, in *M.A.W.*, pp. 160–1; M. H. Jameson in *M.A.W.*, pp. 261–6, 268; Schwabl, 49–60, 68–71.

[2] *Theog.* 453–506. According to Pausanias (c. x, 24, 6) the Delphinians anointed daily a stone that was supposed to be that swallowed by Cronos in lieu of Zeus.

[3] Schwenn, p. 144, assigns ll. 453–62, 468, 471, 472, 474–7, 479, 480, 485, 487–91 to the original *Theogony* of Hesiod; ll. 463–7, 470, 473, 481–4, 492–506 belong, he thinks, to an hypothetical reviser.

[4] Cf. W. K. C. Guthrie, *The Greeks and their Gods*, pp. 40–50; Nilsson, *Minoan-Mycenaean Religion*, pp. 541–83; Schwabl, 15.

peoples. This supersession of an older generation of gods, or rather the displacement of some and the acceptance of others, surely became apart of the folk-memory, and it would appear that Hesiod was thus mindful of it as he constructed his *Theogony* in praise of Olympian Zeus.[1]

The remaining portion of the *Theogony*, after the presentation of this myth, contains three other episodes of cosmogonic significance. The first of these in order of narration in the *Theogony* concerns the destiny of mankind and it will be more appropriately discussed later, together with a similar episode in Hesiod's *Works and Days*.[2] The other episodes have a common *motif*, namely, that of conflict between the Olympian gods, who represent the good order of the universe, and the monstrous forces of disorder. The fact that the second episode follows closely upon the first, and constitutes a kind of anti-climax to it, inevitably raises questions about the origin of the myths involved and of their relation to each other. The first episode, moreover, does not appear to fit well into the context of the *Theogony* at the point at which it occurs, and it seems to imply an antecedent situation of which nothing is told by Hesiod. Thus, we are suddenly informed that the Olympian gods had long been at war with beings described as 'the Titan gods', the identity of whom is not made clear, although once they are referred to as 'the former Titan gods', an epithet that surely implies that they represented some earlier pantheon that had now been discredited.[3] In the mighty conflict that ensues the whole universe is affected by its fury; eventually the Olympian gods, led by Zeus and supported surprisingly also by certain monstrous beings, prevail, and the Titan gods are imprisoned in the gloomy depths of Tartarus.[4] After this original 'Titanic'

[1] The issue here is not, of course, as clear-cut as was once thought, when a line was conveniently drawn between Indo-European and Aegean deities. However, Hesiod is obviously concerned here and in the *Titanomachy* (see below) to describe how the Olympian gods ousted an earlier company of deities. Cf. Schwenn, pp. 127–30; Guthrie, *The Greeks and their Gods*, pp. 50–3; Nilsson, *Minoan-Mycenaean Religion*, pp. 536; *Gesch. d. Griech. Religion*, I, pp. 484–5; Picard, pp. 117–18, 232; H. J. Rose, *Ancient Greek Religion*, pp. 14–15.   [2] See pp. 175 f.

[3] *Theog.* 629–34; see 424: Τιτῆσι μετὰ προτέροισι θεοῖσιν. Cf. Schwabl, 8–10.

[4] *Theog.* 629–819. Schwenn, p. 144, assigns ll. 624–33, 637–9, 643–80, 687–704, 711–9 to the original form of the *Theogony*; the other lines he attributes to the redactor, except ll. 799, 800, the latter being designated 'orphisch'. Cf. Schwabl, 17–19.

173

struggle, it is surprising to read that "when Zeus had driven the Titans from heaven, huge Earth bare her youngest child Typhoeus of the love of Tartarus, by the aid of golden Aphrodite. Strength was with his hands in all that he did and the feet of the strong god were untiring. From his shoulders grew an hundred heads of a snake, a fearful dragon, with dark, flickering tongues, and from under the brows of his eyes in his marvellous heads flashed fire, and fire burned from his heads as he glared . . . A thing truly past help would have happened on that day, and he would have come to reign over mortals and immortals, had not the father of men and gods been quick to perceive it". Then followed another world-shaking struggle, but this time only Zeus and Typhoeus are the contestants. Zeus eventually conquers, and he hurls his monstrous adversary, maimed by his lightning blasts, into the depths of Tartarus.[1]

In these two episodes, as we have noted, there is the *motif* of a primaeval conflict between the forces of order and disorder; however, they appear to derive from two different traditions. The war between the Olympian and the Titan gods seems rather to reflect the memory of a struggle between two rival forms of religion or rather between the protagonists of them. Such a struggle did occur, as we know, between the Aegean peoples and those Indo-European tribes who dispossessed them during the latter half of the second millennium B.C. It would, accordingly, seem that Hesiod has sought to incorporate the memory of this historical happening into his account of the beginning of things, thereby investing it in that quasi-mythical form appropriate to the theogony which he writes in praise of Zeus. This interpretation would seem to be confirmed by the lines with which he concludes the story of the Olympians' victory: "But when the blessed gods had finished their toil and settled by force their struggle for honours with the Titans, they pressed far-seeing Olympian Zeus to reign and to rule over them, by Earth's promptings. So he divided their dignities amongst them".[2] In the episode of Typhoeus we have surely to do with quite a different order of tradition; moreover, the sense of anticlimax which it provides to the story of the

---

[1] *Theog.* 820–68 (trans. Evelyn-White, Loeb ed., p. 139).
[2] *Theog.* 881–5 (trans. Evelyn-White, Loeb ed., p. 143). To the references given in n. 1, p. 173, add Nilsson, *Minoan-Mycenaean Religion*, p. 3, in *H.G.R.*, II, p. 177.

battle with the Titans strongly suggests that the poet inserted it here because it also had to do with divine victory after a frightful conflict.[1] Whence Hesiod drew this tale of the monstrous Typhoeus, who threatened the order of gods and men, affords a wide field for speculation. The idea of such a monster occurs elsewhere in Greek literature and independently of Hesiod;[2] moreover, in the ancient Near East the dragon-myth finds abundant expression in various forms—in a Hurrian-Hittite legend the dragon Illuyanka is overcome by the storm-god,[3] and the part that a primaeval monster or dragon plays in the cosmogonies of Mesopotamia, Canaan and Israel is already known to us. From whatever source or in whatever form Hesiod obtained his story of Typhoeus, it is notable that the monster plays no part in the process of creation as it does in the other cosmogonies which we have studied.[4] In the *Theogony* the myth is only employed to commemorate the power of Zeus, and elsewhere in Greek literature its occurrence has no cosmogonic significance. It would, accordingly, seem that the Greek mind did not instinctively envisage creation as the outcome of a struggle against some opposing force—to that mind creation was rather a developing process, taking the form of the gradual multiplication of constituent entities, including those which menaced good order and were hateful to gods and men.

The *Theogony*, undoubtedly by reason of its theme, contains no account of the creation of man. However, in the course of this poem Hesiod tells the curious story of the deception of Zeus by Prometheus, which has certain fateful consequences for mankind. The account is a complex one, and it would seem that to its composition have gone several traditional *motifs*, which have been fashioned together by Hesiod's peculiar genius and stamped with the impression of his pessimistic philosophy of life.[5] Prometheus is a strange figure in

[1] Cf. Schwenn, pp. 41–5, 145.
[2] Cf. Rose, *Greek Mythology*, pp. 58–60; Kirk-Raven, pp. 65–8.
[3] Cf. *A.N.E.T.*, pp. 125b–126; Gurney, pp. 180–2; T. H. Gaster, *Thespis*, pp. 245–7, 252–3; Güterbock, p. 172; Schwabl, 19.
[4] Cornford, pp. 214 ff. seeks to interpret the battle of Zeus with Typhoeus in a 'Myth and Ritual' context, suggesting that it may be an episode in a single Creation myth ritually enacted at an annual New Year Festival.
[5] Cf. Schwenn, pp. 130–2, who thinks that the Prometheus episode in the *Theogony* is well prepared for by what is said of the other two sons of Iapetus (ll. 507 ff.).

Greek mythology: he is reckoned as a Titan and opposes Zeus; yet he is the benefactor of mankind. His name is significant, meaning the 'Forethinker', and it contrasts with that of his stupid brother Epimetheus ('Afterthinker').[1] Trouble begins when at Mecone, where apparently the original decision was made concerning what parts of a sacrificed animal should be assigned to the gods and what to men,[2] Prometheus so arranged things that men got the better portions— this story looks very much like an aetiological myth explaining the apportioning of a sacrificial victim between the gods and those who make the offering.[3] Whether this be the original nature of the tale, Hesiod uses it to explain the hostility of Zeus towards mankind and the origin of the feud between Zeus and Prometheus. Because men had benefited from the deception which had been practised upon him, Zeus revenged himself by withholding the use of fire from them. Prometheus, however, again defeated him and by a subterfuge gave mankind the gift of fire. Still seeking revenge, once more Zeus devises an evil for the race of men, and this time he succeeds.[4] The divine vengeance takes the form of the creation of woman—Hesiod ignores here the obvious question how mankind had hitherto propagated itself! "Forthwith he made an evil thing for men as the price of fire; for the very famous Limping God formed of earth the likeness of a shy maiden as the son of Cronos willed. And the goddess bright-eyed Athene girded and clothed her with silvery raiment, and down from her head she spread with her hands a broidered veil, a wonder to see; and she, Pallas Athene, put about her head lovely garlands, flowers of new-grown herbs". On the completion of the entrancing new creature, "wonder took hold of the deathless gods and mortal men when they saw that which was sheer guile, not to be withstood

[1] Cf. L. Séchan, *Le Mythe de Prométhée*, pp. 10–33; Guthrie, *In the Beginning*, pp. 82–3; *O.C.D.*, p. 734 ('Prometheus'); Rose, *Greek Mythology*, pp. 54–6.
[2] *Theog.* 533–60.
[3] Cf. Nilsson, *Gesch. d. griech. Religion*, I, pp. 25–6; *P.W.*, xxiii, 1, 660–2.
[4] *Theog.* 561–70. Séchan, pp. 34–5, suggests that Prometheus obtained the fire not only for men to cook their food, but to make their offerings to the gods according to 'le mode prométhéen'. He also thinks that the Prometheus of Hesiod, in contrast to that of Aeschylus, is less the benefactor of mankind than 'L'artisan de la dechéance de l'humanité qui est condamnée de son fait au dur travail et à la souffrance', p. 28.

by men".[1] As the poet continues with his description of the ills which Zeus brought upon men through his creation of woman, he reveals himself to be so thorough a misogynist that his aversion must surely spring rather from his own disposition than from any tradition that he might be retailing. He writes: "of her is the deadly race and tribe of women who live amongst mortal men to their great trouble, no help-meets in hateful poverty, but only in wealth . . . even so Zeus who thunders on high made women to be an evil to mortal men, with a nature to do evil (ξυνήονας ἔργων ἀργαλέων)".[2]

In his *Works and Days*, which he addresses to his unpleasant brother Perses, warning him of the consequences of Strife ('Ερις), Hesiod also tells the story, but with some notable variations. He starts by explaining to his brother the reason for the hard condition of human life. It is because the gods have "hidden from men the means of life (βίον ἀνθρώποισιν)"; if they had not done so, then men might have supplied their economic needs for a whole year by one day's work.[3] He then goes on to elaborate the cause and the form which this divine hostility towards mankind took; in doing so, how-ever, he unconsciously changes the nature of the woe that afflicts men from that of the hard toil of the agriculturalist's life to the evils brought to them by the first woman. The cause of all this he repre-sents as due to the anger of Zeus because Prometheus succeeded by guile in giving to men the boon of fire which he had withheld from them.[4] The repetition of the story of this transaction is very signifi-cant, for it surely witnesses to an appreciation of the basic importance of fire to human culture, and it reveals a curious belief that man acquired the use of fire contrary to the divine will. Hesiod continues his tale by representing Zeus as exclaiming: "I will give men as the price for fire an evil thing in which they may all be glad of heart while

[1] *Theog.* 570-7, 588-9 (trans. Evelyn-White, Loeb ed., pp. 121, 123), The 'very famous Limping God' is, of course, Hephaestus.
[2] *Theog.* 591-602 (trans. Evelyn-White, Loeb ed., p. 123). Cf. Brown, pp. 18-19. O. Lendle, *Die "Pandorasage" bei Hesiod*, p. 92, thinks that, in view of its sophistication, the tale is not derived from some folk-myth, but is the invention of Hesiod "eines Enttäuschten, eines Weiberfeindes".
[3] *Works and Days*, 42-4. "βίος und βίονος immer des Leibes Notdurft und Nahrung", U. von Wilamowitz-Moellendorff, *Hesiodos Erga*, p. 47.
[4] *Works and Days*, 47 ff. No reason is given here for the withholding of fire from mankind by Zeus as in the *Theogony* version. It is said only that Zeus hid fire 'in the anger of his heart' (χολωσάμενος φρεσὶν ᾗσιν).

177

they embrace their own destruction".¹ This evil thing (κακόν), by which the supreme god takes his revenge, is the creation of woman, as in the *Theogony*. Again Hephaestus, the artificer-god, is commissioned to make the new creature, which he does by mixing earth with water (γαῖαν ὕδει φύρειν), and Athene and Aphrodite equip her with the necessary qualities and accomplishments, while Hermes endows her with "a shameless mind and a deceitful nature".² In this version the woman receives a name: it is Pandora, "because all they who dwell on Olympus gave each a gift, a plague to men who eat bread".³ From this point the tale takes on a different character from that in the *Theogony*. Mankind has been living a life free of toil and ills until Pandora is brought by Hermes to Epimetheus, who incautiously accepts her, unmindful of the warning of his brother, Prometheus, that he should take no gift from Zeus.⁴ The evil which the woman brings on mankind does not, however, in this version stem from her own nature but from her act, although it is not clear whether this act was done intentionally or by accident. Pandora had apparently brought with her from the abode of the gods a great jar (πίθος), which contained the baleful gifts of the gods. She removes the lid of this jar and scatters abroad its fatal contents, so causing sorrow and mischief to men.⁵ But, curiously, within the jar Hope (ἐλπίς) is held back, its exit being prevented by the will of Zeus.⁶

¹ *Works and Days*, 57–8.   ʹ*Works and Days*, 60–79.
³ *Works and Days*, 80–3. Cf. Wilamowitz-Moellendorff, p. 50. Lendle, *Die "Pandorasage" bei Hesiod*, is inclined to regard ll. 80–2, giving the name of Pandora, as an interpolation: "es hat den Anschein, dass die Etymologie erst durch eine hesiodeische Formulierung (Eg. 85) angeregt und später in den Text aufgenommen wurde, d. h. vermutlich nicht von Hesiod selber stammt" (p. 54). After a long discussion, Lendle concludes that the association of Hesiod's 'Urweib' with the name of Pandora occurred a little time after the middle of the fifth century B.C. (*op. cit.*, pp. 58–81). On Pandora as an earth-goddess cf. *P.W.*, XVIII, 3, 529–31; Lendle, pp. 65–81.
⁴ *Works and Days*, 83–93. Hesiod refers to mankind as 'tribes of men' (φῦλ' ἀνθρώπων). ll. 90–3 apparently contradict the statement in ll. 42–5, but probably are intended to heighten the drama of what follows.
⁵ *Works and Days*, 94–5: "But the woman took off the great lid of the jar with her hands and scattered all these, and her thought caused (ἐμήσατο) sorrow and mischief to men" (trans. Evelyn-White). Cf. Wilamowitz-Moellendorff, p. 52; *P.W.*, XXIII, 1, 664. According to the *Iliad*, XXIV, 527–33, there were two πίθοι in heaven from which Zeus, arbitrarily, dispensed good and ill lots to men; cf. Brandon, *Man and his Destiny in the Great Religions*, pp. 163–4; Lendle, p. 112.   ⁶ *Works and Days*, 96–9.

178

The battle of the Gods and the Giants. Athena is shown destroying Alcyoneus, while his mother, Earth (Gē) begs for his life. Hesiod distinguishes between the Giants and the Titans; but in this frieze from the Altar of Zeus at Pergamum (2nd century B.C.) they seem to be equated. (See pp. 173–5.) (Photograph by the courtesy of the Staatliche Museen, Berlin.)

PLATE IX

Scene from a pagan
sarcophagus representing
the creation of man by
Prometheus. Minerva is
shown animating the
human body by inserting
the soul, symbolised as a
butterfly, while Lachesis,
one of the Fates,
consults a celestial globe
to determine the infant's
destiny. 3rd century
A.D., in the Museo
Capitolino, Rome.
(Reproduced by the kind
permission of N. V.
Uitgeversmaatschappij
Elsevier, Amsterdam.)

PLATE X

The inclusion of Hope among the many plagues by which the gods planned to afflict mankind, and then its retention in the jar by Zeus when the others escape to work their ill, constitute a problem which permits of no easy solution. The difficulty here is partly lessened when it is recalled that, whereas in the Christian tradition Hope is regarded as one of the cardinal virtues, this was not so among the ancient Greeks, and a catena of quotations can be made from classical writers presenting Hope as a dangerous illusion that prevents men from realistically accepting their lot.[1] However, even with this re-evaluation a problem still remains in that, if Hope was thus an evil entity, why did Zeus restrain it from joining the other ills in plaguing mankind? Some suggestion of an answer may possibly be found in a curious statement that occurs in the following lines: "Of themselves diseases come upon men continually by day and night, bringing mischief to mortals silently; for (ἐπεὶ) wise Zeus took away speech (φωνὴν) from them. So is there no way to escape the will of Zeus".[2] If these lines are intended to explain (although the intention is not clear) the purpose of Zeus in keeping Hope within the jar, then it would seem that there might be some connection between that action and the taking of speech from the ills that do afflict men. In that case it is interesting to note that in Greek the word ἐλπὶς (Hope) can also have the sense of 'anticipation' or 'boding of ill'.[3] Interpreted in this sense, the retention of Hope within the jar could signify a further aspect of the malevolence of Zeus, namely, that he took measure thereby to prevent mortals from anticipating, and so preparing themselves against, the woes that come upon them—a conclusion that would be consistent with the concluding statement: "So (οὕτως) is there no way to escape the will of Zeus".[4]

Hesiod follows this strange story, with its amazing presentation of Zeus as unrelentingly hostile to the race of man, with another that matches it in both its pessimistic estimate of the human lot and its

[1] Cf. P. Shorey in *E.R.E.*, VI, p. 781.
[2] *Works and Days*, 103–5. "Hesiod will sagen, dass die Krankheiten von aussen in den Leib hereinkommt und man davon nichts merkt", Wilamowitz-Moellendorff, p. 53.
[3] Cf. Liddell and Scott, *Lexikon* (9th edition) *in loco*.
[4] On this problem and the various solutions offered see *P.W.*, XVIII, 3, 539–43; Wilamowitz-Moellendorff, pp. 50–2; Lendle, pp. 106–10; cf. Brandon, pp. 166–7.

depiction of divine malevolence. Addressing his brother, he says that he will now summarise another tale (ἕτερόν τοι ἐγὼ λόγον ἐκκορυφώσω), thus seemingly implying that what follows is derived from an existing tradition. He then says that this tale shows how gods and men had a common origin (ὁμόθεν γεγάασι); however, the account that follows in no wise shows how this is so.[1]

The story describes five successive races of mortal men (γένος μερόπων ἀνθρώπων).[2] There is an interesting, and possibly a significant, difference in what is said about the identity of the creators of these races. The first two races are the creations (ποίησαν) of the Olympian gods, acting apparently in concert though no details are given of the process. The other three races are the work of Zeus, acting presumably alone. Since this tale contains Hesiod's most explicit account of the origin of mankind, this element of differentiation is rather puzzling. As we shall see, it is the fifth race that now inhabits the earth and that represents mankind for Hesiod, and he regards it as thoroughly vicious. However, the fact that it owes its origin to Zeus can scarcely be regarded as an explanation of its nature, since Zeus is also the author of the two preceding races, and one of these, that of the heroes, is ranked by the poet as noble and righteous. It is possible that some distinction is intended when the first race is stated to have lived when Cronos was reigning in heaven; but even this point cannot be pressed, because it is the Olympian gods, and not an earlier generation of gods, who make the first race, while nothing is said of the era of Cronos in relation to the second race.

The five races or generations are arranged in a successive chronological series, and, as such, they represent a steady declension in nature and fortune and so further illustrate that deeply pessimistic *Weltanschauung* which we have already seen as characterising Hesiod. The first race is described as "a golden (χρύσεον) race of mortal men". Its members live in a godlike serenity, untouched by toil and grief; they know not the misery of old age, and death comes to them as a sleep. In his account of this first generation it would seem that the poet was attempting to explain the origin of the *daimones*, a kind of demi-god well known in Greek folklore and even in philosophical

---

[1] *Works and Days*, 106–8. Cf. Wilamowitz-Moellendorff, pp. 54–5.
[2] *Works and Days*, 109–201.

speculation; for, when its members die, they become, according to him 'pure spirits' (δαίμονες ἀγνοί), dwelling on earth and benevolent in their attitude towards men.[1] In their place (though why they are supplanted nothing is said) the Olympian gods create another race, of silver (ἀργύρεον) and less noble than the first.[2] But, not only are the members of this race described as inferior in nobility, they are depicted most curiously as taking an abnormal time in reaching maturity, and even then they suffer from their innate foolishness in striving with each other and neglecting to serve the gods; angered by their behaviour, Zeus removes (ἔκρυψε) them; surprisingly, however, it is recorded that after death they are known to men as the "blessed ones beneath the earth (ὑποχθόνοι μάκαρες)" and are honoured—Hesiod possibly seeks thus to explain the origin of the many chthonian genii or demi-gods of Greek popular religion.[3] This silver race is succeeded by a brazen (χάλκειον) race of mortal men,[4] who are made by Zeus apparently from ash-trees (ἐκ μελιᾶν). These are a violent, warlike race; their armament is bronze, and Hesiod adds the significant fact, surely indicative of some degree of historical consciousness, that "there was no black iron". This race destroyed itself, presumably through internecine warfare, and, when its members were seized by black Death, they passed into 'the dank house of chill Hades' and were forgotten. The brazen men are followed by a nobler and more righteous race of heroes, who were recognised as 'demi-

[1] Cf. Wilamowitz-Moellendorff, p. 56; Rhode, *Psyche*, I, pp. 95–9; *O.C.D.*, pp. 251b–252a ('Daimon'). J.-P. Vernant in *R.H.R.*, t. 157, pp. 30–1, suggests that the attribute 'golden' signifies the royal character of their race, to which reference is made in l. 126.

[2] Wilamowitz-Moellendorff, p. 56, thinks that this Silver race was "die erste wirklich menschliche"; it is difficult to understand this view in the light of ll. 141–2.

[3] Rohde, I, p. 101, thinks that Hesiod shows embarrassment in his handling of this second race. "Man nannte später solche gewordene Unsterbliche 'Heroen'. Hesiod, der dies Wort in diesem Sinne noch nicht verwenden konnt, nennt sie mit kühnem Oxymoron: sterbliche Selige, menschliche Götter". Cf. Wilamowitz-Moellendorff, p. 57.

[4] It has been suggested that this third generation was "a race terrible because of their (ashen) spears"; see Evelyn-White, Loeb ed., p. 13, n. 1. Wilamowitz-Moellendorff, pp. 145–6, points out that the ash tree is the first tree to acquire a special significance with the Greeks. In *Theog.* 187 the Μελίαι represent one of the earliest class of nymphs; but the fact throws no light on the derivation of this race from μελιᾶν. Cf. Vernant in *R.H.R.*, t. 157, pp. 36–7, 39.

gods' (ἡμίθεοι) and who fought before Thebes and at Troy. They are the creation of Zeus, and, when they died, he assigned to them a serene abode in the Isles of Blessed on the far shore of Oceanus. The fact that the noble nature of this fourth race breaks the sequence of increasing degradation that runs through the series represented by the others suggests that, if the passage is not a later interpolation, Hesiod incorporated it as a tribute to the memory of the heroic age, howbeit it constituted a contradiction to the logic of this theme.[1] The fifth race, that of iron, is the generation in which the poet laments that it is his lot to live. Its members are afflicted with unceasing toil and sorrow, which render them vicious and degraded. Deterioration will continue until at last children are born showing the marks of old age; then Zeus will intervene to destroy them. Hesiod ends this grim philosophy of history with words of despair: "and there will be no help against evil".

This scheme of the five races or generations is truly unique; it had not been anticipated elsewhere in the ancient Near East, and in Greek literature it appears only in the *Works and Days* and its presence there seems to have exercised little influence on subsequent Greek thought.[2] However, in its pessimistic estimate of human life the conception does appear to give a definitive form to an attitude that first finds expression in Homer and that becomes the main tradition of the Greek *Weltanschauung*. It is peculiar in the fact of its starting with a kind of 'Golden Age' and its presentation of history as a process of deterioration therefrom; as we shall see, many subsequent Greek thinkers had instead a lively appreciation of the brutish beginnings of human life. But what is perhaps most notable about the view of life implicit in this account of the five races, and which is reflected also in the Pandora myth, is the apparent unquestioning acceptance that such was the wretched lot that the gods had ordained for mankind. Hesiod

[1] Cf. Rohde, I, p. 103; J. B. Bury in *C.A.H.*, IV, pp. 477–8. Wilamowitz-Moellendorff, p. 59, notes that we have here the first use of ἥρωες in what to us is the current sense: to Homer the word meant only 'Herr'.

[2] Cf. K. F. Smith in *E.R.E.*, II, pp. 192b–193; A. W. Mair in *E.R.E.*, VI, pp. 669b–670a; Bury in *C.A.H.*, IV, pp. 476–8; Vernant in *R.H.R.*, t. 157, pp. 21–54 (an interpretation in terms of G. Dumézil's theory of the tripartite constitution of Indo-European society); Nilsson in *Lehrbuch der Religionsgeschichte*, II, p. 355 ("So schuf Hesiod eine mythische Entwicklungsgeschichte der Menschheit, die erste Geschichtsphilosophie"); Brandon, pp. 167–8.

seems to see no problem concerning divine justice when he depicts the arbitrary hostility of Zeus towards the race of man; although he bemoans the violence and wickedness of the silver, the bronze and the iron men, he never questions the right of their divine creators to have made them so defective. Doubtlessly we find reflected in this estimate that innate realism of the Greek mind that conceived of deity in terms of the manifestations of power evident in the universe.[1]

Herodotus, the so-called 'father of History', who lived about 430 B.C., has given us a valuable indication of what an educated Greek thought about that aspect of the work of Homer and Hesiod with which we have been concerned here. He writes: "Whence the gods severally sprang (ἐγένετο), whether or no they had existed from eternity, what forms they bore—these are questions of which the Greeks knew nothing until the other day, so to speak. For Homer and Hesiod were the first to compose Theogonies, and give the gods their epithets, to allot them their several offices and occupations, and describe their forms; and they lived but four hundred years before my time, as I believe".[2]

In the second book of his *History*, from which this passage comes, Herodotus is concerned with emphasising the great antiquity of the Egyptians and the fact, according to him, that the names of the Greek gods derived ultimately from Egypt.[3] That such should be his belief, particularly about the part played by Homer and Hesiod, is significant; for it surely implies a recognition that there existed no other important source concerning the origin of things than the writings of Homer and Hesiod.[4] The cosmogonic references in Homer, as we have noted, are very sparse and are chiefly valuable for their indications of the existence of two contradictory traditions that traced the origin of things either to Oceanus, the primaeval waters, or to a

[1] Cf. Brandon, pp. 162–83, 189–90.
[2] II, 53 (trans. G. Rawlinson). For the "spärlichen Reste der nichthesio-dischen theogonischen Tradition" see Schwabl, 22–3, also 32.
[3] II, 52.
[4] Commenting on the question of the existence of a pre-Homeric cycle of tradition, von Wilamowitz-Moellendorff (*Der Glaube der Hellenen*, I, p. 339) says "We can only state its extreme importance: there was a Theogony and a Cosmogony which in some form lay before Homer and Hesiod". The vestiges of such tradition we have noted, and their significance for later Greeks must be evaluated in the light of the statement of Herodotus just quoted.

personification of Night. Hesiod's *Theogony*, on the other hand, is a consciously conceived cosmogony, to which his *Works and Days* provides, as it were, a supplement concerning the original cause of the wretched conditions of human life, as the poet saw them. In constructing this account of the origin of the world and of the human situation, Hesiod clearly drew upon much traditional material; but it is also evident, as we have noticed, that in his presentation of this material he was intent on providing a systematic record of the process of creation. Accordingly, a decisive factor of rationalism has operated in the selection and depiction of whatever traditions were thus utilised, so that these accounts can only be regarded as creation legends in this qualified sense. A similar problem besets us when we turn to consider the remaining evidence of early Greek belief about the beginning of the world.

We may perhaps best approach this problem by noticing a passage from the celebrated comedy of Aristophanes entitled the *Birds*. This passage, which is spoken by the chorus of birds, is, of course, a parody, as is indeed the whole play: "First of all was Chaos and Night and black Erebos and wide Tartaros, and neither Ge (i.e. Earth) nor Aer (i.e. Air) nor Ouranos (i.e. Heaven) existed; in the boundless bosoms of Erebos black-winged Night begets, first, a wind-egg (ὑπηνέμιον... ᾠόν) from which in the fulfilment of the seasons ardent Eros burgeoned forth, his back gleaming with golden wings, like as he was to the whirling winds. Eros, mingling with winged, gloomy Chaos in broad Tartaros, hatched out our race and first brought it into the light . . ."[1] Now, although it is obvious that Aristophanes is parodying Hesiod's *Theogony* here, the idea of a kind of primordial cosmic egg is notable. The concept does not appear in Hesiod, and, while it could be reasonably maintained that it is an obvious invention of Aristophanes in view of the subject of his play, it would seem that there may be another explanation. In the so-called Orphic theogonies the idea of the cosmic egg was apparently well established: from this egg various primordial beings were supposed to have emerged such as Phanes, or Ouranos and Ge.[2] The antiquity and

---

[1] *Birds* 693 (trans. Kirk and Raven, p. 44).
[2] Cf. Kirk and Raven, pp. 41–7; I. F. Burns in *E.R.E.*, IV, pp. 147b, 148a; W. K. C. Guthrie, *Orpheus and Greek Religion*, pp. 92–5; Harrison, pp. 625–9; Schwabl, 37–8, 39; J. Haussleiter in *R.A.C.*, IV, 731–6.

original nature of these Orphic theogonies constitute a problem which has long been discussed by scholars. One of the chief factors of the problem is the fact that the evidence which we have about these systems is provided by writers of a much later period, and, although it clearly preserves earlier tradition, the extant versions are the products of later speculation.[1] However that may be, the fact that Aristophanes provides evidence of the existence of the concept in the fourth century B.C. permits us to think that in this matter the Orphic theogonies may have incorporated an ancient tradition concerning the beginning of things.[2] If this inference be sound, we may well wonder, in the absence of other evidence, as to the original source and form of the idea. Greek mythology provides but one possible parallel, namely, the birth of Helen and of Castor and Pollux from the eggs produced by Leda through intercourse with Zeus in the form of a swan.[3] The parallel is not a very close one, and it can scarcely have provided the prototype of the Orphic concept. A far closer analogy is provided by Egyptian mythology. As we have seen, the idea of a primaeval egg, from which the sun-god emerges, was a very ancient feature of the Hermopolitan cosmogony, and phenomenologically it well affords a prototype of the Orphic egg from which Phanes comes forth.[4] Whether the Greek concept did actually derive from Egypt cannot be shown; it could well have done so, since the idea of the cosmic egg became a traditional *motif* in Egypt, and was still being commemorated there in the early centuries of the present era.[5]

As we noticed earlier in our study of the cosmogonic references of Homer, Night also appears in the Orphic cosmogonies as the original

[1] Cf. Guthrie, *Orpheus*, pp. 69–130; I. M. Linforth, *The Arts of Orpheus*, pp. 291–306; Kirk-Raven, pp. 37–9.

[2] Cf. Guthrie, *Orpheus*, p. 104; Nilsson, *Gesch. d. griech. Religion*, I, p. 648.

[3] Cf. Rose, *Greek Mythology*, p. 230; *O.C.D.*, p. 492 ('Leda'); Haussleiter in *R.A.C.*, IV, 735–6.

[4] See pp. 44–5, 49–50. Cf. Guthrie, *Orpheus*, p. 144, n. 15. The Orphic deity, Phanes personified light, cf. Guthrie, *Orpheus*, pp. 95–7. The earliest mention of Phanes seems to be on a gold leaf found in a grave at Timpone Grande in S. Italy (cf. G. Murray in J. Harrison, *Prolegomena*, pp. 664–6): it is impossible to date these so-called Orphic 'grave-tablets'; it has been suggested that some may be as early as the fifth century B.C. It is interesting to note that Diodorus Siculus (first cent. B.C.) quotes a saying attributed to Orpheus in which Phanes is identified with Osiris and Dionysus (Diod. I, 11.3). [5] See Bonnet, *Reallexikon*, p. 163. Cf. Schwabl, 73 (c).

creatrix; but of this concept, as of that of the cosmic egg, we can justifiably conclude that, even if these concepts were derived from some ancient source, in the Orphic systems they appear essentially as the products of a religio-philosophical form of speculation. As such, therefore, they cannot legitimately be accounted as representative of a true creation legend of early Greece; in fact, as with Hesiod, the Orphic theogonies or cosmogonies, even if they predate the classical beginnings of philosophical speculation, anticipate or adumbrate that fundamentally secular attitude to the cosmic phenomena which characterises the philosophical tradition of Greece.[1] Indeed, to quite an effective degree, the Greek genius for philosophising does actually constitute a barrier to our knowing the authentic creation legends of the Greeks. Homer's allusions to the cosmogonic significance of Oceanus and Night afford us but tantalising glimpses of folk beliefs concerning the origin of the world that were quickly overlaid or transformed by the interpretations of those, such as Hesiod, who sought to provide a seemingly rational cosmogonic system.[2]

Some further insight into this predisposition is afforded by certain enigmatic statements made by later writers about another of those whom Aristotle calls mixed (μεμειγμένοι) theologians, "who do not say everything in mythical form" (μυθικῶς).[3] This thinker is Pherecydes of Syros, who lived during the sixth century B.C. Diogenes Laertius records: "There is preserved of the man of Syros the book which he wrote of which the beginning is: 'Zas and Chronos always existed and Chthonie; and Chthonie got the name of Ge, since Zas gave her Ge as a present [or prerogative]' ".[4] Here it would seem that we have an early example of the rationalising of a mythic tradition by means of etymology. 'Zas' is clearly employed to denominate Zeus, and is possibly meant to establish a relation between the supreme Olympian deity and the earth-goddess Ge, who was known in Cyprus as Za. Chthonie (χθονίη) derives from χθών and is obviously intended to represent the earth-goddess Ge, but stressing thereby the underground aspect of this personification of the Earth.[5]

[1] Cf. Jaeger, pp. 63–6; Kirk-Raven, pp. 46–8.
[2] See n. 4, p. 183. Cf. Schwabl, 4 (40).
[3] *Met*. N4, 1091b8, in Kirk-Raven, p. 48; cf. Jaeger, p. 69; L. Robin, *La Pensée grecque*, pp. 34–5; Schwabl, 25–30.
[4] Diogenes Laertius, I, 119, in Kirk-Raven, pp. 54–5.
[5] Cf. Kirk-Raven, pp. 55–7; Jaeger, pp. 67–8.

Chronos (χρόνος) implies a significant piece of interpretation, for the word means 'Time' and it is surely intended here to represent the ancient god Cronos (Κρόνος).[1] After such evidence of sophistication, it is surprising to learn that Pherecydes wrote an account of the marriage between Zas and Chthonie, in which he not only provided a mythological precedent of the nuptial rite of the Anacalyteria (the 'unveiling of the bride'), but also spoke of 'the winged oak (ἡ ὑπόπτερος δρῦς)'.[2] This mysterious tree seems, from the references made to it by later writers, to have had some cosmogonic or cosmological significance. The puzzle has been discussed by several scholars without the reaching of an agreed solution; recently the suggestion has been made that the oak represents the firm substructure and foundation of the earth, and that its connection with the wedding veil, which was embroidered with cosmic images, indicates that the figure derived from a primitive conception of the structure of the earth.[3]

The case of Pherecydes is more significant for its witness to the complexity of the problem of discovering the earliest forms of Greek cosmogonic imagery than for the information thereon that it actually supplies. From it we may turn for a very brief comment upon the cosmogonic speculation of those Milesian thinkers with whom the beginnings proper of Greek philosophy are to be found. Aristotle, looking back over the course of Greek philosophical speculation, distinguishes between thinkers like Hesiod, whom he calls the πρῶτοι θεολογήσαντες ('the first theologians') and the πρῶτοι φιλοσοφήσαντες ('the first philosophers'). He finds the distinction expressed particularly in the fact that, although both propound specific doctrines (σοφίζονται), the philosophers were careful to support their statements by proof, while the theologians expound their views 'in mythical form' (μυθικῶς).[4] The distinction is a sound one, and for us it may be usefully elaborated by a further statement of Aristotle: "They

[1] Cf. Kirk-Raven, pp. 56–7: the Iranian conception of cosmogonic Time may possibly be older than these writers allow; see pp. 197, 203–5; Jaeger, p. 68. J. Duchesne-Guillemin, *The Western Response to Zoroaster*, pp. 78–9; Schwabl, 39–45.

[2] Grenfell and Hunt, *Greek Papyri*, Ser. II, no. 11, p. 23; Isodorus, *apud* Clement Alex. *Strom.* VI, 53, 5; Maximus Tyrius IV, 4, in Kirk-Raven, pp. 60, 62. Cf. Jaeger, pp. 69–70; Schwabl, 29.

[3] Kirk-Raven, pp. 61–5; Schwabl, 29–30, 74 (d).

[4] *Met.* A 2, 982b11, A 3, 983b6, 983b28, B 4, 1000a4 and 18. Cf. Jaeger, pp. 9–12.

(the 'theologians') assert that the first principles are gods or generated from gods, and say that those beings who did not taste of nectar or ambrosia became mortal! No doubt such phrases conveyed something to them; but with regard to the actual application of these causes, their statements pass our comprehension".[1] As we have seen, with such thinkers as Hesiod, cosmogony was essentially theogony. Instinctively they personified and divinised natural phenomena, explaining their origins in terms of personal relationship. Moreover, in their speculations they seem to have been mindful of earlier traditions and sought to incorporate them, even though moved by an incipient rationalism to modify and adapt them. When we turn to the speculations about the beginning of things by the three famous thinkers of Miletus who inaugurated the tradition of Greek philosophy, we at once sense the presence of a new ethos that manifests itself in a different attitude towards, and a different handling of, the problem of origins. These Milesian philosophers seek each to account for the origin of things in terms of derivation from some single primary material. Thales, famous for his prediction of a solar eclipse in 585 B.C., identified this natural principle (ἀρχὴ τῆς φύσεως), as Aristotle called it, with water.[2] His younger contemporary and pupil, Anaximander, discerned the origin of all in a much more sophisticated, and elusive, concept, namely, the 'Infinite' or 'Indefinite' (τὸ ἄπειρον), which was "the source of coming-to-be for existing things".[3] In turn Anaximander's pupil, Anaximenes, held air (ἀήρ) to be the primordial substance, from which all things were produced by varying processes of condensation and rarefaction.[4] While it is possible to see in Thale's conception of water as the primary material of creation, or in Anaximander's idea that "opposites are to be separated out (ἐκκρίνεσθαι) from the One", vestiges of the earlier

[1] Trans. J. Warrington, *Aristotle's Metaphysics*, p. 104 (Book B, 10, thesis (a)).
[2] Cf. Kirk-Raven, pp. 87-90. See also Robin, pp. 46-8; Jaeger, p. 24.
[3] Cf. Kirk-Raven, pp. 104-118, 126-37. In the only extant fragment of Anaximander the fundamentally important principle of the reciprocity of Nature's processes is stated: "And the source of coming-to-be (ἡ γένεσις) for existing things is that in which destruction, too, happens, 'according to necessity' (κατὰ τὸ χρεών); for they pay penalty and retribution to each other for their injustice according to the assessment of Time" (κατὰ τὴν τοῦ χρόνου τάξιν), trans. Kirk-Raven, p. 117, see pp. 120-1. Cf. Robin, pp. 52-3; Jaeger, pp. 34-5.   [4] Cf. Kirk-Raven, pp. 144-57.

mythological imagery,[1] the cosmogonies of these Milesian philosophers are essentially the products of a ratiocination that is quite divorced from theological interests or presuppositions. They set, moreover, the pattern of subsequent Greek cosmogonic speculation; for, even when myth or mythical imagery is invoked by later thinkers, such devices are consciously conceived parables or allegories and differ fundamentally from the type of creation legend with which we are professedly concerned.[2]

We may notice in conclusion that the earlier cosmogonic traditions of Greece, like those of Egypt, are singularly unconcerned with the question of the origin of mankind. As we have seen, while Homer contains nothing explicit on the subject, Hesiod makes some obscure and apparently contradictory statements which seem to indicate that he knew of no well-established tradition about the creation of man.[3] Generally it would seem that the Greeks set great store by the claim of being auchthonous in the literal sense of the word, and local folklore often commemorated the belief that the inhabitants of a particular area had sprung originally from the soil.[4] However, the local character of such stories, and the very fact that they commemorate such an origin, attest the absence of any generally accepted legend concerning the origin of mankind, or at least of that part of it which lived in Greece. But we may notice that there does appear to have been, despite the silence of Hesiod on so important a matter, some tradition which connected the creation of man with Prometheus. Apollodorus, who made a collection of Greek myths in the first century B.C., states that Prometheus moulded (πλάσας) men out of water and earth, and the belief seems to have been generally current in the Graeco-Roman world, since reference is made to it by other writers and it was represented in plastic art.[5] Another curious legend, which is only attested by later writers, tells how Deucalion, the son of

---

[1] Cf. Kirk-Raven, pp. 90–3; Guthrie, *In the Beginning*, p. 33.
[2] Cf. Jaeger, pp. 71–2; Robin, pp. 30–43; Kirk-Raven, p. 73, Schwabl, 75–6.   [3] See pp. 175–183.
[4] Cf. Guthrie, *In the Beginning*, pp. 23–5; Jameson in *M.A.W.*, p. 267.
[5] Apollodorus, I, vii. 1. See the list of other references to the creation of mankind by Prometheus given by J. G. Frazer in the Loeb ed. of Apollodorus, vol. i, p. 51, n. 5. Cf. Séchan, p. 33; Guthrie, *In the Beginning*, pp. 27–8. There is a representation of the creation of man by Prometheus on a sculptured sarcophagus in the Museo Capitolino, Rome; cf. F. van der Meer and C. Mohrmann, *Atlas of the Early Christian World*, fig. 172; see Plate X.

Prometheus, and his wife Pyrrha, were the only survivors of a flood by which Zeus sought to destroy mankind, and how they re-created the human race by throwing stones behind them which were transformed into men and women.[1] Whether such stories derived from truly ancient tradition, and, if so, in what form, are questions which cannot be answered. However, even if they do derive from some much earlier source, they but witness to the fact, already noticed, that the early Greeks do not seem to have been much occupied with the question of the origin of mankind, or, if they had been, that occupation had not found expression in a legend that was widely known and generally accepted. The reason for this apparent lack of concern is not evident. The Greeks were certainly interested in the past;[2] but, so far as mankind was concerned, their evaluation of the past appears to have been ambivalent. Hesiod, as we have seen, placed the Golden Age in the past:[3] later writers, however, seem to have had a shrewd appreciation of the brutish conditions of life in a primitive society and were conscious of the achievement of human endeavour that contemporary civilisation represented.[4] Certainly there existed no authoritative view of the beginning of things such as that which prevailed among the Jews, and which, carried over into Christianity, was to prove so decisive in fashioning the *Weltanschauung* of the European peoples.[5] This fact is attested by Diodorus of Sicily, who, writing in the first century B.C., could note as he began his great history: "Now as regards the first origin of mankind two opinions have arisen among the best authorities both on nature and history. One group, which takes the position that the universe did not come into being and will not decay (ἀγέννητον καὶ ἄφθαρτον), has declared that the race of men also has existed from eternity (ἐξ αἰῶνος ὑπάρχειν), there having never been a time when men were

---

[1] Apollodorus, I, vii. 2; Ovid, *Metamorphoses*, I, 345–415. Cf. Guthrie, *In the Beginning*, pp. 26–7; Nilsson, *Gesch. d. griech. Religion*, I, pp. 31–2, 200. According to the fragment of Hesiod's *Catalogue of Women* preserved by Strabo (Evelyn-White ed. p. 208), the creation of men from stones by Deucalion only is mentioned, but without the setting given by the later writers.   [2] Cf. Brandon, *Time and Mankind*, pp. 134–141.

[3] Cf. Guthrie, *In the Beginning*, pp. 72, 73, 98; K. F. Smith in *E.R.E.*, I, pp. 195–96a.

[4] E.g. Diodorus Siculus, I, 8. 1–9; Lucretius, *De rerum natura*, V, 925–1457. Cf. J. Baillie, *The Belief in Progress*, pp. 9–19; Guthrie, *In the Beginning*, pp. 74–7, 82, 96.   [5] Cf. Brandon, *Time and Mankind*, chaps. iv, v, viii, ix.

first begotten; the other group, however, which holds that the universe came into being and will decay, has declared that, like it, men had their first origin at a definite time (τυχεῖν τῆς πρώτης γενέσεως ὡρισμένοις χρόνοις)".[1]

Additional note: the origin of death

Greek cosmogonic tradition contrasts notably with that of Mesopotamia and Israel in its apparent unconcern about the origin of death. A similar lack of interest is found in the Egyptian cosmogonies, but the cause thereof, as we have seen, was a very distinctive one.[2] It is significant of the realistic nature of the Greek evaluation of the human situation that already in the earliest documents a fundamental distinction is made between gods and men. The former are essentially ἀθάνατοι ('immortals'), while the latter are characterised as θνητοί ('mortals').[3] The only reason apparently assigned for this basic distinction of nature was that the gods were immortal through their consuming of nectar and ambrosia, which were not available to mankind.[4] Death is personified by both Homer[5] and Hesiod. According to Hesiod, Night gave birth (ἔτεκεν) to Death (Θάνατος), as well as Sleep ("Υπνος), and the two are described as δεινοὶ θεοί ('awful gods').[6] Homer's frequent reference to the 'kēr of death' (κὴρ θανάτοιο) suggests, however, that there was a deep-rooted folk-belief which conceived of death as a grisly demonic being that seized his victims.[7] But, the very fact that in Greek thought death could be imagined in both a horrific and a gentle guise surely indicates that basically it was regarded as an event natural to all forms of life on earth, and as such it was instinctively accepted.[8]

[1] I, 6. 3 (trans. C. H. Oldfather, Loeb ed., vol. i, p. 25). On the cyclic view of the cosmic process see K. F. Smith in E.R.E., I, pp. 196a–200a; H.-C. Puech in *Man and Time*, p. 41, n. 4, 5.   [2] See p. 64.
[3] E.g. Hesiod, *Theog.* 967–8. On the word βροτός, used generally by Homer for 'mortal' (man) see R. B. Onians, *The Origins of European Thought*, pp. 506–7, who connects it with blood, contrasting it with the 'ichor' which flows in the veins of the gods.
[4] See the statement of Aristotle quoted above. Cf. Rohde, I, pp. 73–4; Onians, pp. 292–299.
[5] E.g. *Iliad*, XVI, 454, 672, 682.   [6] *Theog.* 212–13, 758–9.
[7] Cf. Harrison, pp. 174–5; Nilsson, *Gesch. d. griech. Religion*, I, pp. 206–7.
[8] Cf. Brandon in *B.J.R.L.*, vol. 43, pp. 328–30; *Man and his Destiny in the Great Religions*, pp. 179, 189–90. For Death in a gentle guise see the refs. in n. 5 above.

CHAPTER SIX

IRAN: DUALISM IN CREATION

GEOGRAPHICALLY it is difficult to define the ancient Near East
with precision. It is more easily conceived as a cultural area, or rather
perhaps an area of the interplay of certain cultures; as such its geographical bounds vary with the changing historical situation. Thus,
before the reign of David (c. 1000–960 B.C.), Israel cannot be reckoned as a significant constituent of the ancient Near East, nor can
Greece until about the sixth century B.C. The same might fairly be
said of Iran; for in a very real sense the cultural complex of the Near
East did not extend eastward beyond Mesopotamia until the rise of
Cyrus the Great in 549 B.C.[1] The empire that was established
throughout the area by this monarch and his successors, and its
subsequent subjugation and possession by Alexander of Macedon and
his successors, then made Iran an effective constituent of the ancient
Near East for many centuries—indeed until the complexion of that
area of ancient civilisations was transformed by the triumph of Islam.

To the historian of religions the influence of Iran is most notably
manifest in the ancient world of the Near East in two distinctive
forms. Thus it has long been recognised that certain aspects of post-
Exilic Judaism could be most reasonably explained in terms of the
influence of Iranian ideas, and now with the discovery of the so-
called Dead Sea Scrolls notable confirmation has been afforded of
the continuation, or perhaps firm establishment, of this influence in
Judaea.[2] The other form of manifestation is well known, namely,

---

[1] Cf. G. Buchanan Gray in *C.A.H.*, IV, pp. 1 ff.; A. T. Olmstead, *History
of the Persian Empire*, pp. 33 ff.

[2] Cf. Ed. Meyer, *Ursprung und Anfänge des Christentums*, II, pp. 86–120;
K. G. Kuhn in *The Scrolls and the New Testament* (ed. K. Stendahl), pp.
98–100; H. W. Huppenbauer, *Der Mensch zwischen zwei Welten*, pp. 10–13;
A. Dupont-Sommer, *Les Écrits esséniens découvertes près de la Mer Morte*,
pp. 93–7; M. Burrows, *The Dead Sea Scrolls*, pp. 257–62; R. C. Zaehner,
Dawn and Twilight of Zoroastrianism, pp. 51–4; J. Duchesne-Guillemin,
The Western Response to Zoroaster, pp. 86–96.

Mithraism, which became so popular a cult in the later Roman Empire and has been thought by some scholars to have constituted a serious rival to Christianity for the conversion of that Empire.[1] That Iranian ideas could exercise such influence so far from their homeland surely indicates that they were both distinctive and dynamic, which in turn suggests that they were the products of a strongly characterised cultural tradition. The fact that this was so is abundantly attested by a great variety of evidence. The ancient Iranians, who settled in the lofty plateau lands to the east of Mesopotamia sometime before 1000 B.C., were closely related racially and culturally with that other branch of Indo-European peoples which settled in north-western India during the second millennium B.C. and is known to us through the hymns of the celebrated *Rig-Veda*.[2] Of the artistic ability of the Iranians the ruins of Xerxes's great palace at Persepolis is witness enough,[3] while their achievement of empire attests their capacity for well-planned and dynamic action as well as efficient organisation. However, in seeking to evaluate their peculiar genius as it found expression in writing, we are confronted by a curious problem that particularly concerns our special interest of knowing their thoughts about the beginning of things.

This problem is constituted by the fact that the earliest documents preserved in the literary corpus known as the *Avesta* record the utterances of one who was the reformer of his people's traditional religion.[4] Zarathustra, who seems to have been born about 570 B.C.,[5] was conscious of his vocation as a prophet commissioned to proclaim certain newly revealed truths about God and Man. His influence, or that of his teaching, was destined to be decisive for subsequent

[1] Cf. Brandon, *Man and his Destiny in the Great Religions*, p. 291, n. 1: to the references given there on the Indo-Iranian cult of Mithra should be added Zaehner, *Dawn*, pp. 97–144.

[2] Cf. V. G. Childe, *The Aryans*, pp. 16–20, 24–40; Ed. Meyer, *Geschichte des Altertums*, I, 2, pp. 896–903; R. Ghirsham, *Iran*, pp. 73–89.

[3] Cf. H. Frankfort, *The Art and Architecture of the Ancient Orient*, pp. 213–33; Ghirsham, pp. 164–81.

[4] Cf. A. W. Williams Jackson in *E.R.E.*, II, art. 'Avesta', p. 268; J. M. Moulton, *Early Zoroastrianism*, pp. 8–21; W. Eilers in *R.G.G.*, I, pp. 797–800; Zaehner, *Dawn*, pp. 24–29.

[5] On the question of the date of Zarathustra see J. Finegan, *Archeology of World Religions*, pp. 77–83; F. Altheim, *Weltgeschichte Asiens im griechischen Zeitalter*, I, pp. 100–12; H. B. Henning, *Zoroaster: Politician or Witch Doctor;* p. 41; Zaehner, *Dawn*, p. 33.

Iranian religion, for all later tradition appears to bear its impress. But what was the nature and form of his people's religion before he changed it, as it would seem by reforming some parts and suppressing others, is an issue that has provided unceasing debate among the specialists concerned with what is intrinsically a very difficult field of research. For it would appear that, great though the prophet's influence was, the earlier tradition was by no means eliminated, and it finds expression, howbeit in distorted form and coloured by what became known as Zoroastrianism, in the later Avestan and Pahlavī literature. The aspect of this problem that must specially engage us concerns the origin of the fundamental dualism of Zarathustra's cosmogonic utterances.

We may begin our task by citing a passage from the *Gathas*, which by the general consensus of expert opinion are regarded as preserving the teaching of Zarathustra.[1] In this passage the prophet is represented as declaring:

(2) Hear with your ears the best things; look upon them with clear-seeing thought, for decision between the two Beliefs, each man for himself before the Great Consummation, bethinking you that it be accomplished for our pleasure. (3) Now the two primal spirits, who revealed themselves in vision as Twins, are the Better and the Bad in thought and word and action. And between these two the wise once chose aright, the foolish not so. (4) And when these twain spirits came together in the beginning, they established Life and Not-life, and that at the last the Worst Existence shall be to the followers of the Lie, but the Best Thought to him that follows Right. (5) Of these twain spirits he that followed the Lie chose doing the worse things; the holiest spirit chose Right, he that clothes him with the massy heavens as a garment. So likewise they that are fain to please Ahura Mazdah by dutiful actions.[2]

---

[1] The *Gathas* (the 'hymns' or 'songs') form the kernel of a liturgical document known as the *Yasna*. Cf. Duchesne-Guillemin, *Zoroastre*, pp. 163–5; Zaehner, *Dawn*, pp. 25–6, 28–9; Ed. Lehmann in *L.R.-G.*, II, pp. 208–9.

[2] *Yasna* xxx. 2–5; trans. by J. H. Moulton in *Early Zoroastrianism*, pp. 349–50. For other renderings see L. H. Mills, *S.B.E.*, XXI, pp. 29–30; K. F. Geldner in *R-G.L.*, p. 324; Duchesne-Guillemin, *Zoroastre*, pp. 238–9; Zaehner, *Dawn*, p. 42. Duchesne-Guillemin (p. 239) translates the crucial lines of the 4th stanza as follows:
  Et lorsque ces deux esprits se recontrèrent,
  Ils établirent à l'origine la vie et la non-vie.
Zaehner renders them: "And when these Spirits met they established in the beginning life and death . . ."

Ahura Mazdāh, the beneficent Creator of Iran, represented in the form of the winged
sun-disc, a symbol of Egyptian origin. From the palace of Xerxes at Persepolis.
(Courtesy of the Oriental Institute, University of Chicago.)

PLATE XI

A syncretistic
version of the
Temptation of Man.
An Islamic
representation of the
first human pair,
Máshya and Máshyôî,
being tempted by
Ahriman in the guise
of an old man
(Reproduced from
an Islamic
miniature now in
the University
Library, Edinburgh,
by the kind courtesy
of the Librarian).
See p. 207, n. 2.

PLATE XII

A similar statement occurs in another of these Gathic oracles:

(2) I will speak of the spirits twain at the first beginning of the world, of whom the holier thus spake to the enemy: "Neither thought nor teachings nor wills nor beliefs nor words nor deeds nor selves nor souls of us twain agree". (3) I will speak of that which Mazdah Ahura, the all-knowing, revealed to me first in this (earthly) life. Those of you that put not in practice this word as I think and utter it, to them shall be woe at the end of life.[1]

The difficulties that attend the task of translating and interpreting the meaning of the *Gathas* are notorious; however, the sense of what Zarathustra says in these two passages seems to be reasonably clear. We may best begin by noting that, despite the prophet's apparent claim in stanza 2 of the first passage and in stanza 3 of the second to impart a special revelation, it is obvious from the terminology which he instinctively employs that he assumes that his audience is familiar with the basic notions. In other words, it would appear that Zarathustra was addressing those who were already acquainted with the idea of the existence of two primaeval spirits that were opposed to each other from the beginning. It is not clear how these two spirits, designated respectively Spenta Mainyu and Angra Mainyu, were imagined, i.e. whether as abstract principles or in a personified form[2] —in so far as speech is attributed to them, they appear to be personified, but the establishment of 'Not-life' by the Angra Mainyu would seem to imply the operation of an impersonal force or entity. The mention of Ahura Mazdah in the second passage, who for Zarathustra was the supreme deity, raises the question of the relationship of this god to the two primaeval spirits, and the issue is still further complicated by the fact that elsewhere in the *Gathas* the

---

[1] *Yasna* xlv 2–3; trans. Moulton, pp. 370–1. Cf. Mills, *S.B.E.*, XXI, p. 125 f.; Duchesne-Guillemin, *Zoroastre*, pp. 227–8; Geldner in *R-G.L.*, p. 324.

[2] C. Bartholomae (*Altiranisches Wörterbuch*, 1137) defines *mainyu* in this context as " 'Geist' als Bezeichnung unkörperlicher Wesen". The term is rarely employed to denote the dead; but it is used of the gods. 'Spenta' means 'holy' or 'bounteous'; 'angra' signifies 'evil', 'hostile'. Cf. Moulton, pp. 134–6, 145–6; Zaehner, *Dawn*, pp. 42–3. The 'Lie' (*Druj*) referred to in *Yasna* xxx. 4 seems to be hypostatised, and it is used in the *Gathas* frequently (some twenty times) as a designation for the Angra Mainyu; cf. Moulton, pp. 49–50; Zaehner, *Dawn*, pp. 34, 35, 157; Lehmann in *L.R-G.*, II, pp. 230–1.

Spenta Mainyu is essentially associated, if not actually identified, with Ahura Mazdah. Nor is this the sum of the difficulty; for in another oracle Ahura Mazdah is hailed as the father of the Spenta Mainyu, so that logic at least demands that he is the parent also of the Angra Mainyu.[1] The implication, therefore, of these statements of Zarathustra is that already among the Iranians the idea existed of a deity who was the author of two opposing forces or principles, operative in the world and connoting respectively Good and Evil, Life and Not-life.

That Iranian cosmogony thus conceived of the operation of two opposing forces before the coming of Zarathustra has naturally induced scholars to seek further for the origins of this dualism. The quest is hampered by the fact, which we have already noticed, that none of the extant documents predate Zarathustra's mission; however, there are some indications, which may legitimately be interpreted in the light of cognate Indian notions, of an earlier form of this dualism. Some years ago Professor Geo Widengren presented, with an impressive documentation, a case for believing that there was current in ancient Iran the concept of a 'high-god' who personified the phenomena of power manifest in the universe. Because the manifestations of that power were evaluated by men as good or ill, the 'high-god' was imagined as having two sides to his nature, symbolised as light and darkness, life and death, creation and destruction. The conception was embodied in varying forms as a deity with a distinctive name or title. Thus, in both eastern and western Iran, the god Mithra was worshipped as a sky-god who not only incorporated within himself both the light and dark aspects of the heaven under day and night, but was also equally the dispenser to mankind of rain, with consequent fertility and well-being, and of drought, with disease and death.[2] A god of similar ambivalence was Vayu. This deity seems originally to have been a personification of the wind, which also had a double aspect of good and bad. He is pictured as supremely powerful, so that even Ahura Mazdah solicits his help; in cosmological speculation he was regarded as the source of all being

[1] *Yasna* xlvii. 2–3.
[2] Widengren, *Hochgottglaube im alten Iran.* pp. 94–145. Cf. J. Hertel, *Die Sonne und Mithra in Awesta*, pp. 111–22; G. Dumézil, *Mitra-Varuna*, pp. 83–5, 108–12, *Les Dieux des Indo-Européens*, pp. 41–3; Duchesne-Guillemin, *Zoroastre*, pp. 87–95.

and the *anima* of the world.[1] Another 'high-god', equally mysterious, to whom Vayu seems to have been related was Zurvān. This deity connoted Time, and, according at least to later speculation, had a twofold aspect or nature: as Zurvān *akarana* he represented 'infinite Time', and as Zurvān *dareghō-chvadhāta* he was 'Time of long Dominion', which brought decay and death. Considerable discussion of a highly specialised kind has taken place recently about the origin and significance of this divinity.[2] Later we must notice the interesting cosmogonic speculation of which he became the subject in Sassanian times; for the present it will suffice to note that there is evidence of the existence of the name Zurvān, and presumably of the cult of the deity, in the twelfth century B.C.[3] In a recent study Professor R. C. Zaehner has made another interesting suggestion in this connection, namely, that behind the Ahura Mazdah of Zarathustra lies an ancient Indo-Iranian deity connected with the sky who is named Varuṇa in the *Rig-Veda*. In earlier tradition this deity was associated with Mithra, the pair being known as 'the preservers-creators' (*'pāyū-thwōreshtārā'*). In making Varuṇa the supreme god, Zarathustra simply designated him Ahura, i.e. the 'Lord', and added the epithet 'Mazdāh' ('Wise'); then, having no use of Varuṇa's partner, Mithra, he transformed this deity into an attribute or son of Ahura.[4]

It would appear, accordingly, that the Iranians, long before the time of Zarathustra, were disposed to account for the world of their experience in terms of a fundamental dualism of good and evil, or of creative and destructive forces, which they traced back to a single divine source that either embodied these entities as the two aspects of its nature, or, in more anthropomorphic imagery, begot them as his sons. How far such a concept had been elaborated into a proper cosmogony is not known. As we shall see presently, there appears to have

[1] Widengren, *Hochgottglaube*, pp. 188–215; 'Stand und Aufgaben der iranischen Religionsgeschichte', in *Numen*, I (1954), p. 19. Cf. Zaehner, *Zurvān, a Zoroastrian Dilemma*, pp. 82–3; *Dawn*, pp. 148–9.
[2] See Zaehner's massive study *Zurvān, a Zoroastrian Dilemma* (1955), also his *Dawn*, chapters 8–11. Cf. Widengren, *Hochgottglaube*. pp. 266–310; Duchesne-Guillemin, *Zoroastre*, pp. 95–103, *Western Response to Zoroaster*, pp. 58–60; *Ormazd et Ahriman*, pp. 118–34; Brandon, *Man and his Destiny*, pp. 261–2, 280–2, 291–5.
[3] The name *Za-ar-wa-an* is found on the Nuzi tablets: cf. Widengren, *Hochgottglaube*, p. 310; Zaehner, *Zurvān*, p. 20.
[4] Zaehner, *Dawn*, pp. 66–70.

existed some pre-Zoroastrian myth of a Primordial Man.[1] And we may notice too that there are some signs of a dragon-slaying myth, which at once suggests the possibility of a Babylonian prototype in Marduk's conquest of Ti'âmat and its cosmogonic significance. However, in the Iranian sources the name of the dragon never occurs, and the god concerned with the feat, Vṛthraghna, appears to be related to Vṛtrahan, 'the slayer of Vṛtra', which was a title of the celebrated Vedic god Indra. But the dragon Vṛtra, which Indra slew, was not the personification of the primaeval deep as was Ti'âmat; it represented instead the power that withheld the fall of the fructifying rain upon the parched lands.[2]

That Zarathustra regarded his god, Ahura Mazdah, as the sole creator, and not the two primal spirits, the Spenta Mainyu and the Angra Mainyu, as each creating that which corresponded to its own nature as in later cosmogonic doctrine, is clearly stated in another Gathic oracle:

(3) This I ask thee, tell me truly, Ahura. Who is by generation the Father of Right, at the first? Who determined the path of the sun and stars? Who is it by whom the moon waxes and wanes again? This, O Mazdah, and yet more, I am fain to know. (4) This I ask thee, tell me truly, Ahura. Who upheld the earth beneath and the firmament from falling? Who made the waters and the plants? Who yoked swiftness to winds and clouds? Who is, O Mazdah, creator of Good Thought? (5) This I ask thee, tell me truly, Ahura. What artist made the light and darkness? What artist made sleep and waking? Who made morning, noon, and night, that call the understanding man to his deity? (6) This I ask thee, tell me truly, Ahura— whether what I shall proclaim is verily the truth. Will Right with its actions give aid (at the last)? will Piety? Will Good Thought announce from thee the Dominion? For whom hast thou made the pregnant cow that brings good luck? (7) This I ask thee, tell me truly, Ahura. Who created, together with Dominion, the precious Piety? Who made by wisdom the son obedient to his father? I strive to recognise by these things thee, O Mazdah, creator of all things through the holy spirit.[3]

[1] See pp. 199–202.
[2] Cf. Widengren in *Numen*, I, p. 51, in *Atti dell'VIII Congresso internazionale di Storia delle Religioni*, pp. 121–4; Duchesne-Guillemin, *Zoroastre*, pp. 43–7; H. Oldenberg, *Die Religion des Veda*, pp. 132–41; Brandon, pp. 262–3; A. J. Carnoy in *A.O.S.*, xxxvi, pp. 304–5, 310–13.
[3] *Yasna*, xliv. 3–7; trans. Moulton, pp. 367–8. For other renderings see Duchesne-Guillemin, *Zoroastre*, pp. 205–6; M. Molé in *Sources orientales*. I, p. 306; Zaehner, *Dawn*, p. 55. The entities designated in this passage as 'Right' (*Aša*), 'Good Thought' (*Vohu Manah*), 'Dominion' (*Xshatra*), and

This remarkable statement is significant not only for its detailed description of the creative achievement of Ahura Mazdah, but also for its categorical assertion (for the catechetical form surely implies affirmative answers) that Ahura Mazdah created both the light and the darkness. As we shall see, this assertion flatly contradicts the belief of the later form of Zoroastrianism, usually known as Mazdeism, that the evil principle, Ahriman, made, or rather perhaps personified darkness, in opposition to Ohrmazd, i.e. Ahura Mazdah, whose essential attribute is light. It constitutes, moreover, further proof that Zarathustra conceived of Ahura Mazdah as an ambivalent being, thus undoubtedly tacitly following an older tradition of dualism, of which we have seen other indications.

In another of the *Gathas* Zarathustra briefly and enigmatically reveals his knowledge of, and his attitude towards, some ancient myth concerning a Primordial Man. In the passage concerned, after enveighing against the demonic beings whom he calls the *daēvas* and their human followers, whom he accuses of having "defrauded mankind of happy life and of immortality", the prophet exclaims: "In these sins, we know, Yima was involved, Vivahvant's son, who desiring to satisfy men gave our people flesh of the ox to eat. From these may I be separated by thee, O Mazdah, at last".[1] This reference is tantalising in its brevity, for it clearly concerns some well-known figure *in illo tempore*, in that mythical first age when the first fateful acts were done that set the subsequent pattern of things.[2] The nature of Yima's offence is obscure; it would appear from other passages in the *Gathas* that Zarathustra regarded the killing and eating of oxen as the most heinous of deeds,[3] but why such a common

'Piety' (*Ārmaiti*) belong to the company of the six *Amesha Spentas*, which Zarathustra assigns as companions or attributes to Ahura Mazdah. There is reason for thinking that in origin these *Amesha Spentas* were so many Indo-Iranian 'functionellen Götter'. Cf. Carnoy in *E.R.E.*, XII, pp. 863–4; Moulton, 96–7, 110–15, 344; M. N. Dhalla, *Zoroastrian Theology*, pp. 19–39; Widengren in *Numen*, I, p. 23; Duchesne-Guillemin, *Zoroastre*, pp. 57–80, 146–7; Dumézil, *Naissance d'Archanges*, pp. 57–98; Zaehner, *Dawn*, pp. 45–50; Brandon, pp. 263–4, 266–7. There is some trace of a belief in a primordial separation of heaven and earth in stanza 4; cf. Duchesne-Guillemin in *P.W.*, 'Weltschöpfung', 1584.

[1] *Yasna*, xxxii. 8; trans. Moulton, p. 356. Cf. Duchesne-Guillemin, *Zoroastre*, p. 255; Zaehner, *Dawn*, p. 126.
[2] Cf. M. Eliade, *Traité d'Historie des Religions*, pp. 315–7.
[3] *Yasna*, xxxiii. 3–4, xxxix, xlvii. 3, xxxii. 14.

practice was held to be so outrageous can only be understood from the study of some rather complicated comparative material. We must briefly examine the issue, since an important aspect of primitive Iranian thinking about the origin of things appears to be involved.

We learn from the evidence of the later writings of the *Avesta*, notably from the *Vendīdād*, that Yima was regarded in a very different light from that in which he appears in the utterance of Zarathustra which we have just noticed. Thus, in this later tradition, Zarathustra is actually represented as being instructed about Yima by Ahura Mazdah: "The fair Yima, the great shephered, O holy Zarathustra! he was the first mortal, before thee, Zarathustra, with whom I, Ahura Mazdah, did converse, whom I taught the law of Ahura, the law of Zarathustra".[1] In a somewhat earlier text the time of Yima appears as a kind of golden age: "In the reign of Yima the valiant there was neither heat nor cold, neither old age nor death, nor disease created by the *daēvas*. Father and son walked together, each looking but fifteen years of age, or so did they appear, so long as Yima of goodly pastures, Vivahvant's son, held sway".[2] According to the tradition preserved in the *Vendīdād*, Yima was invited to become the prophet of Ahura Mazdah; he declined the office and was instead appointed to watch over the world, which he did so zealously that its inhabitants increased and prospered. But this Golden Age had to come to an end and be replaced by some terrible winters. Faced with the menace of this catastrophe, Yima then became a kind of Iranian Utanapishtim or Noah by devising a subterranean refuge where the seed of all living creatures was preserved until the return of better conditions.[3] This strange legend in its extant form would appear to comprehend a number of mythical themes, perhaps of diverse origin. What, however, seems particularly relevant to our subject is the probability that Yima was in ancient Iranian tradition a kind of Primal Man, who lived in a golden age and was a benefactor and saviour of man and beast. Now, this Yima was undoubtedly the Iranian counterpart of a somewhat similar figure, named Yama, in Vedic mythology, and the two are probably to be traced back to some

---

[1] *Vendīdād, Far.* II, 2; trans. J. Darmesteter, *S.B.E.*, IV, p. 11.
[2] *Yasna*, ix. 5; trans. Zaehner, *Dawn*, p. 93.
[3] *Vendīdād, Far.* II, 3–41, in *S.B.E.*, IV, pp. 11–20. Cf. Zaehner, *Dawn*, pp. 134–5.

common prototype in Aryan or Indo-European mythology. Yama was the Primal Man; and he was also the ruler of the blessed dead, because he "was the first of men that died, and the first that departed to the (celestial) world".[1] It would appear, therefore, that in Indo-Iranian tradition there was some myth of a primordial Man, Yama-Yima, who was revered as both the progenitor of mankind and as a benefactor and saviour to the first generations that peopled the world. This being so, the fact that Zarathustra denounces Yima as perpetrating an heinous crime in teaching people to slay and eat oxen appears the more strange. A clue to the solution of this problem is possibly to be found in another of Zarathustra's recorded utterances, in which he condemns the evil deeds of certain of his opponents: "To his undoing Grehma and the Kavis have long devoted their purpose and energies, for they set themselves to help the liar, and that it may be said, 'The Ox shall be slain, that it may kindle the Averter of Death to help us'."[2] Once again we have to do with language that is obscure to the extreme; however, there can be little doubt that the passage is concerned with the ritual slaying of the Ox as a sacrificial act of an apotropaic kind, namely, to ward off the menace of death or to ensure that life be strong and vigorous. The idea of such a primordial sacrifice at once recalls the famous act of Mithra, the sculptured representation of which formed the focal point of the *mithraea* of the Roman Empire. Indeed in that crucial Mithraic scene, which was thoroughly Iranian in inspiration, the *motif* of Vitality or New Life was vividly symbolised—the tail of the dying animal becomes transformed into an ear of corn, while various creatures seek for the fructifying semen of its genitals.[3] Now, as we have noted, there is no mention of Mithra in the *Gathas*; moreover,

[1] Cf. A. A. Macdonell in *E.R.E.*, XII, pp. 616b–617a; J. Dowson, *A Classical Dictionary of Hindu Mythology*, pp. 373–4; Oldenberg, pp. 532–3; Zaehner, *Dawn*, pp. 132–4.

[2] *Yasna*, xxxii. 14; trans. Moulton, pp. 357–8. The crucial line is rendered by Duchesne-Guillemin (*Zoroastre*, p. 256) as: "Il faut tuer le boeuf, pour faire briller à notre profit l'eloigneur-de-mort". According to Moulton, p. 358, n. 1, the expression 'the Averter of Death', i.e. *Dūraoša*, is in the later *Avesta* the standing epithet of Haoma, the sacred drink which, *inter alia*, was thought to confer immortality. Cf. Zaehner, *Dawn*, pp. 37–9, 88–91.

[3] See e.g. F. Cumont, *The Mysteries of Mithra*, figs. 10, 25, 37, *Les religions orientales dans le Paganisme romain*, planche XII. Cf. Zaehner, Dawn, pp. 128, 130; Brandon, pp. 296–7. See Plate XIII.

there is reason for thinking that in ancient Iranian tradition Yima and Mithra were regarded as twins. It would, accordingly, be legitimate to suppose that there was once current in Iran a myth concerning the sacrifice made by a Primal Man of a Primal Ox or Bull for the purpose of either ensuring or renewing life. Such a sacrifice would, of course, have constituted the prototype of, and the sanction for, the regular offering of a bull, undoubtedly in some New Year festival. To Zarathustra such a practice, and the presuppositions upon which it was based, would obviously have been obnoxious; for they contradicted his exaltation of Ahura Mazdah as the Lord of life and his emphasis upon *post-mortem* beatitude as dependent wholly on the making of a right moral choice. Hence his denunciation of Yima and his inauguration of this cultic practice, which seems nevertheless to have persisted and was eventually so signally perpetuated in the cult of Mithra, the close associate of Yima.[1] In this connection it is interesting also to note that Professor Zaehner recently has even suggested that Zarathustra "may have moulded anew the myth of the two twins (*yimas*) and transformed Mithra into the Holy Spirit [i.e. the Spenta Mainyu] and Yima, in so far as he was a deathless spirit and not merely a man, into the Destructive Spirit [i.e. the Angra Mainyu] who brought death into the world".[2]

Before we leave the theme of the Primal Man as it appears to have existed once in Iranian mythology, we may usefully notice that in a later text, the *Pahlavī Rivāyat*, there appears a myth of a Cosmic Man, from whose body the world and all its denizens were made. This is the only occurrence of such a myth in Iranian literature, and there is much reason for believing that it was derived from India; for in the *Rig-Veda* the sacrifice of Purusha is described, whose various members provided the substance for the formation of the world and the four main castes of Indian society.[3]

The obvious sophistication implicit in this myth of a Cosmic Man characterises the cosmogonic tradition of Iranian religion that finds

[1] Cf. Brandon, pp. 271–3. [2] Zaehner, *Dawn*, pp. 140–1.
[3] Text, and trans. given in Zaehner, *Zurvān*, pp. 360–7; cf. *Dawn*, p. 259. For the Purusha myth see *Rig-Veda*, x. 90, 10–12; cf. Oldenberg, p. 117; J. Gonda, *Die Religionen Indiens*, I, pp. 186–7; H. Jacobi, in *E.R.E.*, IV, p. 156a, M. J. Dresden in *M.A.W.*, pp. 339–40; Duchesne-Guillemin in *P.W.*, 'Weltschöpfung', 1585.

expression in the writings of the Sassanian period (A.D. 208–651) and after. In these later documents orthodox Zoroastrianism, and the heresies that stem from it, have developed into elaborate theological systems in which cosmogonic speculation features prominently, since the basic dualism had to be accounted for in terms of the origin and subsequent development of the world and all that it contains. Strictly speaking such speculation cannot be regarded as constituting 'legends', and it thus lies outside the proper scope of our study. However, since in one notable instance of this speculation an ancient myth may have been employed, and since the cosmogonic scheme itself constitutes the most notable expression of a dualistic *Weltanschauung*, we may fairly end our study of the ancient Iranian view of the beginning of things by a brief account of these two topics.

It would seem that in process of time, as men meditated on that Gathic oracle in which Zarathustra had spoken of the primordial principles of good and evil as 'twins', the question began to be asked how good and evil could be thus related, so implying a common origin. To meet this difficulty it would appear that certain thinkers sought for a transcendental source from which the personifications of good and evil could conceivably have originated. They found such a source in Zurvān or 'Time'.[1] As we have already seen, Zurvān was an ancient deity, who might once have been a kind of high-god; but how far this deity featured in ancient cosmogonic thought is unknown, owing to the nature of the Iranian literary tradition. There is, however, some evidence that already by the fourth century B.C. Greek scholars knew of some Iranian doctrine which attributed the origin of the personifications of good and evil to either Space or Time. Thus, according to Eudemus of Rhodes, a disciple of Aristotle: "both the Magi and the whole Aryan race . . . call by the name 'Space' or 'Time' that which forms an intelligible and integrated whole (τὸ νοητὸν ἅπαν καὶ τὸ ἡνωμένον), from which a good god and an evil daemon were separated out (διακριθῆναι), or, as some say, light and darkness before these. Both parties, however, postulate, after the differentiation of undifferentiated nature (τὴν ἀδιάκριτον φύσιν) a duality of the superior elements (τὴν διττὴν συστοιχίαν τῶν κρειττόνων),

---

[1] Cf. Zaehner, *Dawn*, pp. 175–184.

203

the one being governed by Ohrmazd and the other by Ahriman".[1] The selection of Time, which was essentially associated with Space, as the source of the two opposing forces operative in the creation and direction of the world, surely indicates a considerable faculty for abstract thinking, which in turn suggests a maturity of philosophical reflection.[2] For example, the nature of Time and its cosmogonic significance are carefully set forth in a *Rivāyat*:

And it is obvious, that, with the exception of Time, all other things have been created. For Time no limit is apparent, and no height can be seen nor deep perceived, and it (Time) has always existed and will always exist. No one with intelligence says: 'Time, whence comes it?' or 'This power, when was it not?' And there was none who could (originally) have named it creator, in the sense that is, that it (Time) had not yet brought forth the creation. Then it created fire and water, and, when these had intermixed, came forth Ohrmazd. Time is both Creator and the Lord of the creation which it created.[3]

Just how ancient was this recognition of the primordial significance of Time, personified as Zurvān, cannot on the existing evidence be determined; but, if the testimony of Eudemus is to be trusted, it would seem that in some form such consciousness must have antedated by many centuries the earliest written records of it. Of particular interest to us, however, is a legend which, although preserved only by very late writers, exhibits certain primitive features that might attest its antiquity.[4] It is related that Zurvān offered sacrifice for a thousand years in order to obtain a son who would create the heaven and the earth. But towards the end of this period Zurvān

---

[1] Cited by Damascius in his *Dubitationes et solutiones de Principiis*, in Zaehner, *Zurvān*, p. 446, G.I.; cf. *Dawn*, p. 182; Duchesne-Guillemin, *Ormazd et Ahriman*, pp. 119–20. It may be noted that 'Ohrmazd' is the Parsi name for Ahura Mazdah. 'Ahriman' comes from the Pahlavī *Ahraman*, which derives through the late *Avesta* from the Gathic *Angra Mainyu*.

[2] Cf. Zaehner, *Zurvān*, pp. 88–9, 105–13, 219–42; see also his *Dawn*, chaps. 9–11. Cf. Duchesne-Guillemin, *Ormazd et Ahriman*, pp. 118–34.

[3] *Rivāyat*, in Spiegel, *Die traditionelle Lit. der Parsen*, pp. 161 f.; trans. from Widengren, *Hochgottglaube*, p. 274. Cf. Zaehner, *Zurvān*, p. 410 (8), see also p. 409; U. Bianchi, *Zamān i Ōhrmazd*, pp. 112–17.

[4] See the various versions of the Zurvanite myth given by Zaehner, *Zurvān*, pp. 419–34, see also pp. 60–6; cf. *Dawn*, pp. 212–13, 227–8. Cf. Duchesne-Guillemin, *Zoroastre*, pp. 97–9; H. Corbin in *Man and Time*, pp. 126–31; A. Christensen, *Études sur Zoroatrisme de la Perse antique*, pp. 49–50; Lehmann in *L.R-G.*, II, p. 261; Bianchi, pp. 130–46.

began to doubt the efficacy of the sacrifices, and from this doubt was conceived another son who was to be Ahriman. In due course the two sons, Ohrmazd and Ahriman, were born, the one radiant with light and the other dark and repulsive. Their diverse natures duly found expression in what they created; for Ohrmazd made all that was beautiful and good, while from Ahriman came forth all that was ugly and evil.[1]

This Zurvanite myth does, of course, effectively explain the origin and relationship of the dual principles of good and evil, and as such it could fairly be regarded as a piece of rather sophisticated theological fiction. However, it is important to note that, although Zarathustra's 'twin' spirits are thus conveniently accounted for, Ahura Mazdah (i.e. Ohrmazd) is definitively identified with one of the 'twins' and accordingly represented as of a derivative nature, whereas in the Gathic text it is implied that Ahura Mazdah was himself the pro-creator of the two spirits, the Spenta Mainyu and the Angra Mainyu. If the myth, therefore, is a deliberate invention of a later period, then it must surely follow that Zurvān was chosen on obvious metaphysical grounds for the rôle of the primordial deity, thereby making him the father of Ahura Mazdah, the supreme god of Zarathustra and of later Zoroastrianism or Mazdeism. This conclusion is reasonable; but it would imply a very bold decision on the part of those who thus deliberately gave precedence to an essentially hypothetical Zurvān over the established and long revered deity, Ahura Mazdah. Accordingly, it seems more likely, especially in view of the testimony of Eudemus, that Zurvān had long been associated with the Iranian tradition of cosmic dualism; and perhaps some vestige of the antiquity of the myth concerned is to be seen in the reference to the sacrifice that Zurvān offered to obtain the birth of the demiurge, for in Indo-Iranian thought ritual sacrifice often had a cosmic significance.[2]

Zurvanism was rejected as a heresy by the orthodox believers, who,

[1] According to Zaehner, Dawn, pp. 50-1, 178-9, the dilemma of later Zoroastrianism, which the Zurvanites tried to solve, arose through a mistaken identification of the Spenta Mainyu with Ahura Mazdah.

[2] M. Molé in Sources orientales, I, p. 301, lays great stress upon the cosmogonic significance of sacrifice in Iranian thought: "Les répresentations cosmogoniques iraniennes apparaissent inextricablement liées, à l'origine, à la doctrine indo-iranienne du sacrifice . . . Le sacrifice n'est pas ici un offrande faite à la divinité, mais un acte autonome ayant une fonction cosmogonique et cosmologique propre", cf. pp. 303-4.

whatever its metaphysical difficulties, held fast to the idea of a primordial dualism, of which the protagonists were ever Ohrmazd and Ahriman. Some expressions of this orthodoxy, however, reveal that the authors were mindful of the significance of Zurvān and sought to compromise by representing Zurvān or Time as the helper of Ohrmazd. An interesting example of this attitude occurs in a document attributed to Zātspram, who was high priest of Sirkān in the ninth century. Therein it is related that Ohrmazd, faced by the menace of Ahriman, perceived that it was necessary that the conflict should be limited in time. Consequently, he appeals to Zurvān for help, which is duly given: "Zurvān had power to set the creation of Ohrmazd in motion without giving motion to the creation of Ahriman, for the (two) principles were harmful to each other and mutually opposed".[1]

Logically evaluated, orthodox Zoroastrianism was not absolutely dualistic, because it envisaged the ultimate victory of Ohrmazd over Ahriman. This view of the end of the cosmic process, however, encountered a difficulty that Zarathustra had apparently not noticed, but which obviously disturbed some who followed his teaching in later times and were more sophisticated in their thinking. The difficulty lay in the fact that, if it were held that Ohrmazd was omnipotent and that ultimately Ahriman would be overthrown, why should there be any conflict at all, with its attendant misery and suffering for all concerned—why should not Ohrmazd have annihilated his opponent at the very beginning? An interesting attempt to answer the question, and one which perhaps also shows some consciousness of the significance of the factor of time, is contained in the Dātastān-i-Denik of Mānushchihr, who was the brother of Zātspram. This scholarly high-priest, who was renowned for his orthodoxy, maintained that Ohrmazd had indeed the power to destroy Ahriman from the first and that he also foresaw the harm that his adversary would do, if left unrestrained; however, because his nature was essentially good and just, Ohrmazd could not destroy Ahriman until the latter had, by his evil deeds, provided just cause for his destruction.[2]

It is in the Bundahishn, which was composed sometime after the Islamic conquest of Iran in A.D. 651, that we have the most complete

[1] Zaehner, Zurvān, pp. 341–3; cf. Dawn, pp. 209–210.
[2] See Molé in Sources orientales, I, pp. 309–14. Cf. Zaehner, Dawn, p. 194.

Mithra slaying the Cosmic Bull. As the life-giving blood flows, a dog, a snake, and a scorpion (animals of Ahriman) attack the genitals and the blood of the sacrificial victim. See p. 201. (From a sculptured group in the British Museum. Photo: Mansell.)

PLATE XIII

Zurvān-Ahriman: statue now in the Vatican Museum. The entwining serpent probably represents the tortuous course of the sun's ecliptic. The wings, the sceptre, the signs of the zodiac on the body, and the sphere on which it stands, respectively symbolise the deity's association with time, fate, and cosmic sovereignty. See pp. 197, 203 f. (Photo: Alinari.)

PLATE XIV

orthodox statement of Zoroastrian cosmogony.[1] The work compre-
hends an elaborate chronological scheme comprising four trimillennia,
which represent successive stages in the conflict between Ohrmazd
and Ahriman. It is in fact a combination of cosmogony and eschatology, and it was designed to give the believer a review of the whole
cosmic process from the Creation to the Final Resurrection and
Judgment, which events symbolised the ultimate triumph of
Ohrmazd and overthrow of Ahriman.[2] As such, the work is a consciously conceived theological treatise, and, although it undoubtedly
incorporates much earlier tradition, it cannot properly be regarded as
being a creation legend within the terms of our study. However,
since the *Bundahishn* does represent, as it were, the culminating
expression of the long Iranian tradition of cosmic dualism, it will be
appropriate to close our study of this subject with the carefully conceived description at the beginning of this work of the two opposing
forces operative in the universe: "Thus is it revealed in the Good
Religion. Ohrmazd was on high in omniscience and goodness; for
infinite Time he was ever in the Light. That Light is the space and
place of Ohrmazd: some call it Endless Light. Omniscience and
goodness are the totality of Ohrmazd: some call them 'religion'. The
interpretation of both is the same, namely, the totality of Infinite
Time, for Ohrmazd and the Space, Religion, and time of Ohrmazd
were and are and ever shall be. Ahriman, slow in knowledge, whose
will is to smite, was deep down in the darkness: (he was) and is, yet
will not be. The will to smite is his all, and darkness is his place:
some call it the Endless Darkness. Between them was the Void: some
call it Vāy in which the two Spirits mingle".[3]

[1] *Bundahishn* means 'creation of the beginning', or 'original creation': cf.
E. W. West, *S.B.E.*, V, pp. xxii, xli. Cf. now M. Molé *R.H.R.*, 142, pp. 187 f.
[2] In *Bundahishn* XV, 1–9, the first human pair, Mâshya and Mâshyôî, are
generated from the seed of Gayōmart, the Primal Man. Their original sin
occurred when they ascribed the creation of the world to Ahriman and not
to Ohrmazd. Zaehner, *Dawn*, pp. 136–7, thinks that both Gayōmart and
Mâshya and Mâshyôî are substitute figures for Yima, owing to Zarathustra's
condemnation of the latter. The figure of Gayōmart (the name means 'mortal
life') has been the subject of unceasing discussion among specialists in
Iranian studies: cf. S. S. Hartmann, Gayōmart, *Étude sur le syncrétisme dans
l'ancien Iran*, pp. 37–44; Duchesne-Guillemin, *Ormazd et Ahriman*, pp. 43,
112; H. Güntert, *Der arische Weltkönig und Heiland*, pp. 346–7, See Plate XII.
[3] *Bundahishn*, I, 2–4; trans. Zaehner, *Zurvān*, pp. 312–13. Cf. Zaehner,
Dawn, pp. 248–9; Molé in *Sources orientales*, I, pp. 315–16.

EPILOGUE: THE LEGACY OF THE CREATION LEGENDS OF THE ANCIENT NEAR EAST

THE impression that seems most likely to be left on the modern mind by a survey of these ancient ideas about the beginnings of the world is that of their pathetic naïvety. While we may endeavour sympathetically to understand the motives and the experience that inspired them, the imagery in which they are clothed appears to be essentially fatuous, and often it repels by its gross crudity. It would, accordingly, seem that such primitive cosmogonies can have only an antiquarian interest, with perhaps also the doubtful value of providing material for the psychologist in his speculations about the deeper workings of the human mind. Yet, while all this is in one sense true, some of these ancient conceptions cannot, however, be dismissed as but the childhood fancies of our race, and, so, without current significance.

One such exception at once springs to mind. The legacy of the Hebrew creation story to the culture of the Western world and that of Islam has been incalculable. The fact that Christianity both stemmed from Judaism and accepted the Jewish scriptures as the revelation of God meant that the *Genesis* story of the Creation and the Fall of Man supplied an essential part of the *rationale* of Christian theology. The basic postulate of the Christian doctrine of salvation is that mankind needs saving not only from the consequences of the actual sin of its members, but also from the original sin inherited from its first parents, Adam and Eve.[1] It was because of the fundamental character of this notion that reaction was so profound when the truth of the *Genesis* story seemed to be menaced by the theory of the evolution of species in the nineteenth century. Today, even when few Christians would attempt to defend the literal accuracy of the

[1] Cf. N. P. Williams, *The Ideas of the Fall and of Original Sin* (London 1927), pp. 23–35, 39–163, who shows how the Fall-story of *Gen.* iii gradually ousted that of *Gen.* vi to become the 'official Fall-story of the Christian Church'.

208

Genesis record, the imagery of that dramatic story of the Fall and its fateful consequences is still continuously and essentially invoked in both teaching and devotion. But the influence of the Hebrew creation legend is not confined to those professedly Christian; its influence still continues to permeate Western culture, since it has come to form part of the basic pattern of our traditional *Weltanschauung*. For the old Victorian belief in progress, which we still instinctively hold despite all the disillusionment of the twentieth century, is but a secularised version of the Christian philosophy of history.[1] That philosophy is essentially teleological, in that it sees the passage of time as the field in which the purpose of God is gradually unfolded. History, accordingly, has a *telos* or end, to which it is inexorably moving, as it also had a beginning, when God created time as the essential category of created being. Although our secularised society today has, with varying degrees of consciousness, abandoned the supernatural sanctions of the Christian view of history, the current *Weltanschauung* remains basically teleological. We still instinctively view the passage of time as significant, and we feel that history has a purpose, although we cannot comprehend it—we live convinced that we are part of a process that had a definitive beginning and which moves steadily onwards towards some end that will accomplish its *raison d'être*.[2] It could indeed be reasonably suggested that the *malaise* that seems to afflict Western society today springs from a deep-rooted conflict, of which we are only dimly conscious, between a traditional view of life that stems ultimately from the Hebrew creation story, and that non-teleological evaluation which science alone seems to sanction.

If the Hebrew legacy may thus be judged as fairly obvious, the same cannot be said of that which might conceivably derive from the other ancient cosmogonies which we have studied. Some traces of such legacies can, however, be discerned, and they are worth noting. The first, to which attention may be the more easily directed, is to be found in the idea that creation was the consequence of the victory of the personification of good order over the primaeval forces of disorder. This idea seems to have arisen originally in Babylon,

[1] Cf. J. Baillie, *The Belief in Progress* (Oxford, 1950), pp. 94–6, 130–8; C. Dawson, *Progress and Religion* (London, 1932), pp. 190–201.
[2] Cf. Brandon, *Time and Mankind* (London, 1951), pp. 180–196.

finding expression in the myth of Marduk's struggle with Ti'âmat. From Babylon it seems to have passed into Palestine, and, although it was not incorporated into the *Genesis* creation legend, as we have noted, it became well established in Hebrew tradition and was destined to play an important part in the development of apocalyptic. For the 'crooked serpent', or dragon of the primaeval deep, was in process of time identified with Satan, and, reinforced perhaps by the Iranian belief of the cosmic struggle between Ohrmazd and Ahriman, the concept inspired that qualified dualism which finds such dramatic expression in the *Apocalypse of John* in the myth of the war in heaven and the casting down of Satan and his angels.[1]

It is more difficult to discern what has been, if any, the legacy of ancient Egyptian cosmogonic thought. If the influence of that tradition is to be found in anything, it is perhaps to the concept of Nun that attention must be directed. Although the idea of a primordial deep of waters as the creatrix occurs in Sumerian mythology, it is in Egypt that the primaeval situation was essentially conceived as a motionless waste of waters—a conception that was undoubtedly inspired, as we have seen, by the phenomenon of the Nile's annual inundation. That the demiurge himself originally emerged from this primordial deep, thus making water the source of all things, seems to have been peculiarly an Egyptian notion,[2] and it is reasonable to think that it was from Egypt that Thales derived the idea that water was the primaeval substance from which all was made, while Egyptian influence is demonstrated in what Diodorus has to say about the origins of life.[3] There is one Egyptian concept, however, which, for its metaphysical suggestion, might be expected to have commended itself to Greek philosophy, and thereby to have affected Christian thought. This is the concept of *kheper*, i.e. 'to become'or 'to come into existence', which was personified in the god Atum or Re as 'he who becomes (or exists) of himself'.[4] However, there is no evidence that this truly surprising essay in ontology, considering the great antiquity of its original formulation, had any legacy—possibly the intrinsic

---

[1] *Rev.* xii. 7–9, 13–17. Cf. H. Gunkel, *Schöpfung und Chaos in Urzeit und Endzeit* (Göttingen, 1895), pp. 171–398; R. H. Charles, *The Revelation of St. John* (I.C.C.), I, pp. 313–26.

[2] There must be some doubt as to the antiquity of the Oannes legend of Berossos; see pp. 111–12.

[3] See p. 48. [4] See pp. 22, 25–6, 32–3.

subtlety of the term *kheper* was never made known to, or grasped by, those Greeks who interested themselves in Egyptian culture.

It is difficult to assess, as we have seen, what was the original form of Greek cosmogonic tradition before the incipient rationalism of Hesiod began to set the pattern of Greek speculation about the beginning of things. That the process of creation started with a change in some primordial situation or substance seems to have been a generally accepted axiom of Greek cosmogonic thinking as it was in certain other traditions. But the Greek predisposition to rationalisation soon eschewed the more primitive anthropomorphism that finds expression in Homer and Hesiod, and, in seeking to define a 'First Cause' for the cosmic process,[1] the legacy of Greek cosmogony was mediated through philosophy and not through the mythic concepts of legend.

As we look back across our study of these creation legends of the ancient Near East and seek to assess their witness as a whole, it would seem that they attest most impressively man's essential consciousness of time. For these legends, despite all the strange variety of their imagery, each envisage a beginning to that arrangement of things which we know as the world. This concept, on reflection, is truly a remarkable one for the human mind to have reached, since the general verdict of experience is that natural phenomena constitute, despite certain variations of manifestation, an abiding environment to the life and activities of mankind. Moreover, not only does the earth and the heavens above it, appear eternal, but our ordinary acquaintance with our own species affords no suggestion that the human race had a beginning. Yet, as we have seen, the earliest intuitions of mankind, embodied as they are in these legends, witness to a profound and universal conviction that there was a time when both the world and the human race were not—in other words, that each had a beginning. This concept of a beginning in many instances, as we have seen, also implies some concept of an end to the existing world-order. Hence the fact is significant for any study of man, that already in the earliest written records evidence is found of the ability of the human mind to detach itself from preoccupation with the here-now of

[1] Cf. F. M. Cornford, *Principium Sapientiae* (Cambridge, 1952), pp. 195–6.

present interests, and to envisage a beginning and an end to the whole universe of things. Indeed that imaginative ability that enables the modern astro-physicist to contemplate the almost unintelligibly remote beginnings of the sidereal universe, or the palaeontologist the emergence of the species *homo sapiens*, had been truly, if very crudely, adumbrated by those unknown priests of Heliopolis or of Eridu who composed the first accounts of the origin of the world which they knew. Their records, moreover, and those of their successors in the other cultures with which we have been concerned, reveal also the fundamental teleology of human thought about the universe from the very first—for they all see the universe, not as a fortuitous production, but as the expression of divine purpose, in which mankind has its allotted part.

BIBLIOGRAPHY

Chapter One (The Dawning Concept of Creativity)

Bonnet, H. *Reallexikon der ägyptischen Religionsgeschichte*, Berlin, 1952.
Brandon, S. G. F. *Time and Mankind*, London, 1951. *Man and his Destiny in the Great Religions*, Manchester, 1962.
Breuil, H. *Quatre Cents Siècles d'Art pariètal* (*Les Cavernes ornées de l'Age de Renne*), Montignac, 1954.
Childe, V. G. *Man Makes Himself* (Thinkers' Library edn.), London, 1941.
Clarke, G. *From Savagery to Civilisation*, London, 1946.
'Cosmogony and Cosmology', in *E.R.E.*, VI (1911), pp. 125–79: a series of articles by different writers dealing with the subject in relation to various religions.
Derchain, P. 'Mythes et Dieux lunaires en Égypte', in *Sources orientales*, tome V (*La Lune: mythes et rites*), Paris, 1962.
Edsman, C.-M. art. 'Schöpfung', in *R.G.G.*, V (3. Aufl. 1961), 1469–73.
Eliade, M. *Traité d'Histoire des Religions*, Paris, 1948. *Patterns in Comparative Religion*, E.T., London, 1958. 'Structure et function du mythe cosmogonique', in *Sources orientales*, I (*La Naissance du Monde*), Paris, 1959.
Frazer, J. G. *The Folklore of the Old Testament*, abridged edn., London, 1923.
James, E. O. *Prehistoric Religion*, London, 1957. *The Cult of the Mother Goddess*, London, 1959.
Kuhn, H. *Die Felsbilder Europas*, Zürich/Wien, 1952.
van der Leeuw, G. 'Primordial Time and Final Time', in *Man and Time* (*Papers from the Eranos Yearbooks*), ed. J. Campbell, London, 1958.
Levy, G. R. *The Gate of Horn*, London, 1952.
Lexa, F. *La Magie dans l'Égypte antique*, I, Paris, 1925.
Mainage, Th. *Les Religions de la Préhistotoire: L'Age paléolithique*, Paris, 1921.
Maringer, J. *The Gods of Prehistoric Man*, E. T., London, 1960.
Neumann, E. *The Great Mother: an analysis of the archetype*, New York, 1955.
Neustupný, E. and J. *Czechoslovakia*, London, 1961.
Pettazzoni, R. *Essays on the History of Religions*, E.T., Leiden, 1954.
Pittioni, R. *Die urgeschichtlichen Grundlagen der europäischen Kultur*, Wien, 1949.

Plessner, H. 'On the Relation of Time to Death', in *Man and Time* (*Papers from the Eranos Yearbooks*), ed. J. Campbell, London, 1958.

Russell, B. *Human Knowledge*, London, 1948.

Sethe, J. *Die altägyptischen Pyramidentexten*, I, Leipzig, 1908 (1960).

Wernet, P. 'La Signification des Cavernes d'Art paléolithique', in *Histoire générale des Religions* (ed. M. Gorce et R. Mortier), tome I, Paris, 1948.

Chapter Two (Egypt)

Allen, T. G. *The Egyptian Book of the Dead*, University of Chicago Press, 1960.

Ancient Near Eastern Texts (ed. J. B. Pritchard), Princeton University Press, 2nd ed., 1955 (relevant Egyptian texts trans. by J. A. Wilson).

Anthes, R. "Egyptian Mythology in the Third Millennium B.C." in *J.N.E.S.*, vol. xviii (1959). "Mythology in Ancient Egypt", in *M.A.W.*

Bilderatlas zur Religionsgeschichte (hrg. H. Hass), 2.–4. Lieferung, *Aegyptische Religion* (hrg. H. Bonnet), Leipzig, 1924.

Blackman, A. M. *Luxor and its Temples*, London, 1923.

Bleeker, C.-J. "L'idee de l'ordre cosmique dans l'ancienne Égypte", in *R.H.P.R.*, t. 42 (1962), Strasbourg.

Bonnet, H. *Reallexikon der ägyptischen Religionsgeschichte*, Berlin, 1952.

Boylan, P. *Thoth. the Hermes of Egypt*, Oxford, 1922.

Brandon, S. G. F. *Man and his Destiny in the Great Religions*, Manchester, 1962. 'The Personification of Death in Some Ancient Religions', in *B.J.R.L.*, vol. 43 (Manchester, 1961). 'A Problem of the Osirian Judgment of the Dead', in *Numen*, V (Leiden, 1958). 'Akhenaten, the Heretic King of Egypt', in *History Today*, vol. XII (1962).

Breasted, J. H. *The Development of Religion and Thought in Ancient Egypt*, London, 1912. *The Dawn of Conscience*, New York, 1935.

de Buck, A. *Die Egyptische Voorstellingen betreffende den Oerheuvel*, Leiden, 1922. *The Egyptian Coffin Texts*, vol. II, Chicago, 1935, III, 1947.

Budge, E. A. W. *From Fetish to God in Ancient Egypt*, Oxford, 1934.

Černý, J. *Ancient Egyptian Religion*, London, 1952.

Childe, V. G. *New Light on the Most Ancient East*, London, 1952.

Derchain, Ph. 'L'authenticité de l'inspiration égyptienne dans le Corpus Hermeticum', in *R.H.R.*, t. LXI (1962).

Diodorus Siculus, ed. and trans. by C. H. Oldfather in Loeb Classical Library, vol. i, London, 1946.

Emery, W. B. *Archaic Egypt*, Penguin Books, Harmondsworth, 1961.

Ericksen, W. und Schott, S. *Fragmente memphitischer Theologie in demotische Schrift* (Pap. demot. Berlin 13603), Akademie der Wissenshaften und der Literatur in Mainz, Wiesbaden, 1954.

Erman, A. *Die Religion der Aegypter*, Berlin/Leipzig, 1934. *The Literature of the Ancient Egyptians*, trans. A. M. Blackman, London, 1927.

Erman A. und Ranke, H. *Aegypten*, Tübingen, 1923.

Frankfort, H. *Kingship and the Gods*, Chicago, 1948.

Gardiner, A. H. *Egyptian Grammar*, Oxford, 1927. *Egypt of the Pharaohs*, Oxford, 1961. 'Magic (Egyptian),' in *E.R.E.*, VIII (1915), pp. 262a–9a.

Grapow, H. 'Die Welt vor der Schöpfung', in *Ae.Z.*, 66 Band., Leipzig, 1930.

Horning, E. 'Die "Verurteilten" des aegyptischen Totengerichts', *précis* of paper given at the 10th International Congress for the History of Religions, Marburg, 1960.

Jelinková-Reymond, E. A. E. *Les Inscriptions de la Statue guérisseuse de Djed-Her-le-Saveur*, Le Caire, 1956. 'The Shebtiw in the temple at Edfu', in *Ae.Z.*, 87. Band, 1962, pp. 41–54; 'The Primeval Djeba', in *J.E.A.*, vol. 48 (1962), pp. 81–8.

Junker, H. *Der Götterlehre vom Memphis (Schabaka-Inschrift)*, (Abhandlungen der Preussischen Akademie der Wissenschaften, 1939, Nr. 23), Berlin, 1940. *Pyramidenzeit (Das Wesen der altaegyptischen Religion)*, Zürich, 1940.

Kees, H. in *Religionsgeschichtliches Lesebuch* (hrg. A. Bertholet), 10 (*Aegypten*), Tübingen, 1928. *Der Götterglaube im Alten Aegypten*, Leipzig, 1941. *Totenglauben und Jenseitsvorstellungen der alten Aegypter*, 2. Aufl., Berlin, 1956.

Manetho ed. and trans. by W. G. Waddell, in Loeb Classical Library, London, 1940.

Mercer, S. A. B. *The Pyramid Texts*, 4 vols., New York, 1952. *The Religion of Ancient Egypt*, London, 1949.

Morenz, S. *Aegyptische Religion*, Stuttgart, 1960.

Morenz S. und Schubert, J. *Der Gott auf der Blume*, Ascona, 1954.

Reymond, E. A. E., see Jelinková-Reymond, E. A. E.

Roeder, G. *Hermopolis, 1929–1939 (Ausgrabungen der Deutschen Hermopolis-Expedition in Hermopolis, Ober-Aegypten)*, Hildesheim, 1959. *Die aegyptischen Religion in Texten und Bilden (abbr. Ae.R.T.B.)*, Zürich. Band I, *Die aegyptische Götterwelt* (1959); Band II, *Mythen und Legenden um aegyptische Gottheiten und Pharaonen* (1960); Band IV, *Der Ausklang der aegyptischen Religion mit Reformation, Zauberei, und Jenseitsglauben* (1961).

Rundle Clark, R. T. *Myth and Symbol in Ancient Egypt*, London, 1959.

Sainte Fare Garnot, *L'Hommage aux Dieux d'après les Textes des Pyramides*, Paris, 1954. 'L'Anthropologie de l'Égypte ancienne', in *Anthropologie religieuse* (ed. C. J. Bleeker), Leiden, 1955.

nder-Hanson, C. E. *Der Begriff des Todes bei den Aegyptern*, Copenhagen, 1942.

Sandman-Holmberg, M. *The God Ptah*, Lund, 1946.

Sauneron, S. *Quatre Campagnes à Esna, Esna I* (Publications de l'Institut francais d'Archéologie orientale), Le Caire, 1959.

Sauneron, S. avec Yoyotte, J. 'La naissance du monde selon l'Égypte ancienne', in *Sources orientales*, I, Paris, 1959.

Schott, S. *Mythe und Mythenbildung im alten Aegypten*, Leipzig, 1945.

Schweitzer, U. *Das Wesen des Ka im Diesseits und Jenseits der alten Aegypter*, Glückstadt, 1956.

Sethe, K. *Die ältagyptischen Pyramidentexten*, (abbrev. *P.T.*) 4 Bände, 2. Aufl. 1960, Hildesheim. *Urkunden des Alten Reiches*, Band I, Leipzig, 1903. *Dramatische Texte zu altaegyptischen Mysterienspielen*, I, 'Das "Denkmal memphitischer Theologie" der Schabakostein des Britischen Museums', in *Untersuchungen zur Geschichte und Altertumskunde Aegyptens*, Band X, Leipzig, 1928. *Amun und die Acht Urgötter von Hermopolis*, Berlin, 1929. *Urgeschichte und älteste Religion der Ägypter*, Leipzig, 1930.

Speleers, L. *Les Textes des Pyramids égyptiennes*, 2 tomes, Bruxelles, 1923–4.

Spiegel, J. *Das Werden der altaegyptischen Hochkultur*, Heidelberg, 1953.

Vandier, J. *La Religion égyptienne*, Paris, 1949.

Wilson, J. A. in *The Intellectual Adventure of Ancient Man*, ed. H. and H. A. Frankfort, Chicago, 1946 (also published under title of *Before Philosophy*, Penguin Books, London, 1949); see also under *Ancient Near Eastern Texts*.

Wörterbuch der aegyptischen Sprache, hrg. Erman, A. u. Grapow, H., 5 Bände, Leipzig, 1925–31.

Yoyotte, J. avec Sauneron, J. 'La naissance du monde selon l'Égypte ancienne', in *Sources orientales*, I, Paris, 1959.

Zandee, J. *Death as an Enemy according to Ancient Egyptian Conceptions*, E.T., Leiden, 1960.

Chapter Three (Mesopotamia)

Ancient Near Eastern Texts, ed. J. B. Pritchard. (relevant Sumerian texts translated by S. N. Kramer, and Akkadian texts by E. A. Speiser), Princeton University Press, 2nd ed., 1955.

Bilderatlas zur Religionsgeschichte, hrg. H. Haas. 6. Lieferung: *Babylonisch-Assyrische Religion*, ed. B. Landsberger, Leipzig/Erlangen, 1925.

Bottéro, J. *La Religion babylonienne*, Paris, 1952.

Brandon, S. G. F. *Man and his Destiny in the Great Religions*, Manchester, 1962. *Time and Mankind*, London, 1951. 'The Ritual Perpetuation of the Past', in *Numen*, vol. VII, Leiden, 1959. 'The Personification of Death in some Ancient Religions', in *B.J.R.L.*, vol. 43, Manchester, 1961.

Burrows, E. 'Some Cosmological Patterns in Babylonian Religion', in *The Labyrinth* (ed. S. H. Hooke), London, 1935.

Childe, V. G. *New Light on the Most Ancient East*, London, 1953.

David, M. *Les Dieux et le Destin en Babylonie*, Paris, 1949.

Delaporte, L. *La Mésopotamie: les Civilisations babylonienne et assyrienne*, Paris, 1923.

Dhorme, E. *Choix de Textes religieux assyro-babyloniens*, Paris, 1907. *Les Religions de Babylonie et d'Assyrie* (coll: Mana), Paris, 1945.

Driver, G. R. *Semitic Writing* (Schweich Lectures, 1944), London, 1948.

Ebeling, E. *Tod und Leben nach den Vorstellungen der Babylonier*, Band I (Texte), Berlin/Leipzig, 1931.

Eliade, M. *Traité d'Historie des Religions*, Paris, 1948.
Falkenstein, A. und von Soden, W. *Sumerische Hymnen und Gebete*, Zürich/Stuttgart, 1953.
Fish, T. 'Some Ancient Mesopotamian Traditions concerning Men and Society', in *B.J.R.L.*, vol. 30, Manchester, 1946. 'The Zu Bird', in *B.J.R.L.*, vol. 31, Manchester, 1948.
Frankfort, H. *Cylinder Seals*, London, 1939. *The Art and Architecture of the Ancient Orient*, London, 1954. *Kingship and the Gods*, Chicago, 1948. *The Birth of Civilization in the Near East*, London, 1954.
Furland, G. *Miti babilonese e assiri*, Firenze, 1958.
Gadd, C. J. 'Babylonian Myth and Ritual', in *Myth and Ritual*, ed. S. H. Hooke, Oxford 1933. *History and Monuments of Ur*, London, 1929.
Garelli, P. et Leibovici, M. 'La Naissance du Monde selon Akkad', in *Sources orientales*, tome I (*La Naissance du Monde*), Paris, 1959.
Heidel, A. *The Babylonian Genesis*, Chicago University Press, 1951. *The Epic of Gilgamesh and Old Testament Parallels*, 2nd ed., Chicago University Press, 1949.
Hooke, S. H. *Babylonian and Assyrian Religion*, London, 1953. 'The Myth and Ritual of the Ancient Near East', in *Myth and Ritual*, ed., S. H. Hooke, Oxford, 1933.
Jacobsen, T. in *The Intellectual Adventure of Ancient Man* (ed. H. and H. A. Frankfort), Chicago, 1946. Also published in *Before Philosophy* (Penguin Books, Harmondsworth, 1949). 'Sumerian Mythology' (review article of S. N. Kramer's *Sumerian Mythology*), in *J.N.E.S.*, vol. 5, Chicago, 1946.
James, E. O. *Myth and Ritual in the Ancient Near East*, London, 1958.
Jean, C. F. *La Religion sumérienne d'après des documents sumériens antérieurs à la dynastie d'Isin (-2186)*, Paris, 1931.
Jensen, P. in *Reallexikon der Assyriologie*, art. *apsû-Apsû*, Band I, Berlin/Leipzig, 1932.
Jeremias, A. *Das Alte Testament im Lichte des alten Orients*, Leipzig. 1904.
King, L. W. *The Seven Tablets of Creation*, vol. I, London, 1902. *Legends of Babylon and Egypt*, Schweich Lectures, 1916.
Kramer, S. N. *Sumerian Mythology*. The American Philosophical Society, Philadelphia, 1944. *From the Tablets of Sumer*, Colorado, 1956. 'Dilmun, the Land of the Living', in *B.A.S.O.R.*, vol. 96 (1944). 'Sumerian Literature, a General Survey', in *The Bible and the Ancient Near East* (Essays in honor of W. F. Albright), ed. G. E. Wright, London, 1961 (see also under *Ancient Near Eastern Texts*). "Mythology in Sumer and Akkad", in *M.A.W.*
Kraus, F. R. 'Altmesopotamisches Lebensgefühl', in *J.N.E.S.*, vol. 19, Chicago, 1960.
Lambert, M. 'La Naissance du Monde à Sumer', in *Sources orientales*, Tome I (La Naissance du Monde), Paris, 1959. 'La Littérature sumérienne', in *R.A.*, t. lv (1961).

Lambert, W. G. *Babylonian Wisdom Literature*, Oxford, 1960.
Langdon, S. H. *Babylonian Wisdom*, published in *Babylonica*, ed. Ch. Virolleaud, t. VII, Paris, 1922–3.
Leibovici, M. see under Garelli, P. et Leibovici, M.
Meissner, B. *Babylonien und Assyrien*, Band II, Heidelberg, 1925.
Pallis, S. A. *The Babylonian Akîtu Festival*, Copenhagen, 1926.
Parrot, A. *Archéologie mésopotamienne*, Paris, 1946.
Saggs, H. W. F. *The Greatness that was Babylon*, London, 1962.
Schnabel, P. *Berossos und die babylonisch-hellenistische Literatur*, Leipzig, 1923.
von Soden, W. see under Falkenstein, A. und von Soden, W.
Speiser, E. A. in *the Idea of History in the Ancient Near East*, ed. R. C. Dentan, Yale University Press, 1955; see also under *Ancient Near Eastern Texts*.
Thureau-Dangin, F. *Rituels accadiens*, Paris, 1921.
Ungnad, A. *Die Religion der Babylonier und Assyrer*, Jena, 1921.
Widengren, Geo 'Aspetti simbolici dei templi e luoghi di culto', in *Numen*, vol. VII, Leiden, 1960.
Wiseman, D. J. *Cylinder Seals of Western Asia*, London, n.d.
Woolley, L. 'From Reed Hut to Brick Palace', in *History Today*, vol. V. London, 1955.

Chapter Four (Israel)

Albright, W. F. *The Archaeology of Palestine*, Penguin Books, Harmondsworth, 1949. 'The Old Testament and the Archaeology of Palestine', in *The Old Testament and Modern Study*, ed. H. H. Rowley, Oxford, 1951.
Ancient Near Eastern Texts relating to the Old Testament, ed. J. B. Pritchard, Princeton University Press, 2nd ed., 1955.
Anderson, G. W. 'Hebrew Religion', in *The Old Testament and Modern Study*, ed. H. H. Rowley, Oxford, 1951.
Baumgartner, W. 'The Wisdom Literature', in *The Old Testament and Modern Study*, ed. H. H. Rowley, Oxford, 1951.
Bevan, E. *A History of Egypt under the Ptolemaic Dynasty*, London, 1927.
Bonnet, H. *Reallexikon der aegyptischen Religionsgeschichte*, Berlin, 1952.
Bo Reicke 'The Knowledge Hidden in the Tree of Paradise', in *J.S.S.*, vol. I, Manchester, 1956.
Bottéro, J. 'La Naissance du Monde selon Israel', in *Sources orientales*, t. I (*La Naissance du Monde*), Paris, 1959.
Brandon, S. G. F. *Time and Mankind*, London, 1951. *Man and his Destiny in the Great Religions*, Manchester, 1962. 'In the Beginning: the Hebrew Story of the Creation in its Contemporary Setting', in *History Today*, vol. XI, London, 1961.
Breasted, J. H. *The Dawn of Conscience*, New York, 1935.
Budde, K. *Die biblische Paradiesesgeschichte* (*B.Z.A.W.*, 60), Giessen, 1932.

Burrows, M. *What Means These Stones?*, London, 1957.
Caquot, A. 'La Naissance du Monde selon Canaan', in *Sources orientales*, t. I (*La Naissance du Monde*), Paris, 1959.
Ceuppens, Fr. *Genèse* I–III, Malines, n.d.
Contenau, G. *La Civilisation phénicienne*, Paris, 1949.
De Boer, P. A. H. 'The counsellor', in *Wisdom in Israel and in the Ancient Near East* (H. H. Rowley *Festschrift*), ed. M. Noth and D. Winton Thomas, Leiden, 1955.
Dhorme, E. *Les religions de Babylonie et d'Assyrie*, Paris, 1945.
Driver, G. R. *Canaanite Myths and Legends*, Edinburgh, 1956.
Driver, S. R. *The Book of Genesis* (Westminster Commentaries), London, 1904. *Modern Research as illustrating the Bible* (Schweich Lectures, 1908), London, 1909.
Duchesne-Guillemin, J. *The Western Response to Zoroaster*, Oxford, 1958.
Dussaud, R. *Les Religions des Hittites et des Hourrites des Phéniciens et des Syriens* (Coll: Mana), Paris, 1945.
Eissfeldt, O. *Geschichtsschreibung in Alten Testament*, Berlin, 1948.
Engnell, I. ' "Knowledge" and "life" in the creation story', in *Wisdom in Israel and in the Ancient Near East*, ed. M. Noth and D. Winton Thomas, (H. H. Rowley *Festschrift*), Leiden, 1955.
Epic of Gilgamesh, trans. *A.N.E.T.*, and A. Heidel (see under name).
Fohrer, G. *Das Buch Jesaja*, I. Band, Zürich/Stuttgart, 1960.
Frazer, J. G. *The Folklore of the Old Testament*, abridged edn., London, 1923. *Taboos and Perils of the Soul* (*The Golden Bough*), London, 1936.
Gaster, T. H. *Thespis: ritual, myth, and drama in the ancient Near East*, 2nd ed., rev. New York, 1961.
Gordon, C. H. "Canaanite Mythology" in *M.A.W.*
Gunkel, H. *Schöpfung und Chaos in Urzeit und Endzeit*, Göttingen, 1895. *Die Urgeschichte und die Patriarchen*, Göttingen, 1911.
Heidel, A. *The Babylonian Genesis*, Chicago University Press, 1951. *The Gilgamesh Epic and Old Testament Parallels*. Chicago University Press, 2nd ed., 1949.
Hesiod, *Works and Days* in Loeb Classical Library ed. and trans. H. G. Evelyn White, London, 1914.
Holzinger, H. *Genesis* (Kurzer Hand-Kommentar zum Alten Testament), Tübingen/Leipzig, 1898.
Hooke, S. H. *In the Beginning*, Oxford, 1947. *The Siege Perilous* (*Essays in Biblical Anthropology and Kindred Subjects*), London, 1956.
Huppenbauer, H. W. *Der Mensch zwischen zwei Welten*, Zürich, 1959.
James, E. O. *The Cult of the Mother Goddess*, London, 1959. *Myth and Ritual in the Ancient Near Eeast*, London, 1958.
James, M. R. *The Apocryphal New Testament*, Oxford, 1926.
Jeremias, A. *Das Alte Testament im Lichte des alten Orients*, Leipzig, 1904.
Johnson, A. R. *The Vitality of the Individual in the Thought of Ancient Israel*, University of Wales Press, Cardiff, 1949.

Kautzsch, E. (ed.) *Die Apokryphen und Pseudepigraphen des Alten Testaments*, 2 Bände, Tübingen, 1900.

Kittel, R. *Die Psalmen* (Kommentar zum Alten Testament, Band XIII), Leipzig, 1922.

König, E. *Die Genesis, eingeleitet, übersetzt und erklärt*, Gütersloh, 1919.

de Langhe, R. *Les Textes de Ras Shamra-Ugarit et leurs rapports avec le milieu biblique de l'Ancien Testament*, 2 tomes, Gembloux/Paris, 1945. 'Myth, Ritual and Kingship in the Ras Shamra Tablets', in *Myth, Ritual and Kingship*, ed. S. H. Hooke, Oxford, 1958.

Leenhardt, F. J. 'La situation de l'homme d'après la Genèse', in *Das Menschenbild im Lichte des Evangeliums (Festschrift* zum 60 Geburtstag von Prof. E. Brunner), Zürich, 1950.

Lods, A. *Israël: des origines au milieu du viii e. siècle*, Paris, 1932. *Histoire de la Littérature hébraïque et juive*, Paris, 1950.

MacCulloch, J. A. 'Serpent-Worship' (Introductory and Primitive), in *E.R.E.*, XI (1920), pp. 399–411.

Neumann, E. *The Great Mother: an analysis of the archetype*, New York, 1955.

North, C. R. 'Pentateuchal Criticism', in *The Old Testament and Modern Study*, ed. H. H. Rowley, Oxford, 1951.

Oesterley, W. O. E. 'Early Hebrew Festival Rituals', in *Myth and Ritual*, ed. S. H. Hooke, Oxford, 1933.

Oesterley, W. O. E. and Robinson, T. H. *Hebrew Religion*, London, 1930.

The Old Testament and Modern Study, ed. H. H. Rowley, Oxford, 1951.

Pedersen, J. *Israel: its Life and Culture*, I–IV, in 2 vols., Copenhagen/London, 1926, 1940.

Peters, J. P. 'Cosmogony and Cosmology (Hebrew)', in *E.R.E.*, IV, Edinburgh, 1911.

Pfeiffer, R. H. *Introduction to the Old Testament*, ed. 1948, London, n.d.

Philo *On the Account of the World's Creation given by Moses*, in Loeb Classical Library ed. of Philo, ed. and trans. F. H. Colson and G. H. Whitaker, vol. i, London, 1949.

Pidoux, G. 'Encore les deux arbres de Genèse 3!', in *Z.A.T.W.*, 66 Band. 1954 (1955), pp. 37–43.

Procksch, O. *Die Genesis*, Leipzig, 1930.

von Rad, G. *Das formgeschichtliche Problem des Hexateuchs (B.W.A.N.T.*, iv, 26), Stuttgart, 1938.

Robinson, T. H. 'Hebrew Myths', in *Myth and Ritual*, ed. S. H. Hooke, Oxford, 1933, see also under Oesterley, W. O. E. and Robinson, T. H.

Rowley, H. H. *The Growth of the Old Testament*, London, 1950. *From Joseph to Joshua* (Schweich Lectures, 1948), London, 1950. *The Faith of Israel*, London, 1956.

Schaeffer, C. F. *The Cuneiform Texts of Ras Shamra-Ugarit* (Schweich Lectures, 1936), London, 1939.

Schwarzbaum, H. 'The Overcrowded Earth', in *Numen*, vol. IV, Leiden, 1957.

Skinner, J. *Genesis* (I.C.C.), Edinburgh, 1912.

Soederblom, N. *The Living God*, London, 1933.

Stärk, W. *Lyrik* (*Psalmen, Hoheslied und Verwandtes*), [Die Schriften des Alten Testaments, Abt. 3, Band I], Göttingen, 1911.

Stoebe, H. J. 'Gut und Böse in der Jahwistischen Quelle des Pentateuch', *Z.A.T.W.*, 65 Band, 1953 (Neue Folge, Bd. 24).

Suffrin, A. E. 'Dualism (Jewish)', in *E.R.E.*, V (1912).

Tylor, E. B. *Primitive Culture*, 2 vols., London, 1929 (1871).

Virolleaud, C. *Légendes de Babylon et de Canaan*, Paris, 1949.

Vollborn, W. 'Das Problem des Todes in Genesis 2 und 3', in *T.L.-Z.* 77, (1952), Nr. 12.

Widengren, Geo. *The King and the Tree of Life in Ancient Near Eastern Religion*, Uppsala, 1951. 'Early Hebrew Myths and their Interpretation', in *Myth, Ritual and Kingship*, ed. S. H. Hooke, Oxford, 1958.

Williams, N. P. *Ideas of the Fall and of Original Sin*, London, 1927.

Zaehner, R. C. *The Dawn and Twilight of Zoroastrianism*, London, 1961.

Chapter Five (Greece)

Apollodorus, *The Library*, ed. and trans. J. G. Frazer, Loeb Classical Library, vol. i, London, 1954.

Aristotle *Metaphysics*, ed. and trans. J. Warrington (Everyman Library), London, 1956.

Baillie, J. *The Belief in Progress*, Oxford, 1950.

Brandon, S. G. F. *Time and Mankind*, London, 1951. *Man and his Destiny in the Great Religions*, Manchester, 1962. 'The Personification of Death in some Ancient Religions', in *B.J.R.L.*, vol. 43, Manchester, 1961.

Brown, N. O. *Hesiod's Theogony*, New York, 1953.

Burns, I. F. 'Cosmogony and Cosmology (Greek)', in *E.R.E.*, vol. IV, Edinburgh, 1911.

Bury, J. B. 'Greek Literature from the Eighth Century to the Persian Wars', Chap. XIV in *C.A.H.*, vol. IV, Cambridge, 1930.

Cary, M. *The Geographic Background of Greek and Roman History*, Oxford, 1949.

Charbonneaux, J. 'La Religion égéenne préhellénique', in *H.G.R.*, t. II, Paris, 1948.

Cohen, R. *La Grèce et l'Hellénisation du Monde antique*. Paris, 1948.

Cornford, F. M. *Principium Sapientiae* (*The Origins of Greek Philosophical Thought*), Cambridge, 1952.

Diodorus Siculus ed. and trans. C. H. Oldfather, Loeb Classical Library, vol. i, London, 1946.

Duchesne-Guillemin, J. *The Western Response to Zoroaster*, Oxford, 1958.

Eliade, M. *Traité d'Histoire des Religions*, Paris, 1949.

Fontenrose, J. *Python: a Study of the Delphic Myth and its Origins*, University of California Press, 1959.
Gaster, T. H. *Thespis: ritual, myth, and drama in the ancient Near East*, 2nd ed. rev., New York, 1961.
Glotz, G. *La civilisation égéene*, Paris, 1937.
Goetze, A. 'Hittite Myths, Epics, and Legends', in *A.N.E.T.*, 2nd ed., 1955.
Gurney, O. R. *The Hittites*, Penguin Books, Harmondsworth, 1952.
Güterbock, H. G. "Hittite Mythology", in *M.A.W.*
Guthrie, W. K. C. *The Greeks and their Gods*, London, 1950. *Orpheus and Greek Religion*, 2nd ed. rev., 1952. *In the Beginning (Some Greek views on the origins of life and the early state of man)*, London, 1957.
Harrison, J. *Prolegomena to the Study of Greek Religion*, 3rd ed., New York, 1955.
Haussleiter, J. 'Ei', in *R.A.C.*, IV (1959).
Hesiod, Loeb Classical Library ed., entitled *Hesiod, the Homeric Hymns and Homerica*, ed. and trans. H. C. Evelyn White, London, 1914.
Homer, *The Iliad*, Loeb Classical Library, 2 vols., ed. and trans. A. T. Murray, London, 1932.
Hymn to Demeter, in Loeb Classical Library volume entitled *Hesiod, the Homeric Hymns and Homerica*, ed. H. G. Evelyn-White, London, 1914.
Jaeger, W. *The Theology of the Early Greek Philosophers*, Oxford, 1948.
Jameson, M. J. "Mythology of Ancient Greece", in *M.A.W.*
Kirk, G. S. and Raven, J. E. *The Presocratic Philosophers*, Cambridge University Press, 1960.
Lendle, O. *Die 'Pandorasage' bei Hesiod*, Würzburg, 1957.
Linforth, I. M. *The Arts of Orpheus*, University of California, 1941.
Lesky, A. *Thalatta: der Weg der Griechen zum Meer*, Wien, 1947.
Lorimer, H. L. *Homer and the Monuments*, London, 1950.
Lucretius, *De Rerum Natura*, Loeb Classical Library, ed. and trans. W. H. D. Rouse, London, 1947.
Mair, A. W. 'Hesiod', in *E.R.E.*, vol. VI, Edinburgh, 1913.
Mairuri, A. *The Phlegraean Fields*, Roma, 1937.
van der Meer, F. and Mohrmann C. *Atlas of the Early Christian World*, Edinburgh, 1958.
Nilsson, M. P. *Geschichte der griechischen Religion*, Band I, München, 1941. *The Minoan-Mycenaean Religion and its Survival in Greek Religion*, 2nd ed., Lund, 1950. 'Die Griechen' in *L.R-G.*, Band II, Tübingen, 1925. 'La Mythologie', in *H.G.R.*, tome III, Paris, 1948.
Oldfather, W. O. 'Pandora', in *P.W.*, Band XVIII (3).
Onians, R. B. *The Origins of European Thought about the Body, the Mind, the Soul, the World, Time, and Fate.* Cambridge, 1954.
Opelt, I. 'Erde (II. Griechisch-römisch. a. Gaia)', in *R.A.C.* V (1962).
Ovid, *Metamorphoses*, ed. and trans. F. J. Miller, Loeb Classical Library, vol. i, London, 1916.

Oxford Classical Dictionary, Oxford, 1949.

Picard, C. *Les religions préhelléniques* (Coll: Mana), Paris, 1948.

Puech, H.-C. 'Gnosis and Time', in *Man and Time* (*Papers from the Eranos Yearbooks*), ed. J. Campbell, London, 1958.

Robin, L. *La Pensée grecque et les Origines de l'Esprit scientifique*, Paris, 1928.

Rohde, E. *Psyche: Seelencult und Unsterblichkeitsglaube der Griechen*, 2 Bände, Freiburg, 1898.

Rose, H. J. *A Handbook of Greek Mythology*, London, 1928.

Rostagni, A. *Storia della Letteratura greca*, 13th ed., Verona, 1942.

Schwabl, H. "Weltschöpfung", in *P.W.*, (Sonderdruck, 1958).

Schwenn, F. *Die Theogonie des Hesiodos*, Heidelberg, 1934.

Séchan, L. *Le Mythe de Promethée*, Paris, 1951.

Shorey, R. 'Hope (Greek and Roman)', in *E.R.E.*, vol. VI, Edinburgh, 1913.

Smith, K. F. 'Ages of the World (Greek and Roman)', in *E.R.E.*, vol. I, Edinburgh, 1908.

Stella, L. A. 'La religione greca nei testi miceni', in *Numen*, vol. V, Leiden, 1958.

Thomson, J. O. *History of Ancient Geography*, Cambridge, 1948.

Vernant, J-P. 'Le mythe hésiodique des races. Essai d'analyse structurale', in *R.H.R.*, t. CLVII, Paris, 1960.

Vieyra, M. 'La Naissance du Monde chez les Hourrites et les Hittites', in *Sources orientales*, t. I (*La Naissance du Monde*), Paris, 1959.

Vlastos, G. 'Cornford, Principium Sapientiae', in *Gnomon*, Band 27/1955 (München), pp. 65–76.

Wilamowitz-Moellendorff, U. von *Der Glaube der Hellenen*, 2 Bände, Berlin, 1931. *Hesiod's Erga*, Berlin, 1928.

Chapter Six (Iran)

Altheim, F. *Weltgeschichte Asiens im Griechischen Zeitalter*, 2 Bände, Halle, 1947–8.

Bartholomae, C. *Altiranische Wörterbuch*, Strassburg, 1904.

Brandon, S. G. F. *Man and his Destiny in the Great Religions*, Manchester, 1962.

Burrows, M. *The Dead Sea Scrolls*, London, 1956.

Carnoy, A. J. 'Iranian Views of Origins in connection with Similar Babylonian Beliefs', in *J.A.O.S.*, vol. xxvi, 1916. 'Zoroastrianism', in *E.R.E.*, vol. XII, Edinburgh, 1921.

Childe, V. G. *The Aryans: a Study of Indo-European Origins*, London, 1926.

Christensen, A. *Études sur Zoroastrisme de la Perse antique*, Copenhagen, 1928.

Corbin, H. 'Cyclical Time in Mazdaism and Ismailism', in *Man and Time* (*Papers from the Eranos Yearbooks*), ed. J. Campbell, London, 1958.

Cumont, Fr. *Les Religions orientales dans le Paganisme romain*, Paris, 1929. *The Mysteries of Mithra*, E.T., New York, 1956.

Darmesteter, J. (trans.) *The Zend-Avesta*, Part I *The Vendîdâd (S.B.E.*, vol. IV).

Dhalla, M. N. *Zoroastrian Theology*, New York, 1914.

Dowson, J. *A Classical Dictionary of Hindu Mythology*, 7th ed., London, 1950.

Dresden, M. J. "Mythology of Ancient Iran", in *M.A.W.*

Duchesne-Guillemin, J. *Zoroastre*. Paris, 1948. *Ormazd et Ahriman (L'Aventure dualiste dans l'Antiquité)*, Paris, 1953. *The Western Response to Zoroaster*, Oxford, 1958. "Iranische Kosmogonien", in *P.W.*, "Weltschöpfung", 1582–89 (Sonderdruck, 1962).

Dumézil, G. *Naissance des Anges*, Paris, 1945. *Mitra-Varuna (Essai sur deux représentations indo-européennes de la souveraineté)*, Paris, 1948. *Les Dieux des Indo-Européens*, Paris, 1952.

Dupont-Somer, A. *Les Écrits esséniens découvertes près de la Mer Morte*, Paris, 1959.

Eilers, W. 'Avesta', in *R.G.G.*, Band I, Tübingen, 1957.

Eliade, M. *Traité d'Histoire des Religions*, Paris, 1949.

Finegan, J. *Archeology of World Religions*, Princeton, N. J., 1952.

Frankfort, H. *The Art and Architecture of the Ancient Orient*, London, 1954.

Geldner, K. F. 'Die zoroastrische Religion (Das Avestā)', in *R-G.L.*, Tübingen, 1908.

Ghirsham, R. *Iran*, Penguin Books, Harmondsworth, 1954.

Gonda, J. *Die Religionen Indiens, I. Veda und älterer Hinduismus*, Stuttgart, 1960.

Güntert, H. *Der arische Weltkönig und Heiland*, Halle, 1923.

Hartmann, S. S. *Gayōmart: Étude sur le syncrétisme dans l'ancien Iran*, Uppsala, 1953.

Henning, H. B. *Zoroaster: Politician or Witch Doctor?* Oxford, 1951.

Hertel, J. *Die Sonne und Mithra in Awesta*, Leipzig, 1927.

Huppenbauer, H. W. *Der Mensch zwischen zwei Welten*, Zürich, 1959.

Jackson, A. W. Williams 'Avesta', in *E.R.E.*, vol. II, Edinburgh, 1909.

Jacobi, H. 'Cosmogony and Cosmology (Indian)', in *E.R.E.*, vol. IV, Edinburgh, 1911.

Kuhn, K. G. 'New Light on Temptation, Sin, and Flesh in the New Testament', in *The Scrolls and the New Testament* (ed. K. Stendahl), London, 1958.

Lehmann, Ed. 'Die Perser', in *L.R-G.*, Band II, Tübingen, 1925.

Macdonell, A. A. 'Vedic Religion', in *E.R.E.*, vol. XII, Edinburgh, 1921.

Meyer, Ed. *Ursprung und Anfänge des Christentums*, Band II, Stuttgart/ Berlin, 1925. *Geschichte des Altertums*, Band I, 2, Stuttgart/Berlin, 1913.

Mills, L. H. (trans.) *The Zend-Avesta*, Part III (*S.B.E.*, vol. XXXI), Oxford, 1887.

Molé, M. 'La Naissance du Monde dans l'Iran préislamique', in *Sources orientales*, C.I. (*La Naissance du Monde*), Paris, 1959.
Moulton, J. M. *Early Zoroastrianism*, London, 1913 (published by Messrs. Williams and Norgate).
Oldenberg, H. *Die Religion des Veda*, 2 Aufl., Berlin/Stuttgart, 1917.
Olmstead, A. T. *History of the Persian Empire*, Chicago, 1948.
West, E. W. (trans.) *Pahlavi Texts*, Part I (*S.B.E.*, vol. V), Oxford, 1880.
Widengren, Geo. *Hochgottglaube in alten Iran*, Lund, 1938. 'Stand und Aufgaben der iranischen Religionsgeschichte', in *Numen*, vol. I (1954), vol. II (1955), Leiden. 'The Sacral Kingship of Iran', in *Atti dell'VIII*
Zaehner, R. C. *Zurvān: a Zoroastrian Dilemma*, Oxford, 1955. *The Dawn and Twilight of Zoroastrianism*, London, 1961.

Addenda

Bianchi, U. *Zamān i Ōhrmazd*, Torino, 1958.
Brandon, S. G. F. 'The Propaganda Factor in some Ancient Near Eastern Cosmogonies', in *Promise and Fulfilment* (Essays presented to S. H. Hooke, ed. F. F. Bruce), Edinburgh, 1964.
Eliade, M. *Le Mythe de l'Éternel Retour*, Paris, 1949.
Molé M. 'Une histoire du mazdéisme est-elle possible?', in *R.H.R.*, t. CLXII (1962).
von Rad, G. *Genesis*, E. T., London, 1961.

INDICES

Sources

Modern Authors

Names and Subjects

INDEX—SOURCES

(figures in brackets indicate notes)

Greek Papyri (Grenfell-Hunt), 187(1)
Herodotus II, 52: 183(3); 53: 183(2)
Hesiod, *Cat. of Women*: 190(1)
Hesiod, *Theogony*, 1-103: 167(1); 104-13: 167; 116-38: 167-8; 119: 169(2);
    154-210: 171(3); 187: 181(4); 453-506: 172(2); 212-13: 191(8); 507f:
    175(5); 533-60: 176(2); 561-70: 176(4); 570-7, 588-9: 177(1); 591-602:
    177(2); 629-819: 173(4); 740: 170(2); 746-8: 168(3); 758-9: 191(8);
    820-68: 170(1); 881-5: 174(2)
Hesiod, *Works and Days*, 42-4: 177(3); 47ff.: 177(4); 57-8: 178(1); 60-79:
    178(2); 80-3: 178(3); 83-93: 178(4); 94-5: 178(5); 96-9: 178(6); 103-5:
    179(2); 106-8: 180(1); 109-201: 180(2)
Hymn to Demeter, 268-74, 480-2: 162(1)
Iliad, xiv. 200-04: 164(2); 244-6: 164(3); 256-61: 165(2); xvi. 454: 191(5);
    458: 165(1); 672, 682: 191(5); xviii. 483-5: 162(3); xxi. 194-7: 163(1);
    xxiv. 527-33: 178(5)
Kumarbis (Hittite myth): 171(4)
Lucretius, *De rerum natura*, V. 925-1457: 190(4)
Maximus Tyrius IV, 4: 187(2)
Pausanias, c.X. 24, 6: 172(2)
Ullikummis (Hittite myth): 168(3); 174(3)

HEBREWS

Amos, ix. 3: 153
Baal, II I*, ii. 1-3, 28-30: 120(3); III* A 8-34: 120(2); III* C, 1.4: 120(1)
Clement of Alexandria, *Strom.*, iii. 6.45: 137(2)
Deut. xxxiii. 17: 150
Discourse on Abbatôn, 139(2)
Eccles. i. 4: 137(2)
Enoch lxix. 6: 128(4)
Enuma elish I., 132-142: 150(4)
Epic of Gilgamesh, I, i. 7-9: 142(3); 35-41: 126(5); 36: 128(1); ii. 1: 142(3);
    3-5: 151(4); iv. 34: 132(1)
    II, ii. 10-11: 132(2)
    XI, 180f: 143(2)
Eusebius, *Praep. ev.*, I, 10.7f.: 140
Ezekiel xxviii. 1-14: 126(2)
IV *Ezra* V. 43-4: 137
Genesis i. 2: 47(2), 147; 2-3: 148; 4-5: 148-9; 5b: 149(1); 6-7: 150(3); 6,
    8: 149; 9-10: 147, 150; 11-25: 150(4); 21: 150(4); 26-7: 151; 28-ii.4:
    152
    ii. 4: 122; 5-6: 122-3; 7: 123-4, 146; 8, 9, 10-14: 125-6; 9: 133-6; 15,
    16-17, 18-24: 126; 17: 135; 18-19: 146; 20-3, 25: 127-8
    iii. 1: 128-9; 1b-7: 130-31; 2-3: 134; 5: 135-6; 6: 136; 7: 136; 11: 136;
    12: 131; 14: 128-9; 14-15: 139; 16: 138; 17: 131; 17-19: 139; 19: 138,
    139; 20: 138(2); 21: 140; 22: 136; 22-4: 135, 139
    iv. 1: 138; 2-15: 141; 11-12: 141
    v. 29: 142, 144
    vi. 1-4: 142-3; 5-7: 142-3
    vii. 1 ff.: 143
    ix. 20: 143-4; 21b-28: 144; 22 ff.: 145; 27-7: 145
    xi. 1-9: 121, 140; 1-9, 28 ff.: 145
    xii. 1-3: 145(2)
    xiv. 19: 119
Hesiod *Works and Days*, 42-4: 139(2); 48-82: 131(3)

230

Isaiah xiv. 12-15: 126(2)
  li. 9-10: 155
Job xxvi. 10: 10-13
  xxxiii. 6: 84(4)
  xxxvi. 27: 123
  xliii. 10: 156
Judges vi. 36-40
Keret I, i. 35-7, 43: 119(2)
Numbers xiii. 33: 142
Philo, *On the Creation*, liii. 1152: 137(2); vi. 157-160: 130(1)
Proverbs viii. 22-30: 156(2)
Psalms civ. 5-9: 153-4; 29f.: 148
  lxxiv. 12-17: 154
  lxxxix. 10-12: 155
Rev. xii. 7-9, 13-17: 210(1)
Wisdom ii. 24: 128(4)

IRAN

Bundahishn, I. 2-4: 207; XV. 1-9: 207(2)
Eudemus of Rhodes: 203-4
Pahlavī Rivāyat: 202(3), 204
Vendīdād, Far. II, 2: 200(1), 3-41: 200(3)
Yasna ix. 5: 200(3)
    xxx. 2-5: 194; 4: 195(2); xxxiii. 8: 199(2); 14: 199(3); 201(2);
    xxxiii. 3-4: 199(3); xlv. 2-3: 195; xliv. 3-7: 198; xlvii. 2-3: 196(1);
    3: 199(3)

MESOPOTAMIA

Assyrian creation text, 110
Atrahasis Epic, 88
Babylonian texts (other than *Enuma elish*), 69, 70, 84-5, 89-90, 93(1), 99(3)
Berossus, 107, 111-113, 117
Enuma elish, I, 1-9: 94; 16-20, 41-6: 95; 47-72, 73-85: 96; 87-100, 107-161:
  97
  II 1-91: 97
  III 116-22: 97-8; 120: 114(5)
  IV 1-6, 13-14, 19-26: 98; 35-58, 76-84: 99; 90-1, 93-140: 100; 141-6:
  102
  V 1-4, 11-12: 103
  VI 1-14: 104; 22-6, 29-30: 105; 31-8: 106; 39-58: 108; 59-62, 74-81:
  109; 152-3: 105(2)
  VII 27, 90: 105(2); 90: 108(2)
Epic of Gilgamesh, X, iii. 3-4: 115(2); vi. 26-39: 116
  XI, 88(1)
Seneca, *Nat. Quest.* III, 29, 1: 117
Sumerian texts, 68, 71, 72-3, 74-5, 76-9, 81, 82, 83, 87

INDEX—MODERN AUTHORS

NAMES AND SUBJECTS

hemsut, 36, 38-9
Hermonthis, 19
Hermopolis, cosmogony, 43-52
Herodotus, origin of gods, 183
Hesiod, *Theogony*, 166-77, 183-4, 187
Hesiod, *Works and Days*, 177-83, 184
Hölderlin, J. C. F., 134(1)
Homeric cosmogony, 162-6, 183-4
Hope, significance, 178-9
Horus, 31, 33, 34, 35, 38
ḥw (command), 33, 34, 41
Huh and Hauhet, 46, 55

Igigi, 104(5)
Illuyanka, 175
Inanna, 79, 86
Iranian cosmogony, ritual factor, 201-2, 205(2)
Iranians, origin, 193
irj ('make'), 64
Isis, 23, 24

judgment (*post-mortem*), 40, 57, 64

k3w, 36, 38-9, 60-1
kheper, concept, 18, 32, 41, 63-4, 210-11
Khnum, 60-1, 77, 123-4
Kingu, 97, 105-6, 114
Kramer, S. N., 68, 76, 85
ku-bu, 100(3)
Kuk and Kauket, 46, 55, 148
Kumarbis, 171-2
Kur, 86, 101-2

Lamech's prophecy, 142, 144
languages, origin, 145, 146
Leda, 185
legacy, ancient cosmogonies, 208-12
Leviathan, 120, 153, 154
Light and Darkness, significance, 148-9, 198-9, 203, 207
lotus, cosmogonic symbol, 50-2, 53

magician, creator as (see also 'creation by word'), 121(1)
man, divine origin, 104(2), 107, 151-2
man, image of God, 151-2
man, origin (Egyptian), 23(4), 24, 36, 41, 51, 56-61
(Mesopot.), 76-8, 84, 88, 89-90, 104-6, 110
(Hebrew), 123-4, 151-2
(Greek), 189-190
man, origin evil, 105-7, 182

man, purpose, 43, 56-7, 76-7, 81-2, 104-8, 110, 115, 126, 151
Manetho, 65
mankind, destruction, 57, 87-8, 142-3, 182, 190
divine hostility, 130, 136, 139, 141, 176-183
wickedness, 142
Mami, creates mankind, 88-9, 123
Marduk, appearance, 96-7
creates mankind, 70, 104-8
death of, 92
demiurge, 70, 91, 100-3, 112-13, 149-50
relation to Enki, 96-7, 98, 102, 103, 104-6, 108
Mâshya and Mâshyôî, 207(2), plate XII
masturbation, cosmogonic significance, 22-3, 24, 35-6
Memphis, 29, 30, 31
Memphite theology, 29(2), 30-43, 54
me's, 80-1
Michelangelo, v, 118
Mithra, 196, 197, 201-2
moon's phases, cosmogonic significance, 2(2)
moral order (Egyptian), 39-41, 57
(Iranian), 194, 195, 197
(Mesopot.), 114-15
mortuary cultus, Egyptian, 64
msj (birth), 26, 27, 35, 41, 63-4
mtw.t (semen), 35(2)
Mummu-Ti'âmat, 94(2)
murder, first, 141
'Myth and Ritual' thesis, 92(3), 147(1)

Nammu, creatrix, 68, 69, 70-1, 76, 94
Naunet, 32, 46, 55
Nefertem, 32, 50
Neith, creatrix, 61(1), 62(2)
nephesh, 124
Nephthys, 23, 24
Nergal, 116
New Year festival, 62, 91, 98(1), 106(1), 113-14, 146-7, 175(4)
Nia and Niat, 46(6), 55
Night, creatrix, 165-6, cf. 167, 169, 184, 185-6
Nile, inundation, 14-15, 16, 18-19, 20, 66
Ninḫursag, 75, 89
Ninlil, 83
Ninmah, 77-8
Ninurta, 86, 102

239

Nippur, 81, 83
Noah, *Heilbringer*, 141-2, 143-4
Noah's cursing, 144-5
nudity, significance in *Genesis*, 127-8, 136
Nun, motionless, 17, 47, 54, 63, 148
personified, 17-18, 24, 25, 46, 55, 63
primaeval waters, 16-17, 18, 25, 29, 31, 46-7, 50, 52, 62, 63, 210
Nut (sky), 23, 24, 26-8

oak, winged, 187
Oannes, 111-12
Oceanus, 162-4, 168, 171, 183, 186
Ohrmazd, 199, 204-7
Olympian gods, second generation, 164, 167, 172-3, 174
omphalos, 161
Orphic cosmogony, 184-6
Osiris, 23, 24, 64, 65
Osorkon III, inscription, 16, 17, 62
Ouranos, 167, 169, 170-2
'Overcrowded Earth', myth, 137-8, 143, 152

Palaeolithic art, significance, 7-10
Pallis, S. A., 93
Pandora, 178-9
Petosiris, tomb inscription, 45, 49-50
Phanes, 184, 185(4)
Pherecydes, 186-7
pick-axe, origin, 79, 82
polar ice-caps, theory about melting, 2
pottery, influence, 11-12, 60-1, 77, 123-4
Priestly creation story, 118, 146-52
Egyptian influence, 148
Iranian influence, 149
liturgical use, 146-7
Mesopotamian influence, 146-50
primaeval age (Egyptian), see *sp tpy*
Primaeval hill, 18-19, 20-1, 25, 26, 30
45-6, 47-8, 161, 180-2
Primaeval history, 65, 87-8, 121, 140-6, 156-7, 190-1
Primordial Man (Iranian), 199-202, 207(2)
procreation, Palaeolithic knowledge, 4
significance, 136-8
Prometheus, benefactor of man, 175-6
Prometheus, creates men, 189
propaganda, cosmogonies used (see cosmogony, priestly interest)

providence, divine, 36-7, 38-43, 49, 56-9, 70, 72-6, 79, 82, 84-5, 87, 126, 130, 141, 152, 156-7, 209
Psalm civ and Aton hymn, 153(3)
Ptah as Egypt, 32
as Horus, 31, 38
demiurge, 31-43, 54-5, 64(2)
'Heart and Tongue', 32, 33
in *Pyramid Texts*, 21(1), 29
wr·3, 32, 34
Purusha, 202
Pyramid Texts, evidence, 15-16, 21

Rahab, 155
rain as semen, 170
reed-platform, creative factor, 70
relics, of cosmic egg, 49-50
Re (sun), birth, 26-7, 29, 45, 48, 49-52, 55, 62
rmi.t (tears), origin of man, 51, 55, 56

Sabbath, origin, 152
sacrifice, to create man, 89, 90, 105-8, 110
Satan, identified with Serpent, 128, 210
Sea, creatrix, 68-70, 94, 99, 101, cf. 162-4
serpent, rôle in *Genesis*, 128-30, 139-40
seven-headed, 120, 153, 154
symbol of pleasure, 130(1)
Set, 23, 24, 64
sexual consciousness, fatal, 136-8
Shabaka Stone, 30-43
Shu (air), 22, 23, 24, 27-8, 35, 54, 71, 169
śia (knowledge), 33
Sin, moon-god, origin, 83
Space, Iranian concept, 203-4
Spenta Mainyu, 195-6, 198, 205
sp tpy ('first time'), 19, 48-9, 51, 53, 62, 65
stars, creation (Mesopot.), 103
Sumerian cosmogony, absence of strife, 86-7
Sumerian King List, 87, 88
Sumerians, origin, 67
syncretism, cosmogonic, 54-5, 58, 61(1), 84, 119-20, 123, 125-6, 127-8, 130, 131-2, 140, 147-50, 152-6, 160-1, 163-4, 168(3), 171, 174-5, 187(1), 192, 209-11, see also Pl. XII

240